AMÍLCAR CABRAL

ANTÓNIO TOMÁS

Amílcar Cabral

The Life of a Reluctant Nationalist

HURST & COMPANY, LONDON

First published in the United Kingdom in 2021 by
C. Hurst & Co. (Publishers) Ltd.,
83 Torbay Road, London NW6 7DT
© António Tomás, 2021
All rights reserved.
Printed in Great Britain by Bell and Bain Ltd, Glasgow

The right of António Tomás to be identified as the author of this publication is asserted by him in accordance with the Copyright, Designs and Patents Act, 1988.

A Cataloguing-in-Publication data record for this book is available from the British Library.

ISBN: 9781787381445

This book is printed using paper from registered sustainable and managed sources.

www.hurstpublishers.com

Photographs reproduced with the kind permission of DAC—Documentos Amílcar Cabral/Arquivo da Fundação Mário Soares.

To my beloved uncle,
Aldemiro

CONTENTS

List of Acronyms and Abbreviations	xi
Introduction	1
1. Between Guinea and Cape Verde	17
2. The Years in Lisbon	33
3. Engineer and Clandestine Militant	53
4. Shattering the Walls of Silence	77
5. A United Front	87
6. Modes of Making War	109
7. The Cape Verdean Question	127
8. A State Inside the Colony	135
9. Winning in Politics Without Losing the War	149
10. Towards Independence	169
11. The Killing of Cabral	187
Epilogue	203
Notes	215
Bibliography	233
Index	243

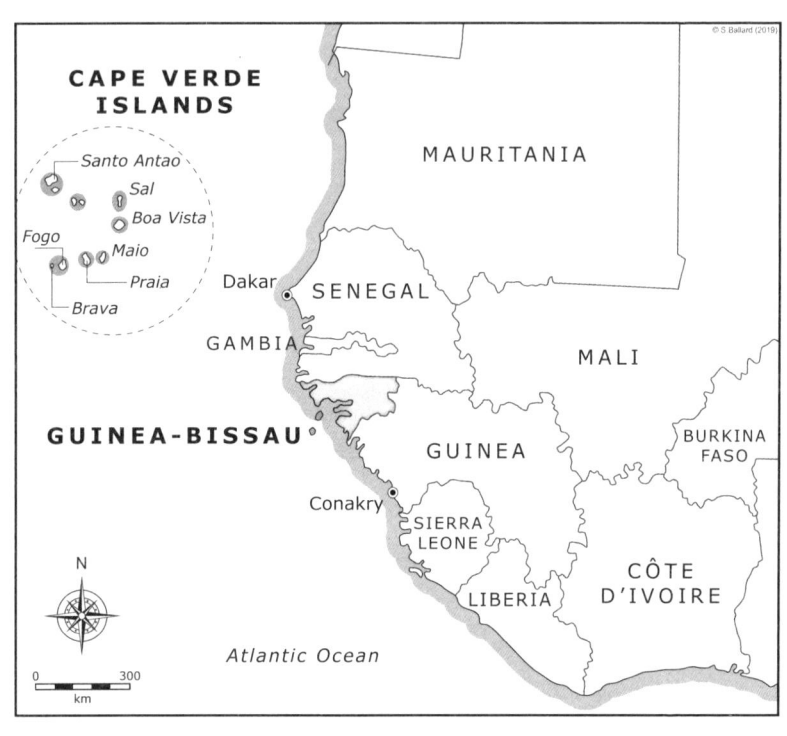

Guinea and Cape Verde

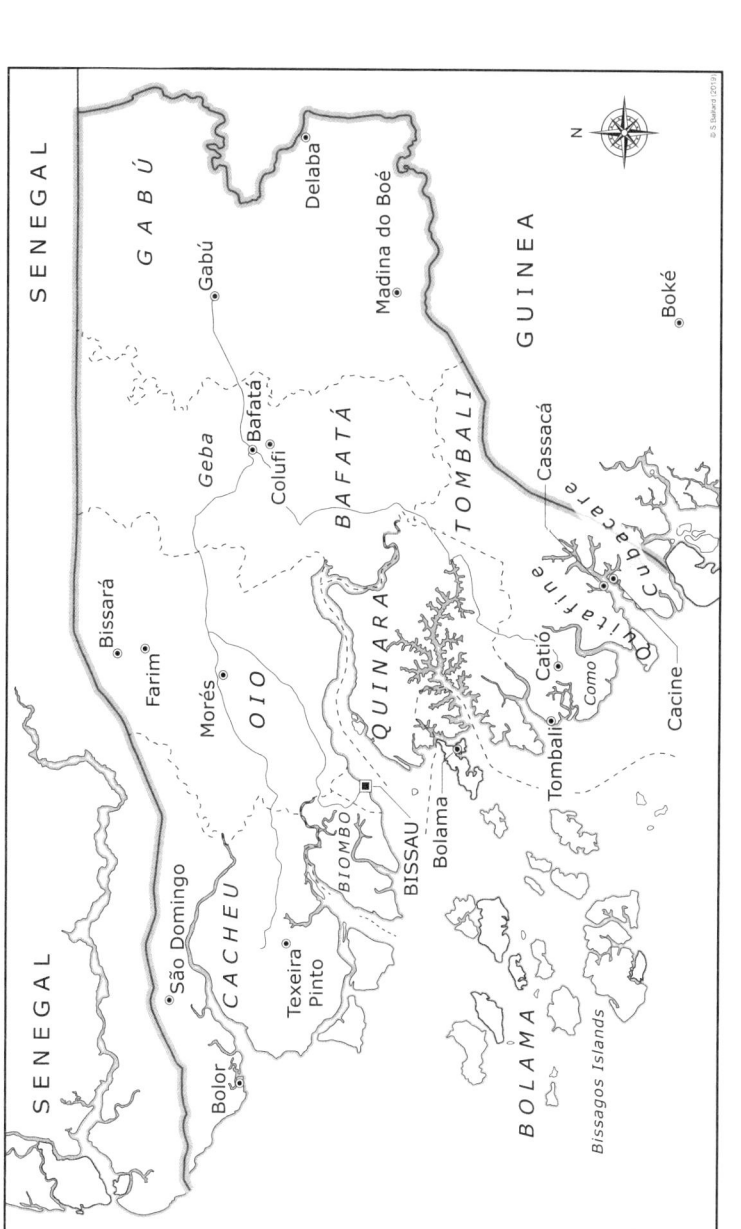

Guinea Bissau

LIST OF ACRONYMS AND ABBREVIATIONS

CBC	Congressional Black Caucus
CEI	Casa dos Estudantes do Império
CEL	Conselho Executivo da Luta (PAIGC)
CIMADE	Comité inter-mouvements auprès des évacués
CNCV	Conselho Nacional de Cape Verde
CONCP	Conferência das Organizações Nacionalistas das Colónias Portuguesas
CSL	Conselho Superior da Luta
CUF	Companhia União Fabril
FARP	Forças Armadas Revolucionárias do Povo (PAIGC)
FLG	Frente de Libertação da Guiné
FLGC	Frente de Libertação da Guiné e de Cabo Verde
FLING	Frente de Libertação Nacional da Guiné
FNLA	Frente Nacional de Libertação de Angola
FRELIMO	Frente de Libertação de Moçambique
FUL	Frente Unida de Libertação
GNR	Guarda Nacional Republicana
GPRA	Gouvernement provisoire de la République algérienne
GRAE	Governo da República de Angola no Exílio
ILO	International Labour Organization
ITU	International Telecommunication Union
MAC	Movimento Anti-Colonialista
MFA	Movimento das Forças Armadas
MLG	Movimento de Libertação da Guiné
MLGCV	Movimento de Libertação da Guiné e Cabo Verde

LIST OF ACRONYMS AND ABBREVIATIONS

MPD	Movimento para a Democracia
MPLA	Movimento Popular de Libertação de Angola
NAACP	National Association for the Advancement of Colored People
NATO	North Atlantic Treaty Organization
OSPAAAL	Organização de Solidariedade dos Povos de África, Ásia e América Latina
OAU	Organization of African Unity
PAI (Guinea and Cape Verde)	Partido Africano da Independência
PAI (Senegal)	Parti Africain de l'Indépendance
PAICV	Partido Africano para a Independência de Cabo Verde
PAIGC	Partido Africano para a Independência da Guiné e Cabo Verde
PCP	Partido Comunista Português
PDG	Parti Démocratique de la Guinée
PIDE/DGS	Polícia Internacional da Defesa do Estado/ Direcção Geral de Segurança
PSP	Polícia de Segurança Pública
RDG	Rassemblement Démocratique de la Guinée
UDC	União Democrática de Cabo Verde
UDENAMO	União Democrática Nacional de Moçambique
UN	United Nations
UPA	União dos Povos de Angola
UPG	União dos Povos da Guiné
UPICV	União dos Povos para a Independência de Cabo Verde

INTRODUCTION

By the end of 1964, Portugal, the most economically deprived, backward nation at that time in Europe, was facing three military insurgencies in Africa. In Angola, the armed conflict had started in January 1961, when hundreds of the FNLA's men attacked farms in the north of the country, killing thousands of Portuguese settlers as well as Angolan indentured workers mostly from the south. In northern Mozambique in 1964, FRELIMO's troops had attacked the Portuguese military positions, and soon made important inroads in controlling areas of the territory. But in Guinea in January 1963, the PAIGC soldiers had occupied isolated positions of the Portuguese army in Tite and launched what would become the most successful military campaign against Portuguese colonialism. The brain behind Guinea's uprisings and operations was the Guinean-born agronomist Amílcar Cabral. The revolution in Guinea has been hailed as one of the defining moments along Lusophone Africa's road to political sovereignty. Contrary to the expectations of the nationalists from the Portuguese colonies, the momentum of the military uprisings stalled the first year after the initial confrontation. Angola is a perplexing case in this regard. Following the uprising of 1960, Portugal implemented a number of sweeping reforms that paved the way for an era of robust economic growth, which not only contributed to quelling the population's thirst for independence, but also drove hundreds of thousands of settlers to the colony. Mozambique, excluding the zones controlled by the guerrillas, was not much different. Guinea was an exception. Guineans were not only challenging the more powerful and better-equipped

Portuguese army, they were also laying the groundwork for the emergence of a postcolonial state. Ultimately, the military insurgency began a process of re-thinking the meaning of revolution itself.

This book is about the man behind this struggle, Amílcar Cabral. It narrates his revolutionary trajectory, from his early life in Guinea to his death at the hands of his own men in the neighboring country of Guinea-Conakry on 20 January 1973. This book is, for the most part, the English version of the biography of Cabral, *O Fazedor de Utopias*, whose first edition, in Portuguese, came out in 2007. However, this version is not simply a translation, even if the overall structure is largely unchanged. It takes advantage of the troves of archival information which have recently been made public and insights from the deluge of studies on Cabral, the last years of Portuguese colonialism, and the anticolonial movement in the former Portuguese colonies. Furthermore, since I have not stopped working on Cabral (publishing papers, presenting at conferences, exchanging emails with readers), this edition has also given me an opportunity to elaborate, correct, and even reflect on issues that were not fully resolved in the Portuguese edition.

Accordingly, restoring Cabral's political dimension is not what animates the writing of this study. To put it another way, the relative obscurity into which Cabral's travails may have fallen is not my main concern. This biography is concerned with the difficulty of how to write about African historical figures and the times and contexts in which they developed their political activities. I have reflected on this question elsewhere, building on the work of the anthropologist and cultural critic David Scott. In *Conscripts of Modernity*, Scott discusses the ways in which postcolonial scholarship uncritically assumes that we still inhabit the same historical times which produced the present day. I approach this conceptual problem by relying on what I call answer-question dialectics. Action, and more specifically political action, is for the most part a response to a very particular question. The insurgency led by Cabral, for example, can be seen as the answer to the problem of colonial exploitation. This, according to Scott, poses a serious conceptual and epistemological problem. For if anticolonial critique were the answer to the problem of colonialism, postcolonial critique should be concerned with the question in itself, and not whether we arrived

INTRODUCTION

at the answer, as if we still live in those historical times. Heeding Scott's advice, I have interrogated in my own work Cabral's diagnosis of the colonial question. Was he right? Did he portray colonialism in the most accurate way?

The question here is how to write about Cabral's times and struggles. As such, I am countering the ways in which a number of topics and motifs have been represented in the literature on Cabral. More specifically, this biography of Cabral intends to address the gulf between the reality of the armed struggle in Guinea and the ways in which it has come to be discussed. Firoze Manji and Bill Fletcher touched on this question when they recently acknowledged that there were significant differences between what Cabral said and what he perhaps would have said if he could speak freely:

> Cabral was not only speaking of his own thoughts but was representing and leading a consensus within, for lack of a better term, a revolutionary movement. He was not, in other words, an individual public intellectual who said or wrote what was on his mind, but instead, and in any case, he had to think of the dynamics that were unfolding within the movement.

The problem here doesn't just flow from Cabral's own representation of the liberation movement in Guinea, but also from the assumption that Cabral was speaking for "a consensus within the revolutionary movement." This passage hints at a major contradiction which will be examined in depth in this biography. On the one hand, it is true that Cabral was not able to speak freely. But on the other, nowhere will one be able to find a process through which a consensus was actually reached in the context of the national liberation movement. Paramount here is not only the issue of internal democracy (or the lack thereof) in the operations of the national liberation movement, but also its consequences. Many writers consider Cabral's war leadership to be exemplary, and it has inspired many studies on revolutionary theory, on the control and administration of liberated zones, and on postcolonial state formation. But the enthusiasm that characterized accounts of Guinea's path to independence is not reflected in the country's present-day situation. In fact, Guinea's descent into one of the most underdeveloped countries in the world started right after independence. Some commentators have suggested that Cabral's murder in 1973 deprived the soon-to-be nation of his problem-solving ingenuity. At the heart of this disjunction is perhaps not the way in which we talk about Guinea's revolution today, but the ways in which it was represented in its own time. To be more emphatic, I am not concerned with contrasting Guinea's present with the promises of the past. This would be cheap criticism, as hindsight allows us a far greater understanding than those that came before us of the complex choices that had to be made. Instead, I will address this question with reference to what Cabral was able to know at different points in time, and what materials he could use in order to make sense of the world in which he lived. This question is important, and I will set out to answer it in this book, thus acting as a corrective to a large amount of what has been written on Cabral.

Earlier biographies of Cabral, by Russian Oleg Ignatiev and Angolan Mário Pinto de Andrade, for instance, tend to depict him as an overconscious nationalist, able to anticipate the course and configuration of historical events well in advance. For them, the fact that Cabral became the leader of the PAIGC, for example, was simply the fulfillment of his calling. They write the life history of Cabral retrospectively. The poems that Cabral wrote in his early days are seen to contain the seeds of the revolt which brought him to nationalism. This is not the approach I will take in this book. Let me give an example. By the mid-1950s, Cabral was back in Lisbon, after a spell in Guinea as an agronomist. Life was going well for him, his wife, and their small child—despite the rampant racism in the city at that time. While he was also involved in nationalist activities, under the alias Abel Djassi, he tried his best to live a double life. Yet in 1960, he had to commit fully to nationalist activism. Those biographers also tend to describe political sovereignty as the ultimate goal of his activism in the late 1940s and early 1950s, when Cabral was still a student in Lisbon. However, I demonstrate in this book that such a conception of independence was not available to them at that time. Only later, particularly after the 1960s, when most African countries had achieved independence, could Cabral assert independence as the primary goal of his struggle.

Accounting for these discrepancies is the fact that a great deal of what we know about nationalism in Lusophone Africa may have been fabricated. Attempts have been made to expose such historical fabrications in books which are for the most part only available in

INTRODUCTION

Portuguese. These studies have tried to bridge the gulf between the accounts of the revolutionary process and what really happened. Curiously, the nationalist Mário Pinto de Andrade not only strongly contributed to the concoction of these misrepresentations, but also, even if involuntarily, tried to debunk them later in his life. In the famous interview with Michel Laban, Mário de Andrade admits that propaganda was an important aspect of the anticolonial strategy in Lusophone Africa. Part of this may perhaps be explained by the schism that existed in these movements between those who made the war and those who publicized it. Cabral was in the second group, and, as Reiland Rabaka has put it, he was a "reluctant soldier": he spent much of the war promoting, but not actually participating in, the fighting. Cabral was not a military man, nor did he have any military training, and even though he was the commander of the rebel forces, he was convinced that the independence of Guinea could only be attained by diplomatic action. As such, Cabral spent a considerable part of the colonial war (from 1964 to 1973) travelling. It was through these trips that his party got almost everything it needed to subsist. But it also meant that Cabral had to depict events in a certain way.

Cabral was an optimist, and much of the materials and information he circulated about the revolution in Guinea painted a rosy picture of events. For him, the revolution was about how Guineans were being exposed to modernity through the national liberation movement, how an African state was being formed through political action in the liberated zones, and how a few hundred peasants were confronting the military might of the colonial army. A great number of Western writers, journalists and activists who visited and wrote about the liberated zones simply repeated the same mantra, either out of idealism, or because of shortsightedness, in part because Cabral's party only allowed them to see certain aspects of the liberated zones. Ultimately, important elements of the movement were swept under the carpet. For instance, Cabral's constant absence bred resentment against him and other Cape Verdeans, and alienated him from the everyday experiences of the freedom fighters. As such, the way we recall the revolutionary process today is largely based on the "facts" which were produced as propaganda.

Commenting on Cabral and his revolutionary movement, the São Tomean nationalist Tomás Medeiros drew a stronger link between propaganda and political leadership. He argues that most of the war-related events were taking place elsewhere and that Cabral could only know what was going on through reports, which produced a great deal of noise. The question is whether this noise has persisted. Key here is to understand what really happened and how these events have been described and conceived. As such, the gulf, as discussed earlier, lies between reality and the description of this reality for the sake of propaganda. What impoverishes contemporary analysis of Guinea's road to political emancipation is that most of the same tropes are still evoked. But as it is no longer necessary to portray the anticolonial struggle in a specific way, our analysis of these historical processes should change in its turn.

Consequently, in this book I focus on archival materials, on the interviews I conducted in 2000—when a number of participants in the events were still alive—and particularly on the evolving debates over the presentation of these questions in Guinea and Cape Verde. As such, this book attempts to capture how the anticolonial war was perceived in the aftermath of independence, when the optimism of this process had largely died down. The aim is to reflect the ways in which the life and work of Cabral is perceived today, outside the academic world. In doing so, I relied on a couple of sources which require a brief discussion. *Cabo Verde: Os Bastidores da Independência* is a good source to start with. Written by the Cape Verdean journalist José Vicente Lopes, the book does not only chronicle the involvement of Cape Verdeans in the nationalist movement, but does so through the voices of those who had taken part in the action. Lopes had the opportunity to interview a many of the nationalists, some of whom have since died. In the same vein, another source to be taken into account is a book by the Portuguese journalist José Pedro Castanheira, *Quem mandou matar Amílcar Cabral?* Accused of having been written for the purpose of absolving General António Spínola of any responsibility for the events that led to the death of Cabral, Castanheira's book nonetheless contains many details which have become standard in writing on this historical period. He was perhaps not only the first author to discuss in detail the three scenarios for the murder of Cabral, which I develop in the last chapter of this book, but he was also one of the first journalists to get access to the PIDE archives when they became available to the public. A considerable amount of the information is prob-

INTRODUCTION

lematic and unreliable, but Castanheira was able to identify the most relevant parts by examining the system the PIDE used to ascertain the accuracy of the information provided by its collaborators. As such, his book is an antidote to the historical fabrications.

Last but not least, the biography of Cabral produced by Julião Soares Sousa is also worthy of note. Although not much is added to what was already known about Cabral, Sousa has done remarkable work in terms of giving documentary substance to a number of events that researchers on Cabral only hint at. He has been able to clarify a number of outstanding questions about Cabral's life, such as the exact date on which he returned to Cape Verde, the place where he attended school, and, more importantly, Cabral's exact location at the time of the "founding" of the PAIGC. He also provides a wealth of new detail on the resentment between Cape Verdeans and Guineans, which contributed to the climate of conspiracy and helps to explain the killing of Cabral. For the most part, this information can only be found in archives in Portugal and in the private communication between participants in the nationalist struggle. Read it carefully, and one starts to understand the unresolved issues within the movement that led to the assassination of Cabral.

* * *

Amílcar Cabral was born in Guinea on 24 September 1924 to Cape Verdean parents, Juvenal Cabral and Iva Pinhel Évora. When he was eight years old, his family returned to the island of Santiago, where he attended primary school. After completing primary school in Praia, Cabral moved with his mother and siblings (the couple had split up) to the island of São Vicente to receive his secondary education at *Liceu* (high school) Gil Eanes, where he finished top of his class. It was during these years, from 1936 to 1944, that he started writing poetry and essays. Critically, it was also during these years that he was confronted with poverty for the first time. To feed her children, Cabral's mother had two jobs, and Cabral and his siblings were forced to perform odd jobs in order to help at home. The São Vicente years also impacted him on a more dramatic level. Because the Cape Verdean islands were cyclically hit by droughts which killed thousands of people, from an early age Cabral saw people starving to death on the streets. This image remained with him for the rest of his life.

AMÍLCAR CABRAL

After a short stint working for the *Imprensa Nacional* (National Press) in Praia, Cabral was awarded a scholarship to attend college in Portugal. In Lisbon, he enrolled at the *Instituto Superior de Agronomia* in 1945, where he obtained a degree in agronomy and met his colleague Maria Helena Rodrigues, who would become his first wife. But the most important aspect of Cabral's life in Lisbon was the political activism he began to be involved with. In Lisbon, alongside other students from Portuguese colonies in Africa, Cabral was exposed to three themes that would mark him profoundly: *Négritude*, Marxism, and nationalism. He wrote and published poems, led the Cape Verdean section of the *Casa dos Estudantes do Império*, and took part in the first cultural actions against Portuguese colonialism. After finishing his studies in 1952, he moved to Guinea-Bissau, his homeland, to take the job of agronomist at the Pessubé Farm. His most important achievement in Guinea was planning and running the first agronomic census in this former Portuguese territory, which gave him plenty of information on how the economy and particularly agriculture was structured in Guinea. During this period he became cautiously involved in subversive political activities, but none that were a concern at the time for the Portuguese secret police, the PIDE.

He relocated back to Lisbon in 1955 and, still on the payroll of colonial agricultural firms, visited Angola many times, using these opportunities to get involved in the emerging nationalist movement there and to connect nationalists in Angola to those in Europe. As previously mentioned, Cabral has long been looked upon as being committed to the liberation struggle from the very beginning. But his decision to leave everything behind and embrace a clandestine life was not taken lightly. It was made after pressure from his Angolan comrades, namely Viriato da Cruz and Azancot de Menezes, who were crucial in the founding of what would later become the MPLA (see Chapter 4). Nor was he the first nationalist to attempt to rally Guineans in Cape Verde in support of the liberation movement. In fact, when Cabral arrived in neighboring Guinea-Conakry, there were already a number of nationalists, particularly from Guinea-Bissau, campaigning in support of the nationalist president, Ahmed Sékou Touré (see Chapter 5). Having developed his ideas in the diaspora, particularly in Portugal, where he was a founding member of the *Movimento Anti-Colonial*, Cabral tried to unify all the

INTRODUCTION

disparate movements into a single front. As such, Cabral was forced to confront a contentious aspect of Portuguese colonialism on the West Coast: the animosity between Cape Verdeans and Guineans. I will come back to this point, for it is central to the book.

Cabral only became fully committed to the nationalist cause in 1960, when he left Portugal and moved to Guinea-Conakry, just after this French colony had become independent under the leadership of Sékou Touré. He then laid the foundations for the establishment of the PAIGC. In the end, Cabral managed to form his united front, using the PAIGC as an umbrella organization for the many other parties and groups fighting for the same goal. He achieved this in two ways: either by silencing the nationalists who did not agree with him, or by integrating them into the ranks of the PAIGC. One of the consequences of such a strategy was that Cabral ended up bringing the growing anti-Cape Verdean sentiment into the party's daily operations.

In January 1963, Cabral ordered the first military actions against Portuguese units in the interior of the country, an assault on a headquarters in Tite, which marked the beginning of the anticolonial war in Guinea. What happened next, at the Cassacá Congress of February 1964, is a cautionary tale against the rose-tinted depictions of the war in Guinea. Most militants were coming from a major confrontation with the Portuguese army, in Como. Cabral had given the order for his units to abandon the island and to join him in Cassacá for the meeting. It was the first opportunity the guerrilla leaders had to examine their progress so far and prepare for the next steps. A number of changes in the structure of the movement were implemented at the Congress. But these are not the reasons Cassacá became a turning point in the history of the party. It was the first time Cabral was confronted with what he later called negative cultural practices. There were a number of warlords who only wanted to fight to liberate their land, and who, once they acquired power, mirrored all the behaviors associated with it. They took village girls as wives, replaced the tribal chiefs, and killed people accused of witchcraft. A number of these chiefs committed war crimes in the process, and Cabral was left with little choice but to condemn them to death.

I would not go so far as Daniel dos Santos in suggesting that the murder of Cabral, nine years later, was the result of the death sentences he authorized in Cassacá. Rather, I would say that Cassacá brought to center stage the question of culture, by separating those who were defined by their culture, the Guineans, from those who were not, the Cape Verdeans. These problems became even more acute as the number of Cape Verdeans in the ranks of the party increased, particularly after 1966. Most Cape Verdeans who joined the movement were cadres, which means that they were not directly involved in fighting or, exposed to the suffering and deaths of loved ones.

Contrary to a number of guerrilla leaders, Cabral was never convinced that armed struggle would bring independence to Guinea and Cape Verde. He used the armed struggle mostly to draw the attention of the international community to the plight of the Guineans under Portuguese domination and to create the structure of the future independent country. Instead, he viewed diplomacy as the most viable path to liberate his countries. From 1963 to 1973, Cabral undertook intensive political and diplomatic activity, and by the time he was killed by his own men, he was in the process of securing the support of a handful of countries for Guinean and Cape Verdean proclamation of independence.

This book tries to bring together, on the one hand, Cabral's personal trajectory and, on the other, his revolutionary ideals and philosophy as he put them into practice. Identity is the question that unites both points. More than any other nationalist of his time, Cabral was obsessed with a collective examination of identity, an interest which underpins all of his writing on subjects such as culture, ethnicity, and class. More importantly, his whole concept of the reasons behind the emerging national liberation movement derives from his quest for identity. While Guineans up until the start of the anticolonial struggle did not have a clear-cut identity, Cape Verdeans, whose collective evolution is the product of the encounter between the Portuguese and Africans, had been obsessed with the question of identity. The literary and cultural movement, *Claridosos*, in the early 1930s, is a case in point.

Cabral was in a privileged position to understand the contribution of the people of Guinea, or of those from the coast of Africa, to the formation of Cape Verde—even though he downplayed the power dynamics. In his view, the penetration of Guinean elements into the Cape Verdean personality took place in a somewhat horizontal way. In fact, during the colonial period, Cape Verdeans saw themselves,

INTRODUCTION

and were seen by the Portuguese, as superior to the Guineans. This explains the pivotal role Cape Verdeans played in the colonisation of Guinea. The islands were used as a base for the occupation of the West African coast, and, since this part of Africa is one of the most inhospitable on the continent—marked as it is by swampy soil and high temperatures throughout the year—the Portuguese relied heavily on Cape Verdeans to control Guinea. They took an active role in the slave trade, and some were involved in the war against the local rulers which was instrumental for Portugal to assert its sovereignty over that region ahead of the Berlin Conference of 1884–5. Things did not change much when the agreement signed at the Conference gave the Portuguese license to lay the groundwork for the modern colonial state.

The role played by Cape Verdeans in the colonization of Guinea is central to understanding Cabral's revolution, but is often overlooked in most writings on Cabral. At the heart of this question is the relationship between nation-state and empire. Most of the writing on Cabral tends to project our contemporary understanding of the nation-state onto Cabral's time. I prefer to follow the thought of Frederick Cooper and Jane Burbank, for whom the framework of empire may be more appropriate for understanding the processes through which nationalism developed. Cape Verdeans moved through the Portuguese empire as quasi-citizens and played the role of subaltern colonizers in Guinea. Even after the effective occupation of Guinea, Cape Verdeans still filled most of the available positions in the colonial administration. As I discuss in Chapter 1, thousands of Cape Verdeans migrated to Guinea, constituting a sort of middle strata between the Portuguese and the natives. However, Cape Verdeans were not seen as colonized, and had a political status that differed dramatically from that of the natives. Cabral's nationalism, then, was caught up in the zone between the empire and the nation-state. While Cabral strived to form two nation-states, the materials he used to do so were salvaged from the wreckage of empire, in that the relationship between Cape Verdeans and Guineans was a by-product of Portuguese colonialism.

Ultimately, Marxism may have provided Cabral with a way out of the abyss. Firstly, Cabral saw colonialism as an ideology, one that masked social reality itself. People were not conscious of their own predicament, but they could be made to understand it, hence the role of the national liberation movement. Secondly, Cabral understood culture, ethnicity, and class as the products of objective reality—the superstructure, in Marxian terms—and if one changed objective reality, culture, ethnicity, and class would change in line with it. To accomplish this, Cabral thought that if Cape Verdeans were made to experience the same kind of ordeal to which Guineans had been subjected, they would be able to understand the real nature of colonialism. But the war was never extended to the Island of Cape Verde, which created a major problem within the liberation movement.

The lack of ideological clarity was compensated for by the care given to matters of war. Cabral did remarkable work in terms of adapting a counterinsurgent methodology to the physical conditions of Guinea itself, as I discuss in detail in Chapter 5. Guinea did not have mountains (traditionally the sanctuary of guerrilla fighters), but it had dense forests, where freedom fighters focused much of their war effort. But Cabral himself was not a combatant, and never entertained the prospect of solving the colonial question by a military victory over the colonial army. Instead, he overestimated the importance of the role of the international community in contributing to the independence of Guinea. While Cabral was making the case for Guinea's sovereignty, the party was engaged in creating state-like structures in the liberated zones. However, the long years that the war took to reach its final phase became a problem, affecting the morale of the combatants and creating enough justification for a conspiracy against Cabral's leadership.

This in turn led to the events of the night of 20 January 1973, in Conakry, the capital city of Guinea, during which Amílcar Cabral, the fighter for the national liberation of Guinea and Cape Verde, was brutally assassinated. The direct perpetrators of this act were his own men, militants of the African Party for the Independence of Guinea and Cape Verde (PAIGC), the party he himself had founded. Unconfirmed suspicions regarding the assassination of Cabral have pointed to a more elaborate and complex plot, involving different branches of the Portuguese army and secret police which, since the beginning of the armed struggle in 1963, had shown a particular interest in decapitating the leadership of the PAIGC as a way to solve the conflict in this then-Portuguese territory.

INTRODUCTION

By the time of his physical elimination, Cabral was hailed as the most serious African revolutionary. This was not only because of his military successes, but due to the administration of the territories recently liberated from the yoke of Portuguese colonialism. Particular attention was given to social areas such as health and education, and the establishment of state structures such as justice, commerce and so on, internationally raising hopes for the future of Guinea once fully liberated from Portuguese colonialism. Cabral's travails, it has to be noted, were taking place against the backdrop of the emergence of what is now retrospectively called Afro-pessimism, when the dream of an independent Africa had veered off course into mismanagement, coup d'états, and ethnic cleansing.

The interplay of three factors—an unresolved assassination, the everyday aspects of an African revolution, and the unfulfilled revolutionary hopes—account for the vivid interest that Cabral has elicited since his assassination. This explains the deluge of works on Cabral and the revolution in Guinea. I have written this book not so much as a scholar, but as someone who was born and came of age in a world in which the emergence of Cabral's theory on decolonization was instrumental.

* * *

I was born in Luanda in the same year in which Cabral was killed, 1973. The revolutionary ideals he championed were shared by his Angolan *compagnons de route*, such as Viriato da Cruz, Mário Pinto de Andrade, Lúcio Lara, and Agostinho Neto. The independence of their countries, Guinea in 1973 and Cape Verde and Angola in 1975, could then be seen as the realization of the emancipationist dreams they had been shaping in the late 1940s and early 1950s in Lisbon, where Cabral's generation had politically come of age. Socialism was chosen as the path for progress and modernity and the same mindset that had been applied during the struggle for independence was transposed to the nation-building. Freedom was limited, the ruling party was the purveyor of the people's aspirations and political dissidents, if not killed, were exiled. The party had in a way replaced the church, and those who dared to challenge its mystifications could expect harsh punishment. During my upbringing, for example, the history of the party, particularly the date its founding, could not be questioned. Those who did, such as the Angolan historian Carlos Pacheco, could only do so from the position of relative security that their exile provided.

When I came of age, particularly when I travelled to Lisbon (Lisbon, again, where everything started), I came to realize that there was a huge discrepancy between the rose-tinted descriptions of the road to independence and what had actually happened. In Portugal, archival documents were being declassified, and the Portuguese, after decades of silence, were finally coming to terms with the trauma of decolonization. The new interpretations of decolonization made me consider the disjuncture between how liberation was celebrated in our countries and the actual events.

In other words, my upbringing in Angola, and the fact that I have come to consider the legacy of and literature on Cabral from this point of view, makes it all the more difficult for me to reconcile events and their presentation. This sentiment was shared by many Cape Verdeans and Guineans of my generation whom I befriended in Lisbon. Portuguese colonialism was evil, but the promise of independence had not been fulfilled. For the Guineans, the ethnic strife that Cabral unsuccessfully tried to resolve had become the glue of the nation-state. And most Cape Verdeans, who had not wished to secede from Portugal, were left with an independence for which they did not fight.

My intention is neither to blindly celebrate the political achievements of these historical figures nor to make them solely to blame for the mishaps that occurred in their country after they were gone.

Instead, this is an attempt to retrospectively reconstruct what would have occurred if the actions shaping the anticolonial struggle were not based on propaganda, but on something closer to the truth. What kind of description of the past can be produced if one disregards propaganda in favor of the real events?

One final point on the notes. I have decided to write this book without inundating it with footnotes, which tempt the reader to interrupt the flow of the narrative to look up particular references. To meet the rigorous standards required by such a book, however, I have pushed all the references to the end in a section called "Notes." This section is intended to provide the exact location the citations are taken from as

INTRODUCTION

well as comments on the bibliography used and contextual information for understanding particular historical aspects discussed in the book.

Finally, I could not conclude this introduction without acknowledgement of the support I was given in order to carry out this project. I am grateful to Mahmood Mamdani, who took a special interest in this project, and who, through the Makerere Institute of Social Research in Uganda, offered me a stipend that allowed me to start working on this book. Being based in South Africa, far from the libraries with the necessary resources for this project, I was forced to rely on a number of people who helped me acquire a vast amount of information, including Luciana Dias, Eurídice Monteiro, Fernando Pereira, Tchiloia Lara, through the Fundação Tchiweka, and Pedro Cerejo.

I am equally grateful to a number of friends, colleagues, and institutions who have invited me to speak on Cabral in the years since the publication of the Portuguese version of this book (*O Fazedor de Utopias: Uma biografia de Amílcar Cabral*). Among these people and institutions, I am particularly grateful to Manuela Ribeiro Sanches, José Neves, Marta Lança, Paolo Israel, Ciraj Rassool, the Center for Humanities Research at the University of Western Cape, and João Rapazote and Manthia Diawara, with the programme AFRICA.CONT (*Câmara Municipal de Lisboa*). I am also particularly grateful to the Stellenbosch Institute for Advanced Studies whose fellowship allowed me to work on the final preparations of the manuscript. STIAS's staff, particularly Cristoff Pauw, Nel-Mari Loock and the director, Edward Kirumira, have helped immensely in creating the perfect environment to fully commit to this project, helping me in every possible way. Last but not least, I am also deeply grateful to my family, particularly my in-laws, who have taken on some of the burdens of childcare over the years. This manuscript has also benefited from the careful attention of my lovely wife, Sylvia Croese, who alongside her own work, and other commitments, found time to revise sections of this book and to check a number of facts. Without her constant love and support, I would not have been able to write this book.

1

BETWEEN GUINEA AND CAPE VERDE

Ever since the "discovery" by the Portuguese of the African territory that would later be called Guinea, and throughout the following centuries, this country on the western coast of Africa was, in the imagination of the Cape Verdeans, the land of opportunities and daring deeds. Hemmed in by the narrow horizons of the poor islands, most Cape Verdeans sought to trade with the natives. In Guinea, at least, they did not have to compete with the Portuguese who, because of the climate, rarely stayed there for long periods of time. Most, particularly in the early days of colonization, were *lançados*, or settlers, made up of Jews—New Christians—and others of African origin such as Senegambians (mostly from present day Senegal) and Sierra Leoneans. By the late nineteenth century, Cape Verdeans had largely become the de facto colonizers of Guinea. Cape Verdeans, or Guineans of Cape Verdean origin, such as Honório Barreto, guaranteed the sovereignty of the Portuguese crown by signing treaties with the local potentates, according to agreements reached by the colonial powers at the 1885 Berlin Conference. Cape Verdeans played an active part in the occupation campaigns. When they were not leading the African battalions themselves, they fought side by side with the Portuguese heroes of the occupations such as Teixeira Pinto. Since these wars were fought with commendable bravery on the part of the Africans, Guinea only became a subjugated territory in the mid-1930s, when the last pacification campaign in Canhabaque was completed.

The involvement of Cape Verdeans in the business of Guinea stemmed from the juridical status of this territory itself. Since the arrival of the Portuguese, the Governor of Cape Verde also oversaw Guinea's affairs from his headquarters in the Island of Santiago. As such, Guinea was formally a colony of a colony. In practice, however, Guinea was administered by the "luzitanized blacks and mestizo traffickers, from Cape Verde." But this state of affairs was soon to change. In December 1878, after a massacre of Cape Verdean soldiers in Bolor, in the aftermath of skirmishes with the *felupes*, the Portuguese political authorities decided to separate Guinea from Cape Verde. On 18 March 1879, in a letter signed by Fontes Pereira de Melo, president of the council, Portuguese Guinea was formally established, and, as a Portuguese overseas territory, would go on to have the right, in the language of the epoch, to its own resident governor and a locally published government gazette.

However, in spite of this legal arrangement, Cape Verdeans kept "colonizing" Guinea. Much of this was due to the fact that the *lingua franca* in Guinea had been created by the Cape Verdeans, testament to the major role of the these islanders in the everyday life of Guinea—unique in the colonial system. For instance, in territory controlled by the Portuguese, colonization hinged for the most part on the emergence of a culturally assimilated group operating between the insignificant number of whites and the large masses of the colonized. In Angola, or Mozambique, they were called *assimilados*—assimilated. In Guinea, however, this was not the case. Cape Verdeans had inserted and established themselves as this intermediary group. By diffusing their own Creole, they became an indispensable link between the Portuguese and the natives.

In this way, Cape Verdeans took hold of the entire life of the province. They made up a large part of the military units and occupied the majority of the posts in public administration. This arrangement, which prevented the emergence of a native elite, suited the Portuguese and the Cape Verdeans alike. Portugal could rely on subaltern colonizers, whose physical characteristics responded better to the demands of the climate, without having the need to send white colonizers to the region. Cape Verde had in Guinea a way to deal with the population surplus or, at least, a way to find a balance between the size of the population and the available food resources. As a school system had developed very early on in the archipelago, many Cape Verdeans were well educated and, with very few opportunities in their own homeland, most of them were forced to migrate. The destinations were either in the New World, in places such as the United States of America and Argentina, or in the Portuguese colonies, such as Angola and Mozambique. However, until the 1950s, Guinea was the most important receiving country for migrants from Cape Verde, before destinations such as France and Metropolitan Portugal became more common.

* * *

Like thousands of other Cape Verdeans, Cabral's parents migrated to Guinea in the first quarter of the century. His mother was born in Santiago on 31 December 1893. She was the daughter of António Pinhel Évora and Maximiana Monteiro da Rocha, both from Santiago. In 1922, at the age of 29, she migrated to Guinea alongside her partner, João Carvalho Silva, and their nine-month-old baby, Ivo Carvalho Silva. Cabral's father, Juvenal, worked for the colonial state and wrote a couple of books full of personal information, which makes the task of tracing his life story far easier.

Juvenal Cabral was born on 2 January 1889, on the Island of Santiago, in Praia, shortly after the death of his father, António Lopes da Costa, at the time a student at the Catholic seminary on the island of São Nicolau. Before da Costa's death, he gave Juvenal Cabral's godmother, Simôa dos Reis Borges, a monetary sum of 600,000 *réis* to cover the costs of his son's education from primary school to priesthood, based on a monthly fee at the seminary of no more than 10,000 *réis*. However, Juvenal Cabral's talents did not blossom in the first years of his life, and few members of his family believed that he was cut out for the priesthood. With Juvenal still unable to speak Portuguese by the age of nine, he went to a village in Beira Alta called Cassurães, where he started his primary education. Eventually, he was enrolled at the seminary at Viseu, alongside a number of other students who would later become very important in Portuguese politics—among them, António de Oliveira Salazar.

Juvenal did not spend enough time in the seminary of Viseu to be ordained as a priest. When drought hit the archipelago, Simôa dos Reis

Borges found herself without the funds to support the education of her godson. Juvenal Cabral was therefore summoned back to Cape Verde in 1907, at the age of 18. He then enrolled at the seminary of São Nicolau, at that time the only education establishment in Cape Verde that granted high-school diplomas. In this way, he became part of the intellectual elite of Cape Verde, who, while having studied at the seminary, did not aspire to the priestly life. This institution trained the vast majority of the clerks who filled positions in the colonial administration of the archipelago, or those who later would go on to work in Guinea or further afield in countries such as Angola and Mozambique.

In the seminary of São Nicolau, Juvenal Cabral jeopardized his final chance to become a priest after being involved in a brawl with a colleague from Guinea. The punishment for this act was not outright expulsion: if he accepted a caning, he could make amends for his bad behavior. However, even when offered the option of taking the beating in private, he refused the punishment. Expelled from the seminary, he lost his one opportunity to obtain a high-school diploma, which would have given him the qualifications needed to apply for a highly sought-after government job in Cape Verde.

Deprived of the possibility of a job in Cape Verde at the level of his personal and social expectations, Juvenal Cabral was left with no other choice but to go to Guinea. In 1911, at the age of 22, he arrived at the most under-developed colony of the Portuguese empire. Only in the 1920s had the Portuguese started to set up public infrastructure, such as proper roads. The reason for this was that even the most reformist of governors such as Jorge Frederico Velez Caroço did not deem this sort of thing a priority. At the time, Guinea was a colony in a permanent state of war, which forced Velez Caroço to spend a great deal of his time and resources on organizing campaigns to "pacify the natives."

It has not been possible to establish exactly when the parents of Cabral first met. What is known is that Iva Évora was romantically involved with Cabral's father, Juvenal, shortly after arriving in Guinea in 1922. Amílcar Cabral was born on 24 September 1924, in the parish of Nossa Senhora da Graça, and only later, probably in 1926, did Juvenal leave his wife Ernestina Soares de Andrade, and join his new family. Although the birth of his first son with Iva was celebrated with some pomp—he gave him the name Amílcar, in homage to Hamilcar Barca, the Carthaginian hero who fought against the Romans—it is not recorded in his memoir, written a couple of years later. However, his account of his journey through Bafatá, where Amílcar was born, provides an interesting point of contrast between his life and that of his son. On the banks of the rivers Geba and Colufi, he writes, the noblewoman of Fá—a black woman from Biafada, hungry for civilization and madly in love—had "given" herself to the Cape Verdean José Valério. Through the symbolism of this sexual act, the Portuguese entered into possession of these territories through the mediation of the Cape Verdeans. A staunch defender of the colonization of Guinea by the Portuguese, Juvenal was far from dreaming that two of his sons, Amílcar and Luís Cabral, would later lead the movement to free Guinea and Cape Verde from colonial domination. But here, as in many other movements, the myth would be kept alive: to them, Guinea would continue to be the land of daring deeds.

In Guinea, Juvenal Cabral had to wait a number of years until he could stabilize his professional situation. Finding jobs was never particularly difficult for him; the problem, due to his temper, was keeping them. He worked in a number of public offices, until he was finally hired at customs, under the directorship of César Correia Pinto, who is described, in Juvenal's memoir, as a fearsome man, a dictator who expected blind obedience from his subordinates. Juvenal could not last long there, even if it were a great loss for him. In colonies such Guinea, which depended heavily on the export of primary goods such as groundnuts, and imported a great deal of finished goods, the customs office was the nerve center of economic life, providing clerks many opportunities to supplement their salaries.

According to what Juvenal Cabral wrote later in his memoir, he left customs because of disagreements with Correia Pinto. His explanations delve into psychology: not having had a father and raised by women who had spoiled him had perhaps contributed to his aversion to any form of authority. But Juvenal Cabral's departure from customs may have been motivated by other events. Cabral had never hidden his admiration for Teixeira Pinto, the "pacifier" of Guinea, who had not hesitated to commit atrocities in order to achieve his goals. If he had kept his praise for Pinto to his close friends, this may not have had any consequences. But Juvenal Cabral made his appreciation public in a newspaper article published in the *Voz de Cabo Verde*. When copies of the newspaper started circulating in Bissau, Juvenal Cabral became the target of insults and threats. He was even asked to write a piece denying the content of his despicable editorial, as many people had deemed it. Pressure was mounting from group of Guineans whose economic positions were improving and who were competing socially with the Cape Verdeans in the colonial administration. These events made Juvenal Cabral's position in the customs office untenable.

With his resignation from customs, Juvenal was forced to accept a modest position as a primary school teacher, which he started in 1913. His first appointment was in the village of Cacine, teaching a class of only six pupils, which, not giving him enough to do, allowed him spare time to read, write, and do some gardening, providing him with a "precious supplement to his meagre salary." In the following years, he was transferred to many schools, in various districts of the colony, such as Bafatá, where Amílcar Cabral was born. His last stop was in Bissau, the capital of the colony, where he and Adelina Correia (another goddaughter of Simôa dos Reis Borges), although unable to attend the wedding in person, were finally married by proxy. This arrangement allowed him to bring forward his retirement in 1932, and to return to Cape Verde as one of the heirs of Simôa dos Reis Borges, who had recently passed away.

It is often said that children inherit character traits from their parents. If this is true, Juvenal had passed some of his to Amílcar. The most interesting of them is perhaps a naïve belief in the power of writing. For both of them, the act of writing was part of the solution to every problem. Those who knew Amílcar Cabral in Conakry remember that he spent part of the war there writing: communiqués, memoranda, letters to various members of the party, essays, and reports on the war situation. In the days before his assassination, he wrote a long document describing in meticulous detail the supposed plan orchestrated by the PIDE (*Polícia Internacional e de Defesa do Estado*) for his physical elimination and the expulsion of Cape Verdeans from the liberation movement. For Cabral, it was as if the mere act of writing about this plot, making his men conscious of such danger, would ward off the possibility of his own death.

BETWEEN GUINEA AND CAPE VERDE

For different reasons, Juvenal Cabral had the same relationship with writing. He wrote a number of articles for newspapers and letters to governors, for example, in which he called attention to the problems of drought and the recurrent food crises in Cape Verde and the ways to definitively solve them. However, Juvenal's epistolary activism was based on a different understanding of colonialism to that of his son. When Amílcar Cabral wrote to Salazar in 1960 to propose negotiations for the independence of Guinea and Cape Verde, for example, he was under the firm conviction that the days of Portguese rule in Africa were numbered. Juvenal Cabral, for his part, believed throughout his life that the biggest problems in Guinea and Cape Verde were caused by the insufficient action of Portuguese colonialism, especially in the domain of education. As such, the appointment of his hero, Salazar, as president of the council was a sort of confirmation that God had listened to his prayers.

* * *

Juvenal Cabral was not the only person in continental Portugal or its overseas dependencies who saw the appointment of António de Oliveira Salazar as an act of divine intervention. In the 1920s, Portugal was going through one of its darkest hours since the proclamation of the Republic in 1910. The country could find no way to balance its public finances and was spending far more than it could produce. These days were marked by political instability, which made it impossible to implement major reforms with long-term effects. For many politicians, and for a large section of the population, only a dictatorial regime could rescue the country from this state of affairs. Consequently, (or at least according to Salazar's successor Marcello Caetano), the military coup of 28 May 1926 was enthusiastically celebrated by much of the population, with the ousting of the liberals generally received with relief rather than shock.

The general to whom the military gave the Presidency of the Republic, Óscar Carmona, invited the prominent Coimbra professor António de Oliveira Salazar to be part of the government. However, he only formally accepted the invitation on 27 April 1928—a month after the presidential elections—after much hesitation and going back and forth. Salazar had been invited as a consensus figure: he was respected by the military, and he was part of Catholic and monarchical circles. More importantly, he was a professor at the most highly regarded university in the country, Coimbra, and a renowned specialist in the academic field of public finance. He would apply a simple formula for governance: a close control over foreign debt and a balanced budget should be the conditions for repairing the public accounts. He would only accept a position in the government if given "veto power for every expenditure of all ministries and vast powers to undertake budget cuts and the fiscal reforms necessary to balance the budget."

Although he was officially the minister of finances, Salazar, in practice, controlled the entire government. He had not been appointed prime minister yet, since some high-ranking members of the military firmly believed that a civilian could not lead a military regime. This hurdle was easily overcome when a group of officials, among them Humberto Delgado, convinced the president of the republic to distinguish Salazar with a *Grã-Cruz da Ordem Militar da Torre e Espada*—never before given to a civilian—which was the equivalent of being made a general. He was given this medal on 28 May 1932 when rumors were circulating that a constitutional reform to end the military regime was underway. In July of that year, Salazar was appointed president of the council, a position he would hold until 1968.

In his plan to stabilize public finances, Salazar had proposed a revolutionary step: the integration of the economies of the colonies in the survival strategies of the regime itself. In those times, in fact, most people in Portugal did not know exactly what to do with the colonies. For centuries, since the arrival of the Portuguese in Africa, these territories had produced an economic surplus thanks to the slave trade. However, with the end of the slave trade in the first quarter of the nineteenth century, the Portuguese colonies became more a source of expenditure than income. At the end of the nineteenth century, for instance, various writers and thinkers, such as the famous writer Eça de Queiroz, argued that the territories Portugal held in Africa should be sold. There were plenty of reasons for such calls. In the first quarter of the twentieth century, the economic crisis that ravaged the colonies seemed almost unsolvable. Inflation was very high, and even the *Banco Nacional Ultramarino* (National Overseas Bank), created in 1864 in order to solve the crises arising from economic stagnation in the colonies, began offering credit and *moeda fiduciária* (paper money) which worsened the situation. The bank was forced numerous times to suspend the transfer of funds from the colonies to the metropole, making the currencies that circulated in Africa not convertible into Portuguese *escudos*. This in turn meant that settlers in Africa could not redeem their remittances in Portuguese currency.

Salazar came to power profoundly motivated to change the economic arena in the colonies. He applied the same recipe he had used to solve the budgetary problems of continental Portugal: financial balance and cutting excess spending. In terms of colonial policy, as the historian Alan K. Smith has stated, Salazar would prefer "stability rather than growth," even to the extent of damaging Portuguese interests in the colonies. The best way to achieve stability was to put an end to the experiment of decentralization, tested out in the last years of the Republic, and to integrate the colonies into the Portuguese economy. He occupied himself with this project during his tenure as minister of the colonies from January 1930 to July 1931. To realize this vision, he worked on the drafting and approval of the *Acto Colonial* (Colonial Act), the piece of legislation which would thereafter govern the integration of Portugal and its colonies. The document stipulates that "possessing colonies" is a historical function and part of the "organic essence" of the Portuguese. The Colonial Act would introduce tighter control over the colonies by the metropole, with Lisbon taking on a number of prerogatives that in the past were under the jurisdiction of the local administration—namely foreign investment, immigration, and employment.

With the promulgation of the Colonial Act, Portugal not only furthered its isolation from the rest of the world, but began to sail against the winds of history. WWI had been a victory against imperialism, and from the ashes of a decimated Europe emerged a new international order, championed by the Americans, particularly the Wilson administration. Having never had traditional colonies, America was striving to secure a world without the fetters of the empire. Politicians from countries such as India, China and Egypt took part in the Peace Conference in 1919 to protect people's right to self-determination. Bowing to their pressure, colonial powers such as England and France started transforming their presence in Africa into regimes of tutelage, and, by the end of 1945, preparing most of the territories they controlled for self-determination. With the Colonial Act, Portugal was attempting to make the case that the territories in Africa under its administration were not colonies, but rather "overseas domains."

The thinking of Salazar and his collaborators, in drawing up the Colonial Act, was based on social Darwinism. For them, humanity was divided into hierarchical categories, with the white/Western man at the top. Armindo Monteiro, one of the most prominent ideologues of Portuguese colonialism, who replaced Salazar as minister of the colonies (in this post from 1931–35), thought that "a great part of black societies, across the African continent, were immobile within [the] old structures of organization," and that the white man had to act fast in order to save these societies from death. For Monteiro, civilization was a long slope, at the top of which only the most skillful society could arrive. As the march of progress was unstoppable, natural selection would run its course. In a dozen or so years, he triumphantly added, the black races which could not scale the slopes of civilization would be wiped from the earth. Salvation was, then, reserved for the races that were able to "understand beauty and discipline and to be subject to them; the races that in the empire will learn how to be Portuguese and who already consider themselves as such."

This mindset had seeped into the infamous *Estatuto do Indígenato* (the Statute of Indigenous Populations). The indigenous, as Adriano Moreira argued, were a category of natives who were not citizens, for they lacked the "erudition and customs" to distinguish them from the masses of the black race. This "deficiency" meant that they could be put to any use which the colonial state thought to be fitting. The view was that just being born was a debt to the state which required paying a tax, also known as an *impost de palhota* (hut tax). Since most indigenous people did not have access to currency, the payment of this tax was made through labor. Although according to the law only the state could recruit laborers under this arrangement, in actual fact a high number of colonial administrators were delivering forced laborers to private enterprises. For example, the thousands of Mozambicans who were sent to mines in South Africa each year were only paid part of their salaries. The other part was paid in gold by the

BETWEEN GUINEA AND CAPE VERDE

South Africans directly to the *Banco de Portugal* (Bank of Portugal). These practices were denounced by international institutions, including the League of Nations and the International Labour Organization (ILO). What the Portuguese, in the words of Salazar, deemed a legitimate way of "civilizing" Africans, was to rest of the western world outright slavery.

Salazar made cheap labor the cornerstone of his economy. The rationale behind such an arrangement was that production costs for primary goods would be significantly lower if the cost of labor was reduced to a bare minimum. Industry in continental Portugal could benefit from cheaper access to colonial products, such as cotton. These products were either converted into manufactured goods in the industries of continental Portugal, or they were simply re-exported. And because of mercantilist laws which increased tariffs on products not made in Portugal, such as clothing, shoes and wine, Portuguese industry had a guaranteed market. But these measures were not enough for Salazar. To close the cycle of exchange between continental Portugal and its colonies, he had to undermine the development of the latter: as late as the 1960s, for example, there were still laws in place which prohibited the setup of certain industries in Africa "while [...] Portuguese [counterparts] did not reach their full capacity." In this way, the *Estado Novo* and the colonization of Africa were so intertwined that the destruction of one, as Cabral would note, would mean the destruction of the other.

* * *

Notwithstanding his rebelliousness, Juvenal Cabral was a man of principle and politically conservative ideals. One of his lifelong habits, which he claimed to have done both in Guinea and in Cape Verde, was to attend the inaugural speeches of colonial governors. Even if he would criticize colonial governors in his letters and newspaper articles for their unfulfilled promises, his way of thinking did not diverge from the general lines of the colonial policy of Portugal. He spoke Portuguese with great care, a language, in his opinion, that should be taught to all natives of Portuguese colonies in Africa. Although he himself ended up writing a book of poems in Creole, *Confissões de Zé Badiu*, he didn't encourage his children to speak in Creole, which he consid-

27

ered to be "fragments of an archaic Portuguese, perverted, having mixed with many barbaric words."

There is no doubt that Juvenal Cabral deeply influenced his son Amílcar, something that is emphasized by almost every person who has written on Cabral, including Mário de Andrade, Oleg Ignatiev and his own brother Luís Cabral. Luís Cabral writes that Juvenal was instrumental in Amílcar's decision to study agronomy. At one point, according to Luís, when Amílcar was vacillating between studying law and studying agronomy, his father convinced him that, given the natural conditions of the archipelago, an agronomist had far more social importance than a lawyer. However, none of those who wrote on Cabral—with the exception of Mário de Andrade—have referred to the even more decisive influence of Iva Pinhel Évora in Cabral's formative years. She was the one who, in the words of Mário de Andrade, bore the weight of protecting "her sons against the adversity of fortune."

In 1932, when Juvenal Cabral returned to Cape Verde with his wife and their newborn son Luís, he also brought with him his first three children from his relationship with Iva: Amílcar, and the twin sisters Arminda and Armanda. Iva had stayed behind in Guinea with her youngest son, António. But this was not due to any desire to stay: only days before she had been due to depart for Cape Verde, she had been robbed, losing every penny of the savings she had accrued through years of managing a guesthouse. It was only after two years of buying and fattening up pigs to sell their meat that she was able to save enough money for the boat ticket to Cape Verde.

On her return to Cape Verde, she was shocked to realize that Juvenal Cabral had not taken good care of the education of their sons. Amílcar, for instance, was ten years old and had not yet started primary school. As the relationship between Amílcar's parents deteriorated, Iva faced more and more difficulties in visiting her children. Pedro Monteiro, a contemporary of Amílcar, remembers that his grandparents often made their house available for Iva to meet her children, interceding with Juvenal Cabral to allow her to visit them. Eventually, on one visit to her children, Iva Évora took the decision to bring them back with her, after discovering that Amílcar had seriously injured one of his eyes while playing, an accident which almost cost him his vision.

With this decision, she took full responsibility for providing for the children. Besides feeding and clothing them, she also had to provide school materials, which, in Amílcar's case, was particularly challenging. In 1936, at the age of twelve, Cabral finally started his studies and finished primary school in one academic year. In October 1936, he was enrolled in first grade, transferred to second grade in January, and finished third and fourth grade before the end of the academic year. In the following academic year of 1937/38, he was already a student at the *Liceu* Gil Eanes.

Financial responsibilities became even more onerous for Iva Évora after Amílcar Cabral started high school, even though he was already contributing to expenses at home by running errands, peddling and, later on, tutoring students of the *Liceu*, including some of his own classmates. However, since Iva had few resources, it is probable that Amílcar Cabral would never have attended the *Liceu* had the educational situation in Cape Verde not changed substantially since the time of Juvenal Cabral. In the decree that abolished the Seminary of São Nicolau, in 1917, the *Liceu* Cape Verde was created (later becoming the *Liceu* Gil Eanes). While keeping sons in the seminary at São Nicolau had required the regular sending of money, as we have seen in the case of Cabral's father, the creation of the *Liceu* in São Vicente made access to education more democratic. From then on, families with less money could not only send their sons, as was the case for the seminary, but also their daughters to school, without being deprived of domestic help.

The democratization of education was not the main goal of creating the school in São Vicente. The initial idea was to abolish the seminary and to use the same facilities for the *Liceu*. However, the decision was later taken to transfer the *Liceu* to São Vicente. This turned out to be a good decision which ultimately benefitted everyone involved. São Vicente had a port, which, although falling into progressive decline because of the end of steamers, was the most cosmopolitan place of the whole archipelago. São Vicente was visited by sailors from all over the world, and it was the main point of entry for foreign newspapers, magazines and books. Unlike the seminary, according to Henrique Teixeira de Sousa, the *Liceu* benefitted from its insertion in the city as it offered students access to an intense academic life. To be a student in the *Liceu* was also to be a member of student associations and to have the opportunity to take part in various sports and cultural activities.

Liceu Gil Eanes was a colonial landmark in terms of education. This was not necessarily because it was the first of similar institutions to be founded in the colonies. The *Liceu* of Luanda, for instance, was founded only a year later in 1918. The major difference was that, whereas in the *Liceus* of Goa, Macau, Mozambique, and Angola the instructors and students were for the most part civilians and military staff from continental Portugal and their sons, almost all of them white, in the *Liceu* Gil Eanes, instructors and students were black and mixed-race (i.e. they were natives of Cape Verde).

In order for her children to study at the *Liceu*—above all Amílcar, whose results in the first years of school showed that he had academic potential—Iva Évora moved her family to São Vicente at the end of 1937. To provide for her family, she worked in a fish-canning factory, where she made the miserable amount of five *tostões* per hour (one *tostão* was a *hundredth* of the *escudo*). But her work there was temporary and she often had to work throughout the night on her sewing machine to bring in extra income to stave off her family's hunger, according to Mário Pinto de Andrade.

During these years, Juvenal Cabral, even if he wanted to, could do very little to support his family. When he became the owner of the property left by his godmother, Simôa dos Reis Borges, on his return to the native land, he built a beautiful mansion in Achada Santa Catarina, with tiles imported from continental Portugal—something that back then very few Cape Verdeans could afford. But this opulent lifestyle could not last, and it was not long before Juvenal Cabral found himself on the verge of bankruptcy. Contributing to this were the regular droughts in Cape Verde, along with his habit of lending money with no guarantees of it being paid back, and his womanizing tendencies. After taking out a number of loans, for which he had to use his property as collateral, he lost his house in Achada. He spent the last years of his life in Praia, in a house too small for the size of his household.

To make his financial situation even worse, Juvenal Cabral was also caught up in a legal case dating back to his time in Guinea. In the school of Bissau, besides teaching, he had also been responsible for the school fund and managing the books. Several times he helped a colleague, a woman from Madeira called Maria Baptista da Câmara, when she, for personal reasons, needed to use these funds. Once, when he needed to send his sick wife Adelina and son Luís to Portugal, where they would receive better treatment, he himself was forced to use the school funds. Later on, according to his own account, he replaced the deducted sum, paying the last installment of 8,500 *escudos* on his return to Cape Verde. However, Maria Baptista da Câmara did not return the documents he had signed when the taking out the sum. Twelve years after leaving Guinea, in 1944, his friend successfully sued him. From then on, Juvenal Cabral had fifty-three *escudos* deducted from his monthly salary of 160 *escudos*, corresponding to one third of his retirement fund.

* * *

Despite having to work to pay for his own studies and help the family, these financial difficulties did not affect Cabral's school performance. During his time at the *Liceu*, he was always among the best students. After finishing fifth grade, he chose to study the sciences, finishing the course in 1944 with an average mark of seventeen—exceptional at that time in the *Liceu*.

Despite his busy schedule, Amílcar Cabral still found time for intellectual stimulation and growth. It was during these years that he wrote his first poems. He put together two notebooks of verses called *Nos Intervalos da Arte da Minerva* [In the Intervals of the Art of Minerva] and *Quando o Cupido Acerta o Alvo* [When Cupid Hits the Target], only posthumously edited, which, as Cabral wrote in the preface of the first notebook, were the "product of a fleeting inspiration, the echo of the voice of a lyre which, played in the intervals of studies, tries to utter a parcel of the feelings of a young heart from a younger generation." In the first of the notebooks, there is also a preface in the form of a letter to a friend which reads: "if today I dare in an almost unconscious act to put my unpretentious poems under the tenebrous wings of the critic, I can't fail to register at the top of the first sheet of my book, as epitome, the following words: for you friend of good and bad times, only to you I have to explain, for the courage you gave me, for the effective support you gave me concerning my literary career (vanity?)." The identity of the person to whom these words are addressed has never been established.

Although a number of commentators claim to have detected political intentions in the poetry of Amílcar Cabral—long before they were to take solid form in nationalistic protest—Cabral never engaged in poetry-writing with any more devotion than other young people of his age. This is the conclusion reached by scholars such as Patrick Chabal, who writes that Cabral's poetry, in its subject matter and form, cannot be told apart from that of other Cape Verdeans of his generation. This is one reason why analyses of the history of Cape Verdean poetry do not include Cabral as a member of any one group: he was too young to be a member of the *Claridosos*, and he did not join the poetic movement of his contemporaries at Gil Eanes—such as Nuno Miranda, Arnaldo Santos, Guilherme Rocheteau, and Tomás Miranda—who founded the publication *Certeza*. This may be explained by his attitude towards poetry, which he saw as a vehicle, an instrument through which political and social ideas could flow. Later on, in Lisbon, he would criticize the Cape Verdean poets for their escapist tendencies and for not taking up contemporary social and political issues. And, perhaps inspired by his friends in Lisbon—poets such as Agostinho Neto and Alda do Espírito Santo, who were trying to fuse poetry and politics—he yearned for a Cape Verde where poets would adhere to Neo-realism, so that they could walk "hand in hand with the people, with their feet nailed to the land."

After completing his secondary studies, Amílcar Cabral, his mother and siblings, returned to Praia. In Praia, Amílcar was hired by *Imprensa Nacional*, as an assistant typographer. He hated the experience for two reasons. Firstly, the work was extremely bureaucratic; and secondly, on account of his vanity, he did not respond well to his writing being corrected by senior officials.

His passage through the *Imprensa Nacional* was only temporary, while he waited for an opportunity to pursue college education in Lisbon. In 1945, he obtained a scholarship and the same year he said goodbye to everyone and moved to Lisbon to study agronomy. At the age of 21, he was already an experienced man and marked by life: a rocky childhood in Guinea and an adolescence full of sacrifices and challenges in Cape Verde. He had already seen people dying of hunger in the streets of Praia. In Lisbon, exchanging experiences with other young people from the Portuguese colonies, Amílcar was to discover the causes to which he would dedicate the rest of his life.

2

THE YEARS IN LISBON

The famine crises which periodically ravaged Cape Verde, killing thousands of people, were of a political, rather than purely geographical, character. This, at least, was an idea on which the majority of Cape Verdean intellectuals at the turn of the century agreed. To put it another way, for them it was a lack of political will, rather than the scarcity of rain or the uneven geographical terrain in some parts of the archipelago—which caused rainwater to run into the sea instead of accumulating in the subsoil—that directly explained the crises. The correct policy was therefore to focus on taking appropriate preventative measures, such as constructing granaries for the storage of agricultural surpluses and dams and tanks for a more efficient use of rainwater. Correct policies should also coordinate the delivery of aid if drought is ultimately unavoidable.

Cape Verdeans, perhaps more than other people, had a good understanding of the relationship between politics and life, or, to put it otherwise, the lifesaving effect that good policies could have. But this relationship was not unconnected to the political status of the archipelago. Although many natives were involved in different areas of administration, Cape Verde was a colony that depended on the colonial central power in Lisbon to implement any substantive policies. In this context, for some, independence was seen as the most viable solution to these problems. However, for many others, the solution lay at the other end of the spectrum: Cape Verde should be an "adjacency" of Portugal, similar to Madeira and the Azores—whose status was effectively that of a province of the European country—giving Portugal greater responsibility for the fate of the Islands.

It was to the backdrop of these debates over the viability of Cape Verde that Amílcar Cabral politically came of age. In this regard, he was only partially influenced by his father. For Juvenal Cabral, as we have seen, contrary to what his son Amílcar later defended, the Cape Verdean question did not stem from colonialism per se, but from the narrowness of colonial policies. Cabral may not have been entirely in disagreement with this point of view, or he likely would not have studied agronomy, which, for Cabral as an African, could only be applied in a colonial setting. Whether he was against or in favor of independence should not concern us at this stage of the biography. The important point to make here is that Amílcar Cabral's anticolonial views evolved in the context of these debates about the viability of Cape Verde. Unity between Cape Verde and Guinea, which would later become the battle cry of the political party founded by Cabral, must be seen from this perspective.

* * *

Significantly, Amílcar Cabral arrived in Lisbon in 1945, the year in which the Charter of the United Nations was signed in San Francisco. Article 73 of the Charter inscribed in international law the inalienable right of people to self-determination. In this context, the question of whether the Portuguese were implementing the right policies in Cape Verde began to be overshadowed by another: whether the Cape Verdeans had the right to be masters of their own destiny. This implied a shift from a model based on trusteeship, which authorized a more developed "civilization" to lift up a lesser one, to one based on identity—that is, the relationship between collective identity and sovereignty. A distinct culture should aspire to the formation of its own political entity: the nation-state. In other words, a culture or civilization should not be determined by another, and should instead aim for political sovereignty. It is no coincidence then that for Cabral and his companions from other Portuguese colonies in Africa, the road to independence had to pass forcefully through culture. It was necessary to sever colonial Africa from Portugal itself. If colonialism had uprooted Africans from their own history, as Cabral would later write, there was only way way it could be overturned: by invoking a history in which colonialism was described as no more than an interruption in the colonized people's story.

In October 1945, Amílcar Cabral was one of the many African youths—white, black and mixed race—who began pursuing further education in Portugal. The arrival of these young men was the result of two important factors: the end of WWII had seen a rise in the price of colonial products, giving the colonial elite the ability to send their offspring to study in the metropolis. But equally, the colonial state could no longer dodge the necessity of educating the native elites to serve as local agents of colonialism. Portugal's tutelage over the colonies forced it to culturally elevate sections of the subjugated populations. But a number of these students were able to come to Lisbon thanks to financial support given by protestant missions in Angola and Mozambique. The vast majority were therefore still descendants of the Portuguese. Whatever the reasons, the number of African students grew rapidly. Mário de Andrade explained this development with a soccer metaphor: at the start of the decade, African students could be counted on one hand, but by the end of the 1950s, it was possible to organize football matches with two teams each of eleven players.

The majority of students who came to Lisbon were from families who could afford to pay for their education. Cabral, on the other hand, relied on funding from two scholarships: the first had been given by the *Liceu* of Cape Verde for his academic merit, with the other granted by the Mission of Overseas Students. He was one of 220 students—including only 20 females, among them Maria Helena Rodrigues, who was Portuguese and would later become his wife—who were accepted that year at the ISA (*Instituto Superior de Agronomia*—School of Agronomy). For his living expenses, he was given a stipend of 500 *escudos*—almost what he paid for a bedroom—which would later be increased to 750 *escudos*. To pay for other expenses, he worked as a tutor during the academic year, and found occasional work in the summer. Despite his financial situation, he never neglected his family responsibilities. Occasionally, he would send money to the family he had left behind in Cape Verde, and later on, he helped one of his sisters, Arminda, to come to Lisbon to study nursing and sewing.

AMÍLCAR CABRAL

Although he was coming from a less-developed educational system and had studied under harsh circumstances, Amílcar Cabral easily became one of the best students at the Institute. This was partly due to his high grades in mathematics, which was one of the subjects with the highest failure rates. He was one of only thirty-three students who passed from the first to the second year; when he moved into the third year, only four colleagues remained who had been with him from the start. In the academic year of 1948–9, he won the Mello Geraldes Prize for the best student of colonial tehnology.

Amílcar Cabral was an open-minded and cordial man, who found it easy to integrate into the institute. For Chabal, this was because culturally and intellectually he was no different from the rest of his (white) cohort. Chabal may be right in that Cabral studied the same books and shared the same cultural references as his Portuguese counterparts. However, we should be careful not to overemphasize this integration. At the end of the day, Amílcar Cabral was black, and in the 1940s, and indeed throughout the whole colonial period, the open defense of racism, and of the moral inferiority of the black man (particularly when not an intellectual), was one of the ideological underpinnings of the Portuguese colonial endeavor. Cabral arrived in Lisbon only eleven years after the anachronistic Universal Exhibition of Porto, held in 1934, where black people had been held as "specimens" representing the various parts of the Portuguese empire, exhibited like animals in a zoo. In 1945, the University of Porto had not yet dismantled the equally anachronistic department of Physical Anthropology, where Mendes Correia taught the superiority of the white man by measuring the brains of black people. No less importantly, many of Cabral's peers had grown up devouring books and films that expounded the purest and most abject forms of racism. The bestselling *Mariazinha em África*, written by Fernanda de Castro—the publication of which was intended to teach Portuguese children the values of empire—described Guineans as "little niggers" and "savages", members of an intermediary state between men and monkeys. All in all, although Amílcar Cabral participated in many activities with his white colleagues from the Institute, to which a number of pictures attest, it was to be expected that he felt more comfortable around his African peers, with whom he more profoundly identified.

THE YEARS IN LISBON

His first interactions with African students, or students coming from Africa, may have taken place at the *Casa dos Estudantes do Império* (CEI). The CEI had been founded through the action of Alberto Marques Mesquita, nephew of the governor of Angola, who in 1944 raised funds from various official institutions, such as the Ministry of Colonies and the *Mocidade Portuguesa* (Portuguese Youth), in order to found what would be called the *Casa dos Estudantes de Angola* (CEA). There were already other *Casas*, namely one created in Coimbra in 1941 by a group of Mozambican students. The example of the CEA was immediately followed and in the following years, other "houses" sprouted up, such as those in Cape Verde, Macau, and India. Fearing the consequences of the free association of students, the Ministry of Colonies encouraged these houses to combine students together into an organization called the *Casa dos Estudantes do Império*. The CEI began its activities under the presidency of Alberto Mesquita in October 1944. It was first located at number one Rua da Praia da Victória, in Arco do Cego, Lisbon, before moving one month later to number 23 Avenida Duque de Ávila, where it stayed until its closure 20 years later. Although there were representatives from every part of the Portuguese empire in the *Casa*, sections were created grouping students by their territorial origins.

In its first year of existence, the CEI facilitated interaction between students coming from Africa. Debates were organized in which members were invited to talk about their homeland, to read poetry, and to sing Portuguese colonial songs. In the same year, a series of conferences on Angola, Cape Verde, Mozambique, and Timor was organized at the Palace of Independence, followed by film showings on several aspects of these regions. A library was set up and a number of radio shows were broadcast through the *Club Radiofónico de Portugal*, under the title of *Portugal Ultramarino*, (Overseas Portugal).

Entering the CEI was almost compulsory for students coming from Africa. The institution had taken on responsibility for providing students with what they needed to complete their studies: it helped students find housing, it ran a canteen that offered affordable meals, and it provided health care. The CEI also contributed to the intellectual development of its members. In the early 1950s, an editorial section was created, led by Carlos Ervedosa, Costa Andrade, Fernando

Mourão and Alfredo Margarido. Here poets such as Agostinho Neto, Mário António, Viriato da Cruz, Noémia de Sousa and Luandino Vieira would publish their first poems and short stories. Cabral, under the *nom de plume* Larbac (an anagram of his surname), published an essay, *Hoje e Amanhã* (Today and Tomorrow).

The bulk of the CEI's membership, however, were white Portuguese people, bringing their own identity issues to the workings of the organization. White anxiety was at the very core of the institution. The colonial state discriminated against the white Portuguese coming from Africa. In the 1930s, there were pieces of legislation which prohibited white people from Africa from achieving the highest positions in a number of professional areas—in politics, administration, and in the military. By the time the CEI came into being in the 1940s, these laws had been repealed, but their effects lived on. To a certain extent it is fair to say that the CEI was concerned with the interests of a subgroup of white Portuguese. The small number of black students from Africa in the *Casa* complained on several occasions that their interests were not represented in the organization. They expressed concerns that the *Casa* assisted only the most vulnerable students, giving them "official representation", but without making efforts to integrate them. This did not mean, however, that they severed their ties with the *Casa*, even though some black students showed an interest in creating an organization which would defend their interests, or at least which would open up a space where they could debate issues affecting them. Quite the opposite. Some years late, for example, Amílcar Cabral would be appointed vice-president of the Cape Verde section. But it was in the margins of the *Casa* that Cabral's group would start to develop a dissident political consciousness.

In the 1940s, black African students constituted a sort of island in Lisbon. Not only because they were represented in the universities in such small numbers, but also because they led their lives independently, outside the privileged places that the majority of white students tended to come from. On account of the meagerness of their stipends or of the funds they received from their families, the housing options available to them were either to live in guesthouses or rented rooms in the poorest neighborhoods of Lisbon, at a time when poverty was a serious social problem. For while Salazar had shielded the country from the destruction that WWII had brought to much of the rest of Europe, it had not been spared the desolation of the post-war period. In general, the war had not been bad for Portugal. Thanks to its neutrality, it received an influx of foreign currency, and the mineral tungsten also flourished on the black market during these years. More importantly, Lisbon was one of the main points of passage for affluent Jews fleeing Europe for the United States, spending some of the money they brought with them there. To explain the destitution in Portugal, British diplomats living in Lisbon used the image of a "man with full pockets and an empty stomach." This discrepancy was evident in how people lived in Lisbon. According to Fernando Rosas, in Alcântara, or Santo Amaro, in the western part of the city—particularly in the neighborhoods of Alfama, parts of Graça, Marvila, Beato, Chelas and Xabregas—many people lived in courtyards and shacks. A Portuguese author of the time, Júlio Martins, wrote that in Lisbon in 1944, thousands of "individuals of both sexes share in large numbers the same room, sometimes the same bed, in such incredible promiscuity." It was in these neighborhoods—such as Alcântara, with its courtyards and overcrowded "islands" (pockets of the city), without electricity, running water or sewage—that many African students such as Amílcar Cabral or Mário de Andrade found a home. However, contrary to Marxist axioms, these students would not find any solidarity among the poor white Portuguese.

The relationship between African youths and lower-class Portuguese was not much better, leading the former to develop strong social bonds producing a pronounced group mentality. In the beginning, this group was made up of Angolans, but Cabral was also let in once he arrived in Lisbon. He was introduced to the group by Mário de Andrade, after they had met in one of the streets of Lisbon, Rua Luís de Camões, an event about which he would later reminisce in conversation with Michel Laban.

It was in this environment of partial isolation from Portuguese society that Amílcar Cabral's group—which later on Mário de Andrade would call the "Cabral Generation"—started nurturing a particular ethos. Looking back on these days, Cabral would later rehearse an explanation for this search for identity. Influenced by the "currents that shocked the world," as he put it, they engaged in a process of "re-Africanization of spirits." This meant for them an attempt to comprehend the Africa that was not taught in the school system for *assimilados*. This gesture, the "re-Africanization of spirits," implied cutting the cultural link with Portugal, so that they could reclaim a culture that predated the arrival of Europeans in Africa: a black heritage.

Hence, the re-Africanization of spirits meant detaching themselves from the history of Portugal—a history in which Africans were simply a chapter in the great story of Portuguese expansion throughout the world. This detaching drew on connections, experiences, and readings of the black consciousness movement. The movement was largely derived from the Haitian revolution of 1804, when this country became the first black independent nation in the world. This momentous historical event sent shock-waves around the world, felt both in slave societies such as Brazil and the USA, and in colonial societies such as those in many African countries. In the territories dominated by the Portuguese, things were no different. In Angola, Mozambique, and Cape Verde, Creole elites founded associations and newspapers to give voice to native protest.

The epicenter of this African Lusophone "protonationalism," however, was Lisbon itself. Before the proclamation of the *Estado Novo*, the liberal political environment of the Portuguese republic saw the creation in Lisbon of some of the most active student organizations, including the *Associação de Estudantes Negros* (Black Students' Association) and the *Liga Académica Internacional dos Negros* (International Academic League for Negros), which from 1911 onwards edited a publication called *O Negro*. The publication relied to a great extent on the materials produced on the subject by the members of the so-called African diaspora in the United States and the Caribbean, which were accessible in English, for those who could read in that language, or, for most, through translations into French. Proof of the connectedness of the global black movement and its counterpart in Portugal is that the São Tomean José Magalhães, one of the most illustrious members of the Creole societies in Lisbon, hosted W.E.B. Du Bois, whom he called the ambassador of "Pan-Africa", for the second session of the third Pan-African Congress, held in Lisbon in 1923. But the protonationalism of the Lusophone creoles had its particularities. The contradictions of the black movement in Portugal in those years were described by Du Bois himself. The sessions of the congress, wrote Du Bois, were attended by the most prominent members of black society in Lisbon, comprised of African students and some professionals, "well dressed, and with courteous manners". But among those who also took part were, for example, the Minister of Colonies Vicente Ferreira, who even served as translator, as well as the former Minister of Colonies Vieira da Rocha. Du Bois says incorrectly that the presence of blacks in the Portuguese parliament was due to the autonomy of cocoa producers from São Tomé, who, by selling their products directly to the British, made important profits, since they could dodge the fixed price established by Portugal. For the African American thinker, this explained how those elites could afford to send their offspring to the schools in Lisbon.

Du Bois, perhaps for not being able to communicate directly with the black Portuguese, could not be further from the truth. The contradictions he pointed out lie elsewhere. In order to dominate the vast majority of blacks in Africa, Portugal had relied on the collaboration of African elites. Honório Barreto, who we discussed earlier, is one of such elites. However, Portugal started to curtail the development of these local elites, as their growing authority began to become a danger to the empire—or at least so it seemed based on experiences in other parts of the continent, where members of these groups started leading nationalist movements. The relevance of this layer then began to dwindle in the 1920s, when Portugal renewed its appetite for colonization and encouraged the migration of whites to the tropics, directly challenging the social prestige of these blacks in the colonies. Even though such a development did fuel resentment, it did not result in open revolts against colonialism. This was not only because of the repressive apparatus of the colonial empire, but also due to the fact that the individuals of this generation had failed to come to terms with their biggest contradiction (one that eludes Du Bois): being simultaneously black and Portuguese.

It is no coincidence that some of the "protonationalists" who engaged with Du Bois in Lisbon would later become the fathers of the first generation of African nationalists. Andrade uses this concept to name those Africans in the Portuguese colonies who took advantage of the freedom granted by liberalism to make citizenship claims. Besides himself, this included Amílcar Cabral and Hugo Azancot de Menezes, to name a but a few. This new generation was developing intellectually in a very different political environment to that of the protonationalists. Although Salazar's colonial policy would not contemplate autonomy for the Portuguese territories in Africa, Cabral's generation had other platforms to voice their claims. There was the UN Charter condemning colonialism in every form, and the emerging black consciousness, particularly in the New World.

For Cabral's generation, black consciousness not only provided the philosophical principles for the "re-Africanization of spirits," but, more importantly, it offered a sense of belonging. In the interactions with a number of African organizations based in Paris, as we will see, they could finally overcome the contradictions that had blocked a nationalist awakening in the previous generation. They no longer had to struggle with their dual consciousness as both black and Portuguese; they could be black and fight for the emergence of their own nationalities. Nationalism in the context of Lusophone Africa, and particularly for the members of this generation, was a matter overcoming this contradiction.

The political and cultural movement *Négritude* was formed in Paris by African students, such as Léopold Sédar Senghor, and West Indians such as Aimé Césaire, who lived in Paris in the 1920s. *Négritude* emerged from the complex and intense discussion between black intellectuals from different parts of the world, French surrealists such as André Breton, and leftist French intellectuals from Marxist tendencies and members of the French Communist Party. It is only from 1949 onwards that the movement crossed the borders of France. Senghor brought together poems written by his friends into into an edited volume called *Anthologie de la Nouvelle Poésie Nègre et Malgache*, insisting that his editor secure a preface from the most famous French intellectual of the time: Jean-Paul Sartre. Satre's introduction goes far beyond what is usual for a preface. He theorizes the movement itself. In the essay "Black Orpheus," Sartre developed an idea that would become a cornerstone of *Négritude*: the idea of anti-racist racism. Using Hegelian concepts, Sartre suggested that racism was the thesis as much as *Négritude* was the anti-thesis. Accordingly, racial consciousness was instrumental to abolishing the idea of race.

The *Anthologie* made a strong impression on Cabral and his friends. After reading it, Cabral conveyed his appreciation in a letter to a friend: "wonderful poems written by blacks from all parts of the French world, poems that speak about Africa, slaves, men, life and men's aspirations." As an indication of the importance of this book for the black students and intellectuals who resided in Lisbon in these years, one need only note that four years after its publication, Mário Pinto de Andrade compiled the poems of his own friends and published the first collection of the work of Portuguese-speaking African poets, the *Antologia da Poesia Negra de Expressão Portuguesa* (Anthology of the Black Poetry of Portuguese Expression).

* * *

The year of the publication of Senghor's *Anthologie*, 1949, is significant for many reasons. Portugal was holding presidential elections, scheduled for 13 February, and it was fast becoming the fiercest electoral campaign ever. For the first time, the opposition, led by a former governor of Angola, Norton de Matos, had been allowed to take part in the process. Although Norton de Matos ended up withdrawing from the ballot—on account of a lack of conditions for free and fair elections—the possibility of change that de Matos (who was aligned to republican ideals) represented, created a certain political opening in Portugal and the colonies. The politicization of Cabral's generation traces its roots to these events.

The political trajectory of Agostinho Neto illustrates this. Neto, who would later become the most politically active member of Cabral's group, arrived in Lisbon in 1949, having transferred from Coimbra University. A card-holding member of the *Partido Comunista Português* (Portuguese Communist Party), he was involved in many risky activities. He found accommodation in the neighborhood of Alcântara, alongside other African students such as Humberto Machado—a student of agronomy—who, together with his wife, Júlia Machado, managed a guesthouse that provided accommodation for Angolans working on the ships that made the regular Lobito-Luanda-Bissau-Lisbon trips. Neto started to build political awareness amongst these crewmembers with the aim of finding a more efficient way to send and receive clandestine materials from Lisbon to Luanda and vice versa. Through crewmembers such as José Van Dúnem, students in Lisbon could engage with subversive literature, such as novels by

Jorge Amado and other Brazilian neo-realists, as well as Portuguese translations of books with Marxist leanings, which, because of the censorship, could not be found in Portugal's bookshops. It was also through these crewmembers that contact between nationalists in Portugal and others in Africa, such as Viriato da Cruz, was made. To camouflage these activities, Agostinho Neto and other Angolans formed the *Clube Marítimo*, which organized cultural activities. Besides the famous Saturday parties, which attracted a large number of African students, the *Clube* also offered these crewmembers literacy classes. Later, in 1954, Mário de Andrade translated and staged with them the play *Maître École*, by the Guinean Keita Fodéba.

The importance of the *Clube Marítimo* is less about the particular clandestine activities they carried out, as many authors have written on, and more about the kind of template it provided for future political activities. The *Estado Novo* restricted individual liberties, prohibiting the formation of labor unions and associations, but tolerated the existence of groups of a sporting and cultural nature. The nationalists could conduct their political activities either through organizations already approved by the *Estado Novo*, such as the CEI, or, and this option was more difficult, under the cover of organizations founded by them which were officially concerned with culture and sports rather than politics. The *Centro do Estudos Africanos*, formed by Cabral and his comrades, fell into the second category. But this was not enough. Part of the reason this center was tolerated by the *Estado Novo* was due to its being open to people who were not necessarily subversive. There were those who were not nationalist, or even students, such as the São Tomean geographer Francisco José Tenreiro. At this time, he was a clerk at the Ministry of Colonies, and author of studies on colonial geography, as well as of a little book of poems called *Ilha de Santo Nome*. Tenreiro moved in other literary circles such as that of the neo-realists, which counted well-established Portuguese writers like Joaquim Namorado and Carlos Oliveira among their members. Later his trajectory would diverge from that of the majority of the other members of the Center, such as Cabral. Whereas Cabral and his companions became involved in nationalist activities and fought for the independence of their countries, Tenreiro became the representative of São Tomé in the National Assembly.

THE YEARS IN LISBON

With the CEA in need of a legal cover, Cabral's group later attempted to integrate itself into the *Casa de África*, an older organization created in the aftermath of the proclamation of the Portuguese Republic in 1910, which brought together African personalities residing in Lisbon. The *Casa de África* was by this point the only survivor of the racialist organizations which had sprouted up in Lisbon at the turn of the century, which, as we have already discussed, Du Bois had contacted on the occasion of the second session of the Third Pan-African Congress. Leading these organizations was the old man and veteran Artur de Castro, seen in governing circles as the spokesperson of the African community in Portugal. Cabral's group met with him to ask for the use of the *Casa*'s facilities for a meeting of the CEA. But de Castro refused. In the heat of this meeting, according to his biographers, Cabral stood up and invited all "honest Africans" to abandon the room, in an episode that has been remembered as Cabral's first political gesture. "Artur de Castro was left totally alone. We broke with the representative of the old generation of the 1920s," Mário de Andrade concluded.

Even if part of this episode has been embellished by Cabral's hagiographers, these events have a very strong symbolism. By inviting his friends to abandon the meeting, Cabral's generation was breaking free of everything Artur de Castro represented: a compromise between the representatives of the African elites and the *Estado Novo*. From this it is possible to see two consequences. It was on the one hand, the moment in which Cabral's group started to undo the aforementioned contradiction of being both Portuguese and black. On the other, after breaking with de Castro, they felt compelled to start developing political activities to eradicate the colonial system outside of the colonial system itself. This double rupture explains the illegality into which the national liberation movements in Lusophone Africa would be pushed.

Deprived of the institutional cover offered by the *Casa de África*, Cabral's group began holding meetings in the home of Januário da Graça do Espírito Santo, where his daughter, Alda do Espírito Santo, one of the members of the group, lived. The residence at no. 37 Actor Vale Street was managed by one of Januário's sisters, known as Auntie Andreza, and was also the meeting point of the São Tomean community in Lisbon.

The group would meet to discuss various topics related to Africa, in the context of the objective interests of the *Centro de Estudos Africanos*. Because of the close surveillance of the PIDE, they had to be careful. In order not to arose the PIDE's suspicion, the discussions took place with loud music in the background. The working plan, elaborated by Francisco Tenreiro and Mário de Andrade, covered themes such as the relationship between man and land in Africa, African philosophies, African social economy, and the problems that blocked "the progress of the black man." The first of these meetings took place in October 1951, when Francisco Tenreiro gave a talk on the geographical structure of the continent. Cabral's talk took place some weeks later, at the end of October, and was about systems of farming and the benefits of the itinerant system.

The Center also provided the opportunity to connect with similar institutions, particularly those in Paris. It was as members of the Center, for example, that Amílcar Cabral, Alda do Espírito Santo, Agostinho Neto, and Mário de Andrade sent their writings to the recently created review *Présence Africaine*, founded in 1947 and directed by Alioune Diop. These writings were included in the section *Les Étudiants Africains Parlent*, to which many African students scattered across various European cities contributed, giving them the opportunity to speak about their problems and their aspirations.

The Center did not record much activity during this time, with political actions taking place irregularly. This was partly for reasons beyond the nationalists' control. In the early 1950s, São Tomé was experiencing labor shortages, largely caused by the difficulties the colonial authorities in Angola were facing in sending *contratados* to the archipelagos. As such, Carlos Gorgulho, the colonel of artillery who had been appointed governor in 1945, devised a way to force the native population to work. The *Forros*, who had always been a privileged group on the islands and had remained free even during the slave period, had a strong aversion to manual labor. In need of construction workers, Gorgulho came up with a number of schemes to force the *Forros* to work for free, one of which was to summon them to workplaces, with the promise that they would be compensated for their time.

During colonial times, there were two categories of colonized Africans, *assimilados* and *indígenas*. *Assimilados* were paid for the work they provided; *indígenas*, however, could be forced to work without pay. The governor's scheme likely saw these *assimilados* arriving at work with the expectation of compensation. Once there, however, they were treated as mere *indígenas*, and denied payment for their labor.

Tensions between the Portuguese and the native population mounted, and, on the night of 31 January, a group of white people were denied entrance to a theater performance, and a fight ensued. Confrontations continued and Gorgulho sent a group of Angolan policemen to arrest the rioters. One of the policemen shot a *Forro* man, triggering an uprising. Gorgulho then called on white colonists to take up arms, convincing them that the rebellion was part of a communist plot. Helped by Angolans and Cape Verdeans, Gorgulho and his white allies killed, raped, tortured, and burned *Forros* alive. The exact number of casualties has never been determined, but hundreds are thought to have perished. Salustino da Graça do Espírito Santo, brother of Januário da Graça do Espírito Santo, accused of being the mastermind of the upheaval, was arrested and deported to Príncipe. However, these events were considered criminal even in the context of Portuguese colonialism. Palma Carlos, a Portuguese lawyer, interviewed a number of survivors, and Gorgulho was summoned back to Lisbon on 17 April, after the minister of the colonies discovered that there had never been any communist plot.

As a consequence of these events, the PIDE reinforced its surveillance over all the nationals of São Tomé e Príncipe, especially those at 37 Actor Vale Street. The surveillance and persecution that followed the massacre in Batepá forced Cabral's group to find more covert forms of political organization in order not to attract attention. Plans to simply leave Lisbon and search for other places to continue their work against colonialism were considered. However, in those years, Cabral and his fellow nationalists were dedicated to political learning. They developed a model for undercover political activities, including, for example, creating small groups to discuss culture, under the cover of cultural organizations recognized by the *Estado Novo*. Politics would come only later, when the most indecisive members were cut off from the group and a climate of confidentiality was created. This technique would later be used by Amílcar Cabral in the formation of the PAIGC, as well as by Agostinho Neto in the formation of the many nationalist groups that would later contribute to the foundation of the MPLA.

* * *

AMÍLCAR CABRAL

The year of 1949 was also important in the life of Cabral for another, more personal, reason. That year, he returned to Cape Verde on vacation for the first time since he had left to begin his studies in Lisbon. For him, this trip was a special moment in his life and career. The main purpose of his trip was to carry out some work for his agronomy studies. During his stay, he was invited to write a series of articles on agrarian issues in Cape Verde, in which he laid out ideas upon which he would later elaborate in his honors thesis on soil erosion in the Alentejo—probably the Portuguese region whose geological and even meteorological make-up was most like that of Cape Verde. Cabral was also returning to the island with the intention of testing out, in a rudimentary fashion, the method he had helped develop in his group in Lisbon.

Cabral returned to his homeland at a time which was also special for the inhabitants of the Islands. In 1949, abundant rainfall finally put an end to the four years of drought, which had resulted in the critical food crisis of 1947–8, with predictable consequences: a section of the population had been reduced to penury and another, no less significant section, had been forced to migrate. The archipelago had a new governor, the Doctor-Captain Carlos Alberto Garcia Alves Roçadas, whose arrival had been anticipated by the fall of the first rains only a few days earlier. A number of Cape Verdeans interpreted the arrival of the energetic and resourceful Carlos Roçadas as a sign that, finally, Portugal was committed to eradicating the food crises in Cape Verde.

Shortly after his arrival, one of his first acts was to found the *Boletim de Informação e Propaganda de Cabo Verde*. The governor had two objectives for this publication. Firstly, he wanted to create a reference magazine, to which the principal intellectuals of the archipelago would contribute. Secondly, he wished to provide the government with the means to communicate its actions to the population. The central pages were always occupied by official activities, such as the inaugurations of various venues that the governor carried out across the archipelago.

Juvenal Cabral and Amílcar Cabral were some of the contributors to this publication, writing on various topics to do with agriculture. By this time, Juvenal had already gone bankrupt, although he was still in possession of some land. His writings on granting agrarian credits were therefore simply a way to advance his own cause. Amílcar Cabral, for his part, started writing a series of articles on agronomy, with the generic title *In Defense of Land*. The first essay, published on 27 September 1949, was written when he was still in Praia.

The articles by Amílcar Cabral can be read as messages to the governor. Cabral, repackaging an old argument, stated that even if problems of drought were of an environmental nature, the means to solve them were eminently political. This was a point of view shared by many Cape Verdeans and Portuguese who visited the archipelago. Juvenal Cabral had been among the first, followed by others such as the doctor Wolfgango da Silva, to defend this line of reasoning in various ways. But Amílcar Cabral would add something else to this debate. He was bringing the authority of a scientist and of a native son, and proposed concrete measures to quell the specter of drought. He recommended drawing up an in-depth public policy plan for the construction of dikes, reservoirs, and water tanks, as well as the afforestation of certain regions of Cape Verde with species better adapted to a dry climate.

The *Boletim* was not the only means by which Amílcar Cabral was given the opportunity to spread his ideas. He also contributed to the Radio of Cape Verde, for which he wrote some texts concerning agriculture, such as one entitled "Some considerations about the rain," which would be published in the first issue of the *Boletim*. Another of his texts was broadcast in which he discussed the relationship between humans and land, an essay he would later present at conferences of the *Centro de Estudos Africanos*. Another was on the cultural similarities between Cape Verdeans, Afro-Brasilians, and Afro-Americans. In this article, he followed the principles of *Négritude*, showing that Cape Verdeans, as blacks, had more in common with other communities in the black diaspora—particularly those that were the result of the Atlantic Slave Trade—than with the Portuguese population in general.

Cabral's hagiographers have contended that his views on culture were so subversive that his radio shows were suspended by the colonial authorities, particularly when they realized that more and more people were drawn to it. At that time, as very few people on the Islands had transistor radios, it was common for many people to gather, by sunset, on Alexandre Albuquerque Square (also known as *Pelourinho*) to follow the shows via a sound system provided by the municipality. Cabral wrote that many of those who used to go to *Pelourinho* to listen to his shows inundated the governor's office with letters when they discovered that the show had been called off.

Regarding this trip, it has also been reported that Cabral's request to give literacy courses to adults was declined. I have found no indication that this request did not take place, but there were other reasons that could have impeded Cabral's plans, such as the sudden illness he contracted. He lost weight so frighteningly that, according to his mother, "this time, we thought he would die." This was all because he followed the advice of a friend to use eau de cologne to shave, instead of the usual alcohol. The result was a terrible "skin allergy," as Cabral informed Mário de Andrade in a letter written on 28 September 1949.

* * *

As previously discussed, Cabral was very popular at ISA. He stood out from the crowd, in part due to being a very good student, but also as one of the few black students in the entire institute. For this reason, he evoked a mixture of feelings, somewhere between repulsion and admiration. During the years he spent there, he built solid friendships with colleagues and professors. One of the people he was close to was Maria Helena Rodrigues, who later became his first wife. They met in their first year, even though they were not in the same class. Only in the third year did they become classmates and inseparable. According to Maria Helena, she and Cabral spent time together partly because she was the only person at the *Instituto* who had no problem with having a close relationship with a person of color. But she would pay dearly for this.

Rodrigues' relationship with Cabral was a source of numerous problems for her. She was born in Chaves, in the northern region of Portugal, Trás-os-Montes, and was the daughter of a physician-captain who had lost both legs in Africa. When the time came for her to go to high school, she obtained two scholarships, which were later extended to study at university. However, when it became known that she was close to Amílcar Cabral and attended the CEI, rumors started circulating that she was a communist. When she announced her intention to marry Cabral, friends attempted to dissuade her. After her marriage, her funding was withdrawn with only a few courses left before graduating. To remedy the situation, the couple increased the number of hours they spent tutoring high school and university students.

Although multiculturalism was the cornerstone of the *Estado Novo* in the years of late colonialism, the marriage rates between black and white people were lower than in Alabama. The number of marriages between black men and white women were even more limited. In this context, the relationship between Amílcar and Maria Helena represented a genuine challenge to the prejudices of those times and was fraught with difficulty from the outset. They had to endure shows of racism on a daily basis, as whites and blacks lived in different social worlds. Azancot de Menezes writes that at that time it was common for the white Portuguese to sneeze at the sight of a black person. In certain parts of Alcântara, close to where Cabral lived, they were frequently verbally abused by workers. In contrast to Maria Helena, who sometimes reacted, Amílcar Cabral rarely lost his temper; workers had difficult lives, he would say, and their behavior was certainly influenced by the envy of seeing someone who, being black and from distant lands, was dating a white, Portuguese woman.

As soon as the financial situation of Amílcar and Maria Helena improved, they decided to get married. They chose 20 December 1951 as the date. As best man, Amílcar chose Telmo Crato Monteiro, a Cape Verdean doctor and colleague in the *Casa*, who had welcomed him when he arrived in Lisbon. At the end of the ceremony, when the best man left, the couple celebrated by eating codfish at the Café Colonial, on Almirante Reis Avenue. They then threw a small party after lunch. Alda do Espírito Santo, Julieta do Espírito Santo, Mário de Andrade and Agostinho Neto came to the apartment of Elisa Horta, secretary of the CEI, who hosted the small celebration. Later, they would rent a room there to spend the first years of their married life.

Juvenal Cabral did not live to see his son marry. He died on 20 March 1951, when Cabral was finishing his studies. The cause of death was a heart attack that he had suffered when, according to witnesses, rumors began circulating in Praia that Amílcar had been detained by the PIDE for talking about politics in a tavern. Curiously, this date coincides with the first imprisonment of Agostinho Neto, who had been detained when, collecting signatures for the Peace Conference, he had knocked on the door of a policeman. When Amílcar's mother

Iva and her twin daughters heard the rumors, they were desperate to know what had happened. They sent him a telegram from Praia, to which he quickly responded. Nevertheless, very few people believed that Cabral was not in prison. Because of this, grief over the death of Juvenal Cabral was stifled by anxiety about the whereabouts of Amílcar, for whom people wept as if he were also dead, as Iva Évora reminisces: "Myself, Arminda and Armanda, went up to the attic in the house and we wept from dawn to dusk. We could not even eat."

Amílcar Cabral found out about his father's death from a telgram sent by his brother. His short telegram in response simply read: "Aware painful fatality united we fight Amílcar." Only years later, when Amílcar's brother met Maria Helena, did she mention how Amílcar had reacted to the death of his father: "He locked himself in his bedroom for many days without talking to anyone."

Cabral's years in Lisbon were formative for a number of reasons. First of all, he had moved to a different reality, to the capital of the empire, and, while a number of things may have seemed different to him, others, such as the poverty he found in Lisbon, reminded him of conditions in Cape Verde. In Lisbon, he also met the comrades with whom he would take up the challenging struggle for the independence of Lusophone Africa. At a personal level, Cabral would marry his first wife, Maria Helena. But more importantly, in Lisbon, Cabral would learn the techniques for subversive work.

3

ENGINEER AND CLANDESTINE MILITANT

In order to earn his agricultural engineering degree, Cabral had to complete an internship and submit a minor dissertation. To complete this assignment, he picked the *Estação Agronómica Nacional* (National Agronomic Station) in the regions of Cuba and Vidigueira in the Alentejo, southern Portugal. He spent a great deal of his time from the end of 1951 to the beginning of the following year doing research on pedology, the science of soil. In 1952, he submitted his dissertation—dedicated to his mother and the day laborers of Alentejo—which was given eighteen out of twenty. This outstanding mark is even more significant if one considers that it was given by Professor Botelho da Costa, known in the *Instituto* as one of the most rigorous and demanding instructors.

Although Cabral used a convincing set of empirical data, the main argument of the thesis was far from being radical. It was something his father, or any other Cape Verdean concerned about the tragic consequences of the food crises on the archipelago, could agree with. At its core, it was not substantially different from what Cabral had written before, such as in his earlier series of pieces called *Em Defesa da Terra* (In Defense of the Soil). Adapting his main concerns to the context of Alentejo, the young engineer could conclude in his final work that although the rain and winds had a substantial effect on soil erosion, human action was the main culprit.

The new element in Cabral's reflections, perhaps, is the relationship he established between capitalism and the destruction of soils, which unquestionably came from his Marxist readings. The main culprit behind soil damage, he wrote, was the property regime—or, in Marxist parlance, the means of production. To support his point, Cabral criticized the attempt to transform Alentejo into the granary of the country through the *Campanha do Trigo*, even though it was evident that the region did not offer the best conditions for the production of cereal. Since Alentejo has a dry climate, irregular rains, and generally dry soils, wheat harvests relied on using all available land, including plains, hillsides and even steep slopes. Although the results of the campaign were positive, for Cabral, and contrary to the *Estado Novo's* propaganda, this success was only temporary, for it involved a harmful use of the soil, which in the long term would bring about the destruction of the moorland itself.

In terms of the means of production, Cabral also criticized Alentejo's economic-agrarian model, as being a direct consequence of the unequal distribution of land. In Salazarist Portugal, agriculture occupied the vast majority of the population, but in Alentejo, only 1.39 per cent of the population held property titles, despite working 80 per cent of the cultivated land. By drawing attention to this contrast, Amílcar Cabral aimed to highlight two facts: first, that this kind of extensive agriculture—based on the concentration of a significant part of the arable land in the hands of very few owners—strangled the rural middle class, formed of *seareiros*, or journeymen. Second, as a large part of this land was subdivided into various lots that were rented out or, at best, worked in partnership schemes, Cabral explained that peasants, indebted and in search of rapid profits, had very few options other than to intensively exploit the soils, in an attempt to maximize profit, without any concern for the exhaustion of the land.

* * *

After graduating in agricultural engineering, the time had come to search for a job. Cabral considered looking for work in Cape Verde, and must have made contacts on his previous visit to Santiago, but such an opportunity failed to materialize. Moving there to work would make the most sense, since all his family were in Santiago, and some of them were struggling financially. Having a well-paid relative in a state-paid job would represent an enormous help. Furthermore, Cabral had become an expert in an area of studies with significant potential for application in Cape Verde. As in Alentejo, Santiago also dealt with high levels of soil erosion. Although not having studied Santiago in the same depth, it was evident there were a number of economic-agrarian issues linking both places. Both were dominated by the same means of production: land was concentrated in the hands of a small number of owners, who then rented it out or exploited it in partnership schemes. Alentejo and Santiago complemented each other, and returning to the latter as an agricultural engineer would allow Cabral to continue his research in his area of expertise.

Having failed to get a job in Lisbon or Cape Verde, the only option left to Cabral was to take a position in his native land, Guinea. So Cabral moved to Guinea to start a new life, as so many Cape Verdeans from the previous generation had done, including his father Juvenal Cabral. But Guinea was the least appealing place for an agricultural engineer trained in Lisbon. Job posts in Guinea were among the least sought-after compared to others in the Portuguese colonies, particularly Angola.

Whatever the reason Cabral moved to Guinea, it became the place where he would actively commit to the nationalist cause. It was during this period that he created what would later become the PAIGC. But contrary to much of what has been written on Cabral, his transition from engineer to revolutionary was not straightforward. Neither was it a move that Cabral had clearly defined: he experienced many moments of anguish and indecision prior to taking the leap. And unlike many members of his group, as we will discuss later, Cabral was not struggling financially, making it even harder to leave behind his secure position. Until the last minute, he maintained a double life, on the one hand working for the colonial regime, while on the other, taking part in illegal activities for its eradication. Consequently, these seven years, from 1952 to 1959, are the among the hardest of Cabral's adult life to reconstruct.

During these years, for instance, it is known that Cabral was involved with a number of nationalist groups, but he rarely talked about it to others. He was the link between nationalists in Luanda and those in Lisbon, but his companions in Bissau were unaware of it. Not even Maria Helena, his wife, seemed to know what her husband was doing. She reacted with surprise, for instance, when Cabral decided to put an end to his double life in 1960 and concentrate his efforts on achieving independence for Guinea and Cape Verde. In the next section, I will expand on this process of transformation from a professional in the colonial administration into a revolutionary.

Amílcar Cabral arrived in Bissau on board the merchant vessel *Ana Mafalda* on 21 September 1952. He was alone, since Maria Helena, who was pregnant with the couple's first child, was due to stop in Cape Verde to meet her husband's family. She wouldn't arrive in Bissau until 5 November of the same year.

Under contract with the Overseas Ministry, Amílcar Cabral was the deputy-director of the Agriculture and Forestry Services, a position putting in him in charge of the *Granja Experimental de Pessubé* (Experimental Farm of Pessubé)—"one of the most extensive and beautiful farms we saw in the colony," as a colonial traveler wrote—occupying an area of 400 hectares, forested with *bissilões* and a vast array of fruit trees. Appointed on 22 September, the day after his arrival, Amílcar Cabral took his responsibilities seriously. Before then, the farm's only role had been to supply a handful of Bissau's inhabitants with fruit and vegetables, as he himself had written in the *Boletim*. But Cabral envisioned transforming the farm into a site for plant experimentation and acclimation.

Amílcar Cabral and Maria Helena Rodrigues settled into the house reserved for the director of the farm, located on the premises of the farm itself: it was "a magnificent house," as Cabral wrote to Maria Helena before her arrival in Bissau. Recently built, it had four bedrooms, two bathrooms, a corridor, two kitchens and two storage rooms. According to the *Boletim*, in a note from January 1953, "the construction of the furniture for the director's residence" was underway, part of which had already been delivered. The farm was located on the outskirts of Bissau, close to the popular informal neighborhoods typical of many African cities, with their unpaved roads and often without basic sanitation or electricity. These areas were less popular with whites, allowing Cabral to be closer to the people he wanted to politically awaken.

ENGINEER AND CLANDESTINE MILITANT

At Cabral's instigation, some of his family moved from Cape Verde to Guinea. The first to arrive was his brother Luís Cabral—who he would live close to for the rest of his life—and for whom he had found a job at *Casa Gouveia*, a company specializing in the purchase of tropical products. Later, António, his youngest brother, joined them, followed by Cabral's mother, Iva, together with the twins Arminda and Armanda.

It was among the Cape Verdean clerks working in the various services of the colony that Cabral found his first group of close friends. Aristides Pereira was one of the first people he met. Although they had known each other since their time at the *Liceu de Cabo Verde*, and had worked together in Praia as clerks before Cabral's departure for Lisbon, they had never been close. They were re-introduced by Sofia Pomba Guerra, a pharmacist and PCP member, sent into exile in Bissau. It was at her home that these two and many other Cape Verdeans—such as Fernando Fortes, Abílio Duarte, and the recently arrived Luís Cabral—met to listen to Portuguese broadcasts on Radio Moscow, or to read forbidden novels and newspapers, such as *Avante!*, the official publication of the PCP.

Cabral quickly became the indisputable leader of this group. In part, this was owing to the fact that he occupied the highest rank in the colonial administration. But he also came with a certain nationalist aura, on account of the many years he had spent in Lisbon and of the type of political activities with which he had been involved there. He was therefore the most experienced person to lead the group. He began by introducing his own clandestine organizational methods, forming small groups to discuss diverse cultural topics such as literature and poetry, while, at the same time, coordinating the most politically mature members to eventually develop more political and risky work. A number of these meetings took place at the farm, Cabral's own residence, with the gramophone turned up to full volume. Helena Iva, Cabral's niece, was sometimes tasked with watching at the door for the possible arrival of the police. If Helena entered the room where the adults were meeting, it was a sign that something unusual was taking place or that somebody had unexpectedly arrived. At this moment, conversations would be stopped and everyone would get up and dance.

The situation, however, was far from amusing, and was becoming increasingly more dangerous, especially after a number of Guineans joined the group. The lives of Cape Verdeans and Guineans were worlds apart: the former were considered "civilized", while the latter, the majority of the population, were for the most part "natives"—with everything that entailed in the colonial state. Aristides Pereira, who arrived in Guinea in 1948, succinctly explained what it meant to belong to one or the other group. "In Bissau, by 6 pm there was the whistle to remind the native workers employed in the city that they had to abandon the precinct […] With this in mind, whether we liked it or not, any Guinean would see me as a sell-out to the colonists because I was in a whites-only zone." This social engineering, in the case of Guinea, was intended to isolate the various social groups.

Pereira's reflections neatly capture the intricacies of Portuguese colonialism, and the ways in which members of the subjugated population were assigned to different groups, occupying distinct positions in the colonial structure. I have already shown the particular place of Cape Verdeans in Guinea, who sometimes even replaced the colonizers themselves. Furthermore, Cape Verdeans were not subject to the *indigenato*, the Native Law, whereas Guineans were—testament to their separate social worlds. Hence, while the activities of a group of Cape Verdeans meeting at Sofia Pomba Guerra's house (such as listening to Radio Moscow) could be enough reason for the police to intensify surveillance, a meeting of this type of group in and of itself would attract little suspicion. On the other hand, the presence of a native Guinean within a group of Cape Verdeans would immediately prompt the police to question the exact nature of an encounter which assembled people from such diverse social backgrounds.

So although it was easy for Cabral to mix with Cape Verdeans, he was very aware of the risks posed by his efforts to contact Guineans of inferior social standing. This forced him to find new ways to approach them, such as by offering to coach Guinean soccer teams. It was only through this kind of contact that political work could develop and evolve. It was by carrying out political work among Guineans that Cabral prepared one of his first more daring subversive actions: a plot to kill Carlos Gorgulho, governor of São Tomé. When the news got out that Gorgulho was to be transferred from São Tomé to Guinea after the Batepá massacre of 1953, Cabral allegedly gave Bacar Cassamá the order to assassinate him as soon he disembarked at the Port of Bissau.

ENGINEER AND CLANDESTINE MILITANT

Cabral's experiences in Lisbon provided the template for carrying out political work in Bissau. Much like his attempt to take over the *Casa de África* in Lisbon—as a way to develop illegal activities under the cover of an organization recognized by the regime—Cabral and his companions submitted an application to the colonial administration in Guinea to set up a sports and cultural club. The preparatory meetings, as explained above, were full of risks, since they gathered together Cape Verdeans and Guineans, and were easily infiltrated by the police. When it came to signing the application form that was to be sent to the colonial services, Cabral initially refused to add his name. He alleged that because of his past in Lisbon, adding his name to the documents alongside that of the other signatories would only weaken the project. Very few people agreed with this position, however, considering it a mere gesture of cowardice. In the end, Cabral signed the document. The project, however, was turned down by the authorities.

As far as I see, there is no evidence to support the theory that Amílcar Cabral had deliberately chosen Guinea to complete his nationalist project. But there is a profound link between his métier and the kind of nationalism he became involved in from then on. The more of a nationalist he became, the less he was involved in colonial agricultural engineering. In other words, the less time Cabral committed to being an engineer, the more he was able to immerse himself in the nationalist struggle. These two aspects of his life, at least at this stage, were interlinked. It was largely because he was an agricultural engineer that Cabral became a unique type of nationalist. By the time the anticolonial struggle started, he had acquired a knowledge of the geography, economy, and sociology of the people of his country which was far greater than that of many other nationalists at similar stages of their movements. Contributing to this was the fact that Cabral was the main architect of the first agricultural census in the province, his most ambitious professional project yet. This work would give him the opportunity to get to know the agrarian structure of Guinea and would put him in direct contact with the most powerful leaders of the various ethnic groups. Above all, it would make him conscious of the importance of natural conditions in organizing everyday activities: without this experience, as we will see later, it would have been very difficult to lead an armed revolutionary movement in Guinea.

Guinea's first agricultural census was carried out in 1947 by Portugal in conjunction with the UN's Food and Agriculture Organization (FAO). The following year, a four-member committee was established in Bissau to study and plan the task. However, the work of this committee was limited to presenting a report on the number of people and the amount of resources required to undertake the project. The delay in actually starting this project was probably due to the fact that there were no agricultural engineers in Guinea at that time who could carry out such an assignment. But Cabral was the right man for the task: he was young and strong, important attributes for a job which consisted of five months of travelling, from August to December, around the 36,000 square kilometers of the country, visiting over 2,248 farmers.

The first step for Cabral was to put together his own team, who would follow and support him throughout the process. Upon completion of the fieldwork, helped by Maria Helena, he analyzed the data and produced a final report. The idea of the census was to show, using a quantitative method, as the FAO required, what Cabral already knew in a more or less intuitive form: which sections of the population dedicated themselves to agriculture, the techniques they used, how the production of certain crops was distributed across ethnicities, and how land tenure and the distribution of profit were organized.

It was thanks to this work that Cabral found the language needed to instruct his men on how to mobilize the population. Peasants must be informed that the agricultural problems in Guinea were the result of the introduction of the colonial means of production. The Guinean economy was mostly based on the production of three crops: rice, groundnuts, and different types of maize. Although all ethnic groups produced rice, the Balanta—a group from the southern part of the country, who would go on to be some of the most unreserved supporters of the war effort waged by the PAIGC—were the group whose economy was most based on monoculture. While some groups used the method of consociation, through which different crops could be planted in the same soil, the Balanta depended almost exclusively on the production of rice. As rice was not an export crop, mostly supplying the internal market, their profits were dismal.

In contrast with the Balanta the Fulani were almost exclusively involved in the production of groundnuts. Because of weak domestic demand, almost all their produce was exported, making them seemingly more prosperous. However, unlike the Balanta, who despite their meager profits could trade their rice for other products, the Fulani were forced to sell their crops at prices fixed by the concessionaire *Casa Gouveia*. Furthermore, since groundnuts were an export product, they were less protected from price fluctuations in international markets.

In the conclusion of his report, Amílcar Cabral made various suggestions to correct the weaknesses his inquiry into Guinea's agriculture had found. It was necessary, he wrote, that the various ethnic groups specializing in monoculture diversify their crops, making them less dependent on the barter system for the Balanta, and less at the mercy of price fluctuations on the international market for the Fulani. He also noted that more diverse production, adding vegetables and fruits, would provide peasants with access to a richer and more varied diet.

These conclusions were not without political motivation and could be read as veiled attacks on the colonial policies in Guinea. Unlike in Angola and Mozambique, where the concessionaires had expropriated the land of the natives and forced them into salaried labor, in Guinea the exploitation took place under different principles, namely through engineering fixed prices. The natives produced their own crops, but they were forced to sell them at a price set by the concessionaires. The greater value placed on some crops, to the detriment of others, skewed the agricultural system. Since groundnuts were the most in-demand crop, for example, a large part of the province was dedicated to producing them. Therefore, only a change in the agrarian structure would alter the system. This was more in the domain of politics than agriculture.

Cabral learned two other lessons from the census, equally as important as the knowledge gained about the economic reality in Guinea. First, activity in Guinea should be organized according to the meteorological calendar. As work on the census began in August, during the rainy season, it was necessary that the less humid northern regions were the first to be surveyed. Only after this could Cabral's units move into the Bissau region, where they would catch the end of the rainy season. At the end of the year, they moved to the southern part of the country, to the Balanta region, where outside the dry season, travelling was virtually impossible. During the rains, roads in the south became impassable, with floods and mud preventing cars from moving about. Being in the south during those times was also dangerous for health-related reasons, as without proper medication the likelihood of contracting malaria was very high. The second lesson worth noting was the importance of constant innovation. What was discouraging at times was not so much working under difficult conditions, but constantly being forced to look for alternative solutions. This was the case, for example, when an unforeseen rise in river levels prevented them from transporting material, or when a boat assigned to the team was suddenly sent elsewhere to perform another activity.

Cabral did not stay much longer in Guinea after submitting the final report. His hagiographers, namely the Russian Oleg Ignatiev and his own brother Luís, have written that Cabral left the province on the orders of the governor Melo e Alvim, on account of suspicions that he was involved in clandestine activities. In his book, Ignatiev goes even further, describing an episode in which the governor summoned Cabral to his office and gave him a choice to either to "totally stop his [clandestine] activities, or to abandon the province. Otherwise he would let him be put in jail". According to these narratives, Cabral was thus expelled from Guinea, although he was granted permission to return to the country once a year to visit his family.

It is possible, however, that another series of events prompted Cabral to leave Guinea. Work on the census had left Amílcar and Maria Helena physically weak, due to them having carried out much of the work during the rainy season and on account of the poor sanitary conditions in many of the places they had visited. After presenting the final report, Cabral contracted malaria, and his health did not improve despite medical treatment. Consequently, on 18 March 1955, the couple took an Air France flight to Lisbon. This narrative is confirmed by the PIDE, which states that Cabral and his wife left the province in compliance with a report by the Medical Board. Maria Helena was so ill that she was told never to return to Guinea.

This does not mean that Cabral did not develop activities that might arouse suspicions. Quite the opposite. A PIDE report produced years after Cabral's stay in Bissau is definitive: according to the police, Cabral had tried to "rouse the natives against the presence of Portugal in the region, soliciting, for this reason, the company of other natives for the foundation of a Sports and Recreational Association of Bissau." But Cabral's choices were not all political, and it is important to also consider the personal motivations that may have guided his actions.

Once back in Lisbon, in March 1955, Amílcar and Maria Helena moved into a spacious apartment on Infante Santo Avenue. Unlike Bissau, a very small city where it was difficult to maintain discretion, Lisbon afforded Cabral more freedom to develop his clandestine activities. Just as in Guinea, his work served as a cover. For work-related reasons, he could travel throughout Europe and to other parts of the Portuguese colonial empire, such as Angola, linking up the emerging hubs of Lusophone nationalism. In this way, as we will see, during these years Cabral became the lynchpin of the incipient nationalist movement in the Portuguese colonies.

* * *

On his return to Lisbon, Cabral tried to find a new job. He applied for positions in various public organizations but was not called for any interviews. Through his former colleagues and professors at ISA, he found some consultancy work, all in the private sector. Working for the company Mercantil Lda, Cabral developed a study on the possibility of sugarcane production in Guinea. The same firm solicited his services again between 1958 and 1959, this time to study the viability of sugar beet production in continental Portugal. He eventually found more stable work in the *Brigada de Estudos e Defesa Fitossanitária dos Produtos Ultramarinos* (Brigade of Phytosanitary Studies and Defense of Overseas Products), a section of the *Junta de Investigações do Ultramar* (Overseas Research Board), whose director, Baeta Neves, was one of his former teachers. Between 1956 and 1960, he provided intermittent services to this organization, managing the storage section, which gave him the opportunity to write a handful of studies on the question of the conservation of colonial products, either in continental Portugal or in overseas provinces.

As part of a group chaired by Botelho da Costa—and other former teachers and colleagues, such as Ário de Azevedo—Amílcar Cabral also took part in various projects in his capacity as a pedologist. Most of his commissions involved travel to Angola and the clients were colonial companies which produced crops with high prices on the international markets of those times, such as sugarcane, coffee, and cotton. As such, between 1955 and 1956, Cabral was able to travel to Angola for the first time in order to collect data for the development of a soil map for Cassequel Properties, paid for by the Agricultural Society of Cassequel. He worked for *Fazenda Tentativa* and for *Fazenda São Francisco* on similar projects, in assignments that took place in 1956 and 1957, respectively. Between 1957 and 1958, he returned to Angola for the agrological census of *Fazenda Nhia*. At the end of the following year, he was once again in Angola, this time to take part in a study of soils and coffee-growing in the farms of Amboim and Seles, which had been commissioned by the Angolan Company of Agriculture. This was to be his last assignment for institutions, even if private, linked to the colonial regime.

In late 1959, Amílcar Cabral met with Ário de Azevedo, his former professor at ISA, who had become a close friend and colleague in the various projects he had been involved with since his return to Lisbon, especially those that required travel to Angola. The reason for the meeting, which took place in a restaurant in Setúbal, was to discuss the details of his next mission to Angola. But Cabral told Azevedo that he was no longer interested in such work. He wanted to abandon the commissions in order to "give a different direction to his life." More than forty years after these events, Ário de Azevedo was still convinced that Cabral's plans were motivated by the various injustices he had suffered since his placements in Alentejo and in Bissau, and later, Lisbon. These problems were related to the prevalence of racism at that time. Being a black engineer meant that most of the time Cabral had to carry a document with clear instructions on how he should be treated (where to sleep and what to eat, for instance) on his travels to Africa. In a piece written by Azevedo on the agronomic career of Cabral, he concludes by asking "what would have happened if the doors of investigation had not been closed but opened more early to Cabral?" suggesting that Cabral's desire for a change of life direction was simply motivated by professional disillusionment. What he ignores however, as do many others, is Cabral's involvement in the formation of the movement for the liberation of Lusophone Africa.

Whichever perspective is used to analyze this transformation, there is one clear fact: Cabral traded in a stable life, with a profession that allowed him well-paid work—in spite of highs and lows and moments of misunderstanding—for the trials and tribulations of nationalism and revolution in Africa—with no fewer uncertainties and misunderstandings. However, to reduce the cause of this transformation to mere professional frustrations is both to underplay the seriousness with which he devoted himself to the nationalist project, and also to overlook the ways in which he had prepared and anticipated this change. His development into a nationalist did not take place overnight but was a process which had involved much doubt and hesitation.

* * *

The independence of Guinea-Conakry in September 1958 was an event that changed Cabral's life, for he saw it as a clear indication of a radical change in history and a sign that Portuguese colonialism in Africa could also become a thing of the past. Luís Cabral provides a vivid description of the euphoric reaction of his brother to the event. Luís had recently married Lucette Andrade and was in Lisbon to enjoy his leave of absence, *licença graciosa*, which allowed him to attend academic examinations for the fifth grade of the *Liceu*. According to Luís, this was one of the happiest times of Amílcar's life: he enjoyed a stable family environment and had overcome the financial difficulties of his time as a student. Testament to this was the spacious apartment he lived in with his family, which boasted an ample terrace with a view of the Tejo river. This well-being was also reflected in his appearance:

> [H]e was grooming a fine moustache, dressing in the latest fashion and, when he went out, he dressed in a beautiful brown raincoat with a matching cap. When he smoked one of his exquisite pipes with his usual self-confidence, he had all the appearance of an elegant young intellectual for whom life was going well.

The independence of Ghana, in 1957, and particularly the political events in the French colonies began to have an effect in the centers of the colonial powers themselves. Algerians had taken up arms to fight for their own liberation in November 1954. The colonial power's indecisiveness in the face of an Algerian revolution had prompted a handful of *pied-noirs* to seize government buildings in Algiers, which pushed France to the brink of a civil war. General Charles de Gaulle, the hero of the French liberation from the Nazis in 1945, seized the opportunity and threatened to stage a coup, erupting back onto the political stage. Overcoming resistance from a number of members of parliament, particularly the socialists, de Gaulle was appointed head of the state under two interrelated conditions that he himself had imposed. The first was that he would govern for seven years with extraordinary powers for the first six months. The French constitution had to be revised to allow such sweeping changes, and France entered into a new political era, the Fifth Republic. Since Algiers was the epicenter of the constitutional crisis, de Gaulle, even before his appointment as the president of the council of ministers (prime minister) on 1 June 1958, had already announced his intention to visit the territory.

Only three days after his inauguration on 4 June, de Gaulle travelled to Algiers to announce what had already been established in the new constitution: all African subjects of France would be called to choose between independence or integration into a "community" in which the African states would have autonomous governments, but leaving France in control of portfolios such as foreign affairs, defense, economic policies, education, justice, transportation, and communication. France would also reserve for itself the right to keep troops in these territories, allegedly for the protection of French expatriates, who could also be given orders to use force in case it was necessary to suppress any form of internal resistance. De Gaulle, using his personal influence and trying to give form to the elements of the *loi-cadre* (Reform Act) integrated into the constitution, was attempting to revive the old principle of the French Union.

However, the French project of constitutional neo-colonialism did not get off the ground. On 20 August, de Gaulle began an African trip, to Abidjan, Brazzaville, Antananarivo, Conakry and Dakar, and then back to Algiers, to present the two options to the colonies—either to join the French federation, or to push for independence in the referendum the French were to vote in on 28 September. Ceremonies and engagement with the communities in these places went according to plan, until de Gaulle arrived in Conakry on the afternoon of 25 August. He was received by Sékou Touré, former trade unionist and leader of the *Parti Démocratique Africain*, and at that time representative for his country in the French parliament. In front of crowds who elbowed their way forward to see the French president,

Touré stated that Guineans would rather choose poverty in independence than opulence in slavery. Visibly shocked, de Gaulle was forced to improvise a speech in which he stated that Guinea was free to choose independence by voting no in the referendum. In fact, Guinea was the only country that voted no to the new constitution, and, on 29 September, it became independent.

The afternoon of 27 August in which Touré secured the destiny of Guinea was broadcast worldwide, capturing the imaginations of many Africans across the continent. And beyond the continent too, if we take into account the descriptions provided by Luís Cabral on how these events were celebrated in the apartment at Infante Santo. This was the occasion at which Cabral uttered one of the sentences cherished most of all by his hagiographers: "Now, I have a homeland. I can pack my things and return to Africa for good." Even if this description is not accurate, and even if Cabral did not say these words at that precise moment, the sentence captures a feeling shared by many African nationalists living in Europe who felt that the time had come to go back to Africa.

* * *

Ário de Azevedo and Luís Cabral both provide explanations for events in Cabral's life at this time. For the former, the need for change in Cabral's life was motivated by professional frustrations, whereas for the latter, it was a response to the opportunities opened up by the independence of Guinea. Both suggest that these changes were for the most part spontaneous. These differing interpretations may be caused by the fact that Cabral was careful to conceal certain aspects of his life. Ário de Azevedo, and other colleagues, for instance, were not aware that during his travels to the centers of sugar beet production Cabral contacted friends that had already left Lisbon.

Early debates and deliberations about forming a single front against Portuguese colonialism probably took place during Cabral's trips to visit Mário de Andrade and Marcelino dos Santos in Paris. This group would initially be called *Movimento Anti-Colonial* (MAC). The set-up of this organization, far more modest in its objectives and activities than described by the Angolan nationalist Lúcio Lara, only took place later when a "delegation of the Democratic Movement for the Portuguese

Colonies in Paris, in the person of Marcelino dos Santos, visited Lisbon in the first semester of 1957 by invitation of the African nationalists residing in Portugal. From the conclusions of this meeting the Anticolonial Movement is founded." Agostinho Neto, Noémia de Sousa, Humberto Machado, as well as Eduardo dos Santos (not to be confused with the later Angolan president) and Lúcio Lara, almost all of them residing in Lisbon, also took part in these meetings.

Cabral was the most financially stable of the group. On various occasions, he had to send his friends "small" amounts of money. Cabral's help was more than welcome, as his companions in Europe at that times were facing problems of political or financial precariousness, if not both. Agostinho Neto, for example, spent as much time in jail as he did on the outside. Marcelino dos Santos and Mário de Andrade lived in Paris, the former supported by his family and the latter barely able to cover his expenses with the meager salary of his job as secretary of Alioune Diop's magazine *Présence Africaine*. It was only Cabral who could freely travel under the cover of being an agricultural engineer on assignments for colonial companies. Thanks to him, Angolans—especially the nationalists in Luanda and Lisbon—were able to keep in touch.

Up to this point Amílcar Cabral had been very discreet. Despite the meetings at his house or in his car, albeit in constant motion to dodge the police, and even though he was close to people with police records and visited others in prison—such as Agostinho Neto—he had never been summoned by the PIDE. Every year his record with the PIDE was updated with the same brief commentary: "morally and politically nothing was found against him." However, this period of grace would only last until 30 December 1958, three months after he had decided to return to Africa.

The apparent bubble of security that Cabral lived in began to burst when the Angolan nationalist Viriato da Cruz arrived in Lisbon. Da Cruz was coming from Luanda, where he had been living until then and had taken part in the creation of what was very probably the first political party to be founded in Angola, the *Partido Comunista Angolano* (Angolan Communist Party). After his arrival in Lisbon, with the police on his tail, Viriato da Cruz, for whatever reason sought shelter at the home of Amílcar Cabral, whom he must have met during the various trips the latter had made to Angola. This created a double problem for Cabral, for it was not only the PIDE that was after da Cruz. The Angolan nationalists residing in Lisbon found it unacceptable that a "cadre of the interior" had come to Portugal without looking for them. To resolve matters, Lúcio Lara approached Cabral, who, according to the former, somewhat hesitantly confirmed that "Viriato da Cruz was really hiding at his place but that for conspiratorial reasons he asked for secrecy." Lara was not convinced and, according to himself, succeeded in demonstrating to Cabral the "dubious situation" he found himself in "as member of the directorate" they had created. Cabral then agreed to take da Cruz to a meeting to resolve the "awkwardness" of the situation, which took place at the home of Lúcio Lara. Besides those already mentioned, others who took part in this meeting were Agostinho Neto, Eduardo dos Santos and Ruth Lara, Lúcio Lara's wife.

In one of the meetings with this group, Cabral was assigned a very dangerous mission. During a trip to Angola, between August and September 1959, he was given the task of recruiting eleven youths to be sent to Tunisia, where they were to receive training in guerrilla tactics. The idea was that once they were back in the country, they would form the "core operational group to jumpstart the armed struggle." The offer had been made by Frantz Fanon, at that time adviser to the GPRA, who, during the second Congress of Black Writers and Artists in Rome between 26 March and 1 April 1959 met with the Angolan representatives, namely Viriato da Cruz, Lúcio Lara and Mário de Andrade, in the basement of a small coffee bar. Fanon, who was yet to write his famous *The Wretched of the Earth*, explained to them that he meant to export the "Algerian model" of anti-imperialist struggle to Angola, as a way to scatter the forces of NATO, which supported France in the war against the Algerian nationalists.

Amílcar Cabral had not been the group's first choice. The directorate had already asked Noémia de Sousa to undertake the mission. But, for family reasons, she was not available. As Cabral was to go to Frankfurt shortly after the Congress (under the cover of one of his trips to study the viability of beetroot planting in continental Portugal), he was asked in de Sousa's place. In Luanda, however, Cabral could not find any of the individuals he was meant to contact. The PIDE had conducted a raid, imprisoning and torturing hundreds of nationalists. They were later put on trial in the famous *Processo dos 50* (Trial of the 50).

It is likely that this experience in Luanda may have triggered in Cabral the certainty that the time had come to return to Africa. In the report he sent in September 1959 to his friends at the MAC, written from "somewhere in Africa," he discussed the details of the massive operation undertaken by the police to imprison, threaten, and bribe members of nationalist cells. As such, he concluded, there were no reasons for the members of the MAC to stay in Europe. Time had come to move to Africa, where they should create the conditions to develop more serious work for the independence of their countries.

On his return from his last trip to Luanda, he visited the Republic of Congo, "to see the possibility of work for our trusted people". He visited also Accra, the capital of Ghana, instead of Guinea as scheduled, having not been given guarantees that his passport would not be stamped at the airport. To his companions in the MAC, echoes of these trips came from other sources, such as the correspondence with AK Barden, an official in the cabinet of Ghana's prime minister. According to Barden, Cabral had taken advantage of his short stay in Ghana to "prepare a document on the inhuman atrocities that the indigenous citizens (*sic*) of Angola were submitted to by the Portuguese regime," adding that this document was being analyzed with careful attention. The proof of Ghana's interest in the Angolan question arrived a couple of days later, when, according to Viriato da Cruz, Kwame Nkrumah gave a speech in which he made reference to the case of Angola, based on the information provided by Amílcar Cabral. Da Cruz was convinced that the information used was based on Cabral's report since, "as president, he would not mention the case without the basis of an Angolan source (*sic*)".

Cabral's courage was recognized by the members of the MAC. For Lúcio Lara, Amílcar Cabral deserved praise for the "intelligent and patriotic manner in which he had undertaken his mission". However, Cabral was also the target of some criticism. Lara, for example, criticized him for having made reference to the MAC, in a letter sent to the *Parti de la Fédération de l'Afrique* of Mali, as being a structure that instead of people, comprised all the nationalist movements.

This doubt concerning whether the MAC should represent people or organizations provides interesting clues to understand the emergence of anti-Portuguese nationalism. What was the importance of this group of former students in Lisbon in the overall structure of African nationalism in the Portuguese colonies? Was it the case that the MAC, in practice, had anticipated the formation of the MPLA and the PAIGC? The action plan that Viriato da Cruz wrote for the MAC may shed light on some of these questions. The MAC was to contact the organizations of the Portuguese colonies; discuss with those organizations the conditions for their representation in the MAC; for the MAC to be transformed into a council; and to include in this council representatives of all organizations. However, the MAC ended up being dissolved, and the work of bringing together the nationalist forces would be continued by the PAIGC and MPLA.

His work colleagues were not the only ones Amílcar Cabral kept ignorant of his involvement in clandestine nationalist groups. Even though his colleagues at the MAC could count on him to undertake tasks as the "messenger," linking up the groups in Angola and Europe, they were probably unaware of the efforts of Amílcar Cabral to create a nationalist movement in his native land. According to the official PAIGC narrative, Amílcar Cabral had been driven from Guinea by governor Melo e Alvim and he was only authorized to visit the country to see his family. It was thus under this pretext that Cabral twice visited Bissau. During his first stay, he founded the *Partido Africano para Independência*—which would later on become the PAIGC—and, on his second visit in 1959, in the aftermath of the events of Pidjiguiti, he convened the famous meeting of cadres in which the party decided to change its strategy. He gave the order to end direct confrontations in the big cities, which would certainly lead to civilian casualties, and advised his men to leave Bissau and seek refuge in neighboring countries such as Senegal and Guinea-Conakry, where they should organize themselves to start the anticolonial war.

However, one can also draw attention to a number of other events which help explain the circumstances under which the PAIGC was created. The falsification of the founding dates of the nationalist movements has been a common feature in Lusophone African countries. In Angola, Mozambique, and Guinea, for example, political organizations would choose a date of origin which came before their actual founding. This was perhaps because of the fact that colonial powers would only recognize and deal with "legitimate representatives of the people." In most cases, this simply meant the oldest organization in the struggle for the liberation of a given territory.

Leaders of national liberation movements came under pressure to present their organizations as the first to be established, so as to devalue the emergence of others. The fact that Cabral referred to these movements as groups instead of as people in his report—for which Viriato da Cruz had admonished him—speaks to the fact that there were no nationalist and political organizations, such as the MPLA and the PAIGC, at that time. However, in vying for international support, they had to label themselves as the first, which in most cases also meant being the "legitimate force of the people's aspirations."

Furthermore, it is not conceivable that the PAIGC was founded under the circumstances often described if one takes into account the conditions under which these young nationalists operated at the time. Political activism in the context of the *Estado Novo* regime was labeled a crime, so those wishing to subvert the colonial order were immersed in a climate of fear, mistrust, and even paranoia. In the clandestine meetings in which political and subversive issues were discussed, it was often impossible to distinguish true nationalists from those who were there as PIDE informants.

Luís Cabral is perhaps the Guinean nationalist who most painstakingly attempted to provide the party with the formality of a date of birth. In his book, he describes in great detail the founding of the party as having taken place on the afternoon of 19 September 1956, in an apartment shared by Aristides Pereira and Fernando Fortes. However, there are no references to the party in the correspondence between members of the MAC in the period from 1956 to 1960. In the letters that survived, Cabral never refers to the existence of nationalist groups in Bissau. This is all the more surprising as there were a number of opportunities to do so. When he returned from Bissau, for example, he refers to the massacres in Guinea and mentions "the determination of the people", but he makes no reference to any anti-colonial activism taking place.

The reason for this omission may simply be that the PAIGC did not exist at that time. Abílio Duarte, considered one of the founders of the party—although he was not in Bissau on the date attributed to its establishment—denied various times that the events took place in the

ENGINEER AND CLANDESTINE MILITANT

way in which they were later described. Aristides Pereira, more recently, has shed some light on this confusion. The date for the founding of the party was chosen retrospectively, when he and Cabral were asking for the support of the Senegalese president, Léopold Sedar Senghor, in Dakar. Senghor believed that a Guinean party with PAI as its acronym had to be a branch of a Senegalese political formation which he had declared illegal. This led to the need to find a founding date which preceded the formation of the Senegalese party—only later would the letters "GC" be added to the acronym. It is therefore plausible that the PAIGC was only actually formed in 1959, on the occasion of Cabral's last trip to Bissau.

In sum, in the context of the MAC, Amílcar Cabral did not represent any political force of Guinea. Or at least not to the knowledge of his friends. It was in fact Hugo de Menezes who took the initiative of creating a party in Guinea. Menezes, who inexplicably appeared at the end of the 1950s representing the MAC in the PDG of Sékou Touré, decided of his own volition to include Guineans in his organization, with the simple reasoning that, as he argued, out of all the Portuguese colonies, Guinea was the one whose struggle for independence most interested his host. His gesture was simply one of anticipation, since Sékou Touré himself had already considered forming a nationalist organization to work for the independence of Guinea. Testament to this interest were the privileges that Menezes' group were granted: the right to create newspapers and broadcast radio shows and a loan to be "repaid after the independence of Guinea".

A nationalist group had existed in Guinea since 1956, which, although not formally organized, was striving to be so. This is an indication of one of the many contradictions that the PAIGC would face right from its inception. It was, at its founding, essentially a party of Cape Verdeans (or descendants of Cape Verdeans) with scant local membership, founded in Guinea, for the purpose of liberating both countries. Another contradiction was that Cape Verdeans were also a cog in the machine of colonial domination, in that they constituted an intermediary group between the natives and the central power. As we have already discussed, the different social statuses of Cape Verdeans and Guineans—who lived under different legal systems, with Cape Verdeans considered citizens and Guineans largely considered "natives"—they could only interact with each other fleetingly.

Notwithstanding these structural limitations, the leadership of this group of nationalists tried to work among groups living in urban centers. Although it remains unclear, it is probable that the PAIGC was involved in the radicalization of protests by dockers at the Port of Bissau on 3 August 1959, when these workers decided to stop their activities and demand an increase in their salaries. According to the priest Henrique Pinto Rema, there had already been skirmishes between the police and the sailors of *Casa Nosoco* on 8 March 1956—before the alleged foudning of the PAIGC—when the sailors "refused to receive their salaries and did not allow the exit of *Casa Gouveia*'s boats." This was the incident, according to Rema, which forced the police—who had been warned about the situation at the Pidjiguiti docks—to go to the place armed. After a short struggle in which two officers and seven agents were injured, the police shot at the protesters, who could only fend off the bullets with sticks, oars, and iron bars. As a result, fifteen Guineans died and another fifty were injured, not counting the corpses that were carried away by the waters of the Geba river.

These events convinced Cabral of the impossibility of developing peaceful means of protest such as those that were being employed in the British and French colonies. The police had already shown how they would quell any acts of this nature. According to the historiography of the party, this is the moment, during his last stay in Bissau in September 1959, that Cabral called for the "historic" meeting of cadres, in which every available member should be present. In this meeting, a decision was taken to change the strategy of the party. Urban actions with strikes and protests would only cost human lives, as had been demonstrated. Armed force was the only way to adequately respond to the violence of the Portuguese. For this, it was necessary to organize the party outside of the urban centers. Accordingly, Cabral ordered the militants to abandon Bissau, where only a small structure should stay, in order to work on recruiting young people to be sent to guerrilla preparation camps. According to Aquino de Bragança, this marks the moment in the history of the party where it passed from mere protest nationalism to revolutionary nationalism.

However, at this stage, Amílcar Cabral and other elements of the PAIGC leadership did not have the capacity to mobilize Guineans. As

ENGINEER AND CLANDESTINE MILITANT

we have already seen, the colonial state not only curtailed the right of association, but was also deeply suspicious of any interaction between people of different social groups, such as Cape Verdeans and Guineans. To overcome this problem, before leaving the country, Amílcar Cabral met with Rafael Barbosa, a Guinean, and at that time one of the most active members of the underground networks of Bissau. Cabral persuaded him to use his connections and his ability to mobilize others in order to help the party smuggle those young people interested in taking part in the guerrilla campaign out of the city. From this encounter, according to Luís Cabral, a structure emerged which brought together the groups represented by Amílcar Cabral and Rafael Barbosa—the Front for the Liberation of Guinea and Cape Verde. There were already many young people wanting to leave Bissau, such as Victor Saúde Maria, who would later become one of the most distinguished party cadres. According to Saúde Maria, Cabral convinced them that it was still too early to leave Bissau—a position which seemed to contradict the decisions of the historic meeting of 1959—since the conditions to receive them had not yet been put in place in Conakry. Cabral bought Mussa Fati, one of these prospective freedom fighters, a sewing machine to help him make some money while he was waiting for the time to leave. After consultation with Rafael Barbosa, Cabral left Bissau for Lisbon, stopping off in Dakar, Senegal, on the way, to meet with Guineans and Cape Verdeans who were organizing a nationalist movement there.

4

SHATTERING THE WALLS OF SILENCE

In the late 1950s, Cabral's personal security and physical integrity had become a major concern after the risks he had taken in order to accomplish his clandestine missions to Africa. Information on Cabral's illicit activities had reached the headquarters of the PIDE. It was only a matter of time before he would receive an arrest warrant, as the police began to piece together the puzzle of his suspicious activities. On his return to Lisbon, after visiting Bissau for the "meeting of cadres", as well as going to Dakar to meet the nationalists residing there, Cabral probably realised that his freedom to move around like this was coming to an end. But he had to take this risk and return to Lisbon one final time before embracing a clandestine life.

Cabral had a number of administrative tasks to attend to before he could leave Lisbon for good, such as securing all the cash he could from the banks—as Cabral was, according to his friends, the "only one in a position to help others." There were also other more urgent and painful matters related to his family and marriage. Cabral's wife Maria Helena in all likelihood knew very little about his political activities. Cabral left Lisbon without telling her a thing. It was only a number of weeks later on 20 December 1959 that he sent her a letter explaining his situation and asking her to hold out with "the girl and life." Maria Helena immediately wrote to Lúcio Lara, who tried to "calm her down." But he could not keep her from packing her things and travelling to join Cabral in Paris. The couple spent four days, 21–25 January, at Hôtel de la Paix, on Blainville Street. Cabral, "depressed and quite worried," managed to convince his wife to return with their daughter to Lisbon, "where they would be better off than anywhere else." Maria Helena had departed Lisbon for a leave of absence of a month, Cabral writes, alleging that her husband was sick, but she would return to put their accounts in order and "settle the matter for good."

Perhaps on account of this domestic crisis, Cabral was the last of the MAC members to arrive in Tunis, the capital of Tunisia, where from 25 to 29 January 1960 the Second All-African People's Conference was taking place. This was a major event in the history of Africa, for it is also referred to as the second preparatory meeting (the first had taken place in Accra) for the founding of the Organization of African Unity (OAU) three years later on 25 May 1963. For Cabral and his group, Tunis was the first opportunity to raise awareness of the colonial situation in Lusophone Africa. Represented in this forum were not only the recently liberated African countries—or those that would achieve independence over the course of 1960—but also a number of others, such as the People's Republic of China, the Federal Republic of Germany, India, Sweden, the Soviet Union, Yugoslavia, and even the United States of America, through the American Committee on Africa.

As Cabral would soon find out, denouncing Portuguese colonialism was no easy task in these early days. Portuguese colonialism was for the most part simply ignored, or considered benign, since many people had the idea—thanks to works of colonial propaganda—that the Portuguese were effectively building multiracial societies in Africa. Cabral illustrated this through a conversation with one of the delegates at the meeting, in which he tried to explain to him the real situation in the Portuguese colonies. His interlocutor simply responded: "you don't have any problems; you get along with the Portuguese."

Nevertheless, the meeting in Tunis was a milestone for the liberation of Lusophone Africa for at least two reasons. Firstly, notwithstanding the indifference to the situation in the Portuguese colonies, it was in Tunis that the first victory against Portuguese colonialism was achieved: the representatives adopted a resolution condemning Portuguese colonialism, the first document on the topic signed by

African countries, many of them only recently liberated. Secondly, with the exception of Agostinho Neto who was imprisoned in Lisbon, Tunis provided an opportunity for this group of African nationalists to reunite for the first time on African soil. Even more importantly, Tunis marked the first time that they emerged as representatives of a nationalist organization, in this case the MAC.

Properly speaking, Tunis marked the beginning of nationalism in the Portuguese African colonies. There, the group decided to break up the MAC, resolving a contradiction that had provoked a great deal of debate among them, as the MAC was a nationalist organization bringing together individuals. At the Tunis conference, the individual members of the MAC were pushed by a number of delegates and organizations to represent their own countries. Receiving assistance would be dependent on this move. Consequently, it was in Tunis that Cabral and his colleagues signed the first documents with the names of their nationalist organizations, such as the MPLA and the PAIGC. At the end of the conference, the MAC was dissolved and, in its place, as a sort of coordinating organization, they founded the African Revolutionary Front for the National Independence of the Portuguese Colonies (FRAIN).

As Tunis was the next level in the struggle against Portuguese colonialism, Cabral's friends soon found African states in which to settle and from there to start the fight for the liberation of their own countries. Viriato da Cruz, Mário de Andrade, and Hugo de Menezes went to Conakry, while Lúcio Lara and his family headed to Morocco, after being granted political asylum there. Cabral, however, would first go to London, where, in a symbolic fashion, he was initiated into life as a freedom fighter.

Cabral's stay in London in February 1960 continued the work he had started in Tunis: shattering the wall of silence regarding the Portuguese colonial question. London was a particularly interesting place for such an undertaking. Like France, Great Britain was conceding, or about to concede, independence to its colonies in Africa. Cabral therefore wanted to make the British audience aware of the path chosen by Portugal: instead of leaving Africa, Portugal was reinforcing its military presence, particularly in Angola and Mozambique, and violently repressing any independentist claims. Angola was a case in point, as in the previous year of 1959, hundreds of people had been accused and sentenced on charges of terrorism.

The trip to London was the last time that Cabral would travel using a passport which bore his real name—from then on, he would travel with many other passports displaying different nationalities and names. He had so far been adept at hiding his identity, using various aliases including Abel Djassi and Abel Silva. This was probably one of the reasons that the PIDE took so long to implicate him in activities considered criminal. For some of his close associates, however, the reason Cabral refused to use his own name was simply cowardice. In a letter in which he was asked about his use of an alias, Cabral argued that there was no reason not to use one, explaining that the "organizations" they were forming, while still weak, were not "private matters". Cabral added that no significant gain would come from using his own name, since "our comrades know that I am abroad and know who I am, and all the prestige that we can get has to come from our work and from our organizations, not from us as individuals." He also suggested that using his name at that time would be putting his companions and his family members at risk, since "the demands of the struggle and the need to act freely forced me to be away, in the certainty that it would be an unnecessary sacrifice for them."

* * *

In those years, Cabral was still totally unknown in the British capital and in African and diplomatic circles there. The few contacts he had were probably given to him by Hugo de Menezes, with whom he had spent time weeks before in Tunis. Mainza Chona from Zambia and Kanyama Chiume from Malawi, members of the powerful Committee of African Organizations—a body that brought together nationalist organizations from various British colonies represented in London—were among these contacts. Along with many other African nationalists, they wee staying in an eighteenth-century mansion situated at number 200 Gower Street, which served as a sort of passing house for nationalist activists from Africa. This was where Cabral spent his first nights in London. It is possible that this arrangement had also been facilitated by Hugo de Menezes, who had lived on Gower Street, or at least had used this address to receive his mail, during his time in the British capital.

SHATTERING THE WALLS OF SILENCE

In London, Cabral met a number of people related in various ways to nationalist organizations in Africa, such as João Caracciolo Cabral from the Goa League, who would later represent the FRAIN in the British capital. More importantly, Cabral would make acquaintance with Basil Davidson, one of the most genuine and generous supporters of nationalism in Lusophone Africa. Davidson was a journalist and writer who had worked for the British secret services in the Balkans during WWII, helping organize resistance to the Nazis. He then moved into writing and journalism, and in 1955, published *African Awakening*, an essay-cum-travelogue on Angola and the Congo. This book came to provide first-hand insight into two of the most inaccessible African countries at a time in which around half the continent was about to become independent, and two which had been largely ignored by the world press. By travelling to these countries, which were under the domination of Belgium and Portugal, documenting the appalling working conditions, and, above all, describing the hope at the prospect of impending independence, particularly in Congo, Basil Davidson became, as Cabral put it, the first Western man to try to break down the wall of silence around the Portuguese colonies.

For Davidson, one imagines it was riveting to have a native of Guinea make the case for the independence of Lusophone Africa. Davidson translated and prefaced Cabral's pamphlet entitled *The Facts About Portugal's African Colonies*, edited by the Union of Democratic Control. This document was the first major indictment of Portugal's colonialism written by a native of the Portuguese colonies in Africa. Its opening is reminiscent of how Jean-Paul Sartre starts the preface for Fanon's *The Wretched of the Earth*, sharing with the reader the number of people worldwide living under colonialism. Likewise, for Cabral, numbers counted, and according to him, there were 11 million Africans who lived under the domination of Portugal, the most backward and agrarian country in western Europe, with the lowest education rates. For Cabral, Portuguese colonialism was based on what he called "European migration", which consisted of the implementation of legal measures to facilitate the occupation of African territories by metropolitan whites. These settlers were given the best plots of land in Angola and Mozambique, which consequently drove thousands of Africans out of their own homes. Those Africans, left with few other alternatives, either settled for poorer plots of land to dedicate themselves to the production of colonial crops to sell at fixed prices to the concessionaires, or surrendered themselves to the colonial state's labor schemes—akin to slavery.

The Portuguese labor regime, whose origins preceded the arrival of Salazar in power, had been theorized by a number of the so-called *ilustres coloniais*, distinguished colonial thinkers. For António Ennes, for instance, the "natural laziness of Africans" should be fought through the transformation of labor into a legal obligation. This philosophy is the basis of the abject *indigenato* system, which divided the colonial society into two groups, the "civilized" and the "natives". In the Portuguese colonies, the civilized only accounted for one percent of the population. They were considered to have comparable levels of culture and knowledge to the Portuguese and were accordingly granted by the state rights only citizens could enjoy. The remaining population did not benefit from any rights, for the simple reason that, according to racist laws, they did not have "the knowledge, the habits and social presuppositions necessary for the full application of the private and public law of Portuguese citizens."

In the thinking of Cabral, shattering the wall of silence meant separating the myths of Portuguese colonialism in Africa from the reality. For as Cabral suggests, Portuguese colonialism depended to a great extent on maintaining the mythology around it. In the 1930s, paternalism, with its Darwinian undertones, was the cornerstone of Portuguese colonialism, claiming that without Europe's intervention, Africans were condemned to stagnation, if not to barbarity and extinction. Later, however, this framework could no longer be justified, as in many parts of the continent Africans were engaged in administering their own countries. It was in this context that the theories of the Brazilian sociologist Gilberto Freyre gave new life to Portuguese colonialism through the creation of a new myth—that of luso-tropicalism.

For Freyre, Brazil was a unique society in the world and its formation was a result of the smooth blending of different elements, namely the African, the native Indian, and particularly the Portuguese, who had contributed their affectionate and malleable character. The outcome of this, Freyre argued, was not only the establishment of a racially diverse society, but also the creation of a milder colonial process, if compared to other territories in the Americas colonized by the Spanish, French, British, and Dutch. The Portuguese *Estado Novo* saw in Freyre's work an opportunity to repackage the Portuguese presence in Africa. Freyre himself was invited to travel through Portuguese colonies and write about the colonial experience in Africa, which he diligently did in books such as *Aventura e Rotina* (Adventure and Routine). He argues that even if the Portuguese were not "mixing racially" as they did in Brazil, they were still blending culturally. With the *Estado Novo's* appropriation of the concept of luso-tropicalism, colonial propaganda went even further than Freyre himself to make the case for the existence of a multiracial society in the colonies.

Countering luso-tropicalism theoretically was probably the most serious concern among these nationalists, for living in Lisbon they could sense the extent to which practice diverged from propaganda. Mário de Andrade, under the pseudonym of Buanga Fele, had already addressed this issue for *Présence Africaine*. Andrade did not only demolish Freyre's argument in *Casa Grande and Sanzala*, but he also accused the Brazilian sociologist of selling his work to the Portuguese regime. In the pamphlet, Cabral also takes up the critique of luso-tropicalism, writing that while the presence of the Portuguese in Africa had resulted in some racial diversity, it was more talked about than real. For racial miscegenation had stopped in the early 1920s with the migration to Africa of large contingents of metropolitan whites. Hence, the numbers were manifestly inferior to what was claimed in propaganda: out of 10 million inhabitants in Angola and Mozambique, only 60,000 appeared in the census as mixed race, which corresponded to less than 1 per cent of the population. In his attempt to explain Portuguese colonialism, Perry Anderson wrote that in the year 1958 in Angola, only one marriage between a white man and a black woman had taken place, a situation that could not be compared even to that of South Africa during apartheid, but more closely resembled that of the racially segregated states of Mississippi and Alabama.

Separating myth from reality equally meant denouncing the falsehoods of luso-tropicalism. For as Cabral attempted to demonstrate, in all of Portugal's colonies, racism was hypocritically practiced, with the Portuguese justifying their permanent presence in Africa by their "capacity" to mix with black people and form a multiracial community.

This was, of course, a fallacy, but nonetheless it was a significant factor in Portuguese colonial policy. In the colonies with a significant white population, such as Angola and Mozambique, there were cinemas, cafes, and restaurants exclusively frequented by whites. Mixed-race couples were laughed at and few would show themselves in public. Perry Anderson added that in hospitals, white and black people stayed in separate wards, and hotels only gave jobs to whites. The Portuguese politician Almeida Santos tells in his memoirs of an episode in which, during a trip to Mozambique as a member of the academic choir *Orfeão Académico de Coimbra*, he refused to go to a ball hosted by the general-governor because two mixed-race sisters of his colleagues were refused entry. However, as Cabral also hinted, the more pervasive and subtle form of discrimination was economic. Wages for most black people did not grant them sufficient income to use public transport regularly or to rent a house in central urban areas.

If colonialism in all its forms and manifestations was condemnable—an undisputed notion in most of the civilized world—Portuguese colonialism, according to Cabral, was even more so, as Portugal was not even equipped to colonize. The survival of colonialism was anchored in the artificial differentiation between the colonizers and the colonized. Privileges were distributed on that basis. The colonized population was deprived of political and civic rights unless they could transition to the intermediary level of *assimilado*. However, in order for this to happen, the applicant had to prove economic stability, conditions of habitability, the capacity to pay taxes, and proof of military service. With a note of irony, Cabral asserts that had these regulations applied in continental Portugal, half the Portuguese would not qualify as *assimilado*. For he concludes, "if Portugal could have a civilizing influence over any people, it would be a kind of miracle. Colonialism, a dying phenomenon, has never depended on miracles to survive."

In this document, Cabral could use the information he himself gathered during the time he spent in Africa, as well as many other sources of information condemning Portugal's practice with the same vehemence. For data on the labor question in Angola, Cabral used Henrique Galvão's explosive report, whose information was collected during his time as colonial inspector and representative for Angola in the National Assembly, in 1947. Galvão was not the first to denounce such practices, and his document came in a long tradition of foreigners denouncing poor, if not criminal, labor conditions in the Portuguese colonies. Galvão's report is still in a way quite constructive, for he argues that labor conditions in Angola were the main reason for Angolans to migrate to Congo or Zambia, where they could receive better salaries. Those who stayed in Angola were simply condemned to malnutrition and physical decay, which was the cause of the high rate of child mortality.

While clearly stating the problem of colonial exploitation, Cabral's document was too vague in terms of what was being done in order to improve the situation that he was denouncing. His pamphlet *The Facts About Portugal's African Colonies*, for example, states that it is presenting the position of organizations fighting against Portuguese colonialism, but these organizations are never named. He also mentions his desire for a peaceful resolution to the colonial situation: force was only to be used if Portugal refused to negotiate the right of self-determination, in order to "assist the peoples represented" by the nationalists. However, he did not give any explanation for what was meant by the "use of force".

By then, Cabral was aware that his time of anonymity was over. Before the publication of *Facts*, he gave a press conference in London, the content of which was broadcast by some international agencies and picked up by some journals of reference, such as the French newspaper *Le Monde*. The results were immediate, as Viriato da Cruz enthusiastically comments in a letter: "the press conference Abel (Amílcar Cabral) gave was broadcast by news agencies across the world. It made the news in the Congos and Nigeria. In short, the case has alarmed the Portuguese."

Cabral was right to point out that while the echo of the press conference did not have any impact in the Portuguese press—its content was obviously not cited in any of the Portuguese newspapers—the secret police was paying attention. While the PIDE had not been able to prove that Cabral was involved in subversive activities during his time as a student in Lisbon, things changed after London. A few months after his intervention in London, on 30 July 1960, the PIDE produced an extensive report under the title "Subversive Activities in Africa." The police had found out that Cabral, agronomist and member of the

FRAIN, had been involved in the brutal events of Bissau, the massacres of Pidgiguiti in 1959. The report added that Cabral, on his way to Lisbon, had visited numerous African countries, such as the Belgian Congo, Ghana, the Republic of Congo, Senegal, and the Republic of Guinea. These trips, according to the report, were part of a strategy to convince African and Asian countries to take a position against Portuguese colonialism, since all these countries had, or were about to have, seats in the General Assembly of the United Nations.

In London Amílcar Cabral had accomplished a number of things, personally and in terms of his nationalist activism. He had clarified his position, since he was no longer working for the colonial state, and had fully taken on his revolutionary status. In this way, at least temporarily, he had also freed himself from the weight of family responsibilities that could limit his movements. More importantly, he had tapped into a diplomatic possibility, by conceiving of himself and the organizations he represented as an interlocutor in the process of negotiations with Portugal for independence. For the rest of his life he would favor this solution, even if the Portuguese colonial empire only came down through a protracted colonial war and revolution.

5

A UNITED FRONT

After a short stay in London, between February and March 1960, Cabral finally returned to Africa. He settled in Conakry, the capital city of the recently liberated Guinea-Conakry, which was under the leadership of Ahmed Sékou Touré. He came with the mission of setting up a base for his party, the PAIGC, and was largely operating under the auspices of the FRAIN, alongside Angolan nationalists such as Mário Pinto de Andrade and Viriato da Cruz, who represented the MPLA. In these first years of nationalist activities, Cabral's operations took place in the two countries bordering Guinea-Bissau: Guinea-Conakry and Senegal, especially in the cities of Conakry and Dakar. These places demanded different strategies for mobilization. In the Guinea of Sékou Touré—which would later become one of the bloodiest dictatorships on the entire continent, where only the laws of force and naked power prevailed—Cabral installed the movement's military units and civilian services. The Senegal of Senghor—which had a political system with some semblance of democracy, despite its flaws—would be used by Cabral as a platform for actions of a more humanitarian and civic nature.

Cabral had settled in Conakry with the expectation of a job at the Ministry of Rural Economy. Guinea by then had been depleted of its skilled labor force. Since Guinea had been the only French colony to opt out of the Francophone federation, France, as Irving Markovitz has written, "true to her promise, eradicated her presence to the extent of pulling telephones off the walls and medicines out of the hospitals." Suddenly, Guinea was deprived of teachers in most secondary schools, as well as qualified clerks and doctors. To alleviate the pressure, Touré opened the country up to massive foreign aid. Leftist intellectuals and technocrats from Europe, and to a lesser extent from Africa, moved to Guinea to fill the available positions. Maria Helena, who had finally joined her husband, alongside their daughter, found a job as a high school teacher.

Although the couple had reconciled after Paris, Cabral's marriage to Maria Helena would not last much longer. Cabral persuaded Maria Helena to settle in Rabat, Morocco after she became pregnant with their second daughter. The idea was that she would benefit from better health care in Rabat. However, when Ana Luísa was born, on 14 August 1962, Cabral made no effort to reunite his family. According to Luís Cabral, having Maria Helena in Rabat was not only convenient for Cabral himself, but for the party as well, as this allowed its leader to spend time outside of Conakry and develop work that demanded concentration, while enjoying the company of his family. Even though Cabral's marriage had been in crisis since he had decided to leave Lisbon, Luís, very generously, assumed responsibility for the separation: "[W]hen taking such a decision [implying that the decision was in a way collectively taken], we did not take into account the profound links of Lena [Maria Helena] with the struggle which she had shared from the beginning."

Living in different countries, Cabral and Maria Helena began to gradually grow apart personally, as well as politically. Maria Helena found her own way, working alongside other Portuguese refugees in Rabat against the dictatorship of Salazar. The couple formally divorced in 1966, although in Cabral's intimate circle of friends there were still those who tried to salvage the marriage by proposing, for instance, a romantic trip to the Soviet Union. But it was too late and, at the end of that year, Cabral married Ana Maria Voss e Sá, originally from Guinea, who had studied in Czechoslovakia with financial support from the PAIGC.

* * *

A UNITED FRONT

In truth, Cabral was not the first nationalist from the MAC who sought to organize Guineans around a nationalist project. Hugo de Menezes had preceded Cabral, as Cabral writes a couple of decades later when reminiscing about his reception in Conakry. De Menezes, a doctor from São Tomé who had grown up in Angola, studied medicine in Lisbon and became a nationalist before moving to London. Disparagingly, Cabral adds that he then moved to Conakry, where he organized the first nationalist cells in that African country. When Cabral arrived, he was referred to in radio announcements as the first to launch the "cornerstone for liberation." He was invited to various events in celebration of his arrival, with long speeches and beer, organized by the so called *Movimento de Libertação dos Territórios sob Domininação Portuguesa* (Movement for the Liberation of the Territories Under Portuguese Dominance), a subsidiary of the MAC in Conakry. Cabral introduced himself as the general-secretary of the PAIGC, a party formed in the interior of Guinea, and open to every fellow countryman interested in working for the independence of this Portuguese colony.

While the PAICG was not the first political formation to appear in Guinea-Conakry, in less than three years, Cabral managed not only to neutralize all existing political formations in the neighboring country, but also to transform his movement into the only nationalist formation that was internationally recognized. How did this happen? What strategies did Cabral use? The unity between Cape Verdeans and Guineans, which would later become the party's Achilles' heel, was at that time one of its biggest advantages in comparison to other nationalist movements.

Cabral's position was that the PAIGC should not only fight for the liberation of the two countries, Guinea and Cape Verde—as some other formations would also put forward—but that once independence had been achieved, they should constitute a single country. For Cabral, this unity was anchored in two sets of arguments, one more fundamental, representing the embodiment of a historical process, and the other more contingent and provisional. Cape Verdeans were the product of the slave trade insofar as its population was formed by slaves taken from West Africa, particularly Guinea. In this way, unity as a political tactic seemed so self-evident to him that he did not make any real effort to justify or theorize it. This lack of explanation is interesting, particularly in the context of his attempts to explain so many other questions, such as the problem of class and the relationship between culture and the struggle for national liberation, among others.

But unity for Cabral also had a more circumstantial and contingent meaning. When Cabral was making the case for the independence of Guinea and Cape Verde, unity was an African catchword. In the 1960s, as Luís Cabral noted, the slogan "Africa must unite" was very popular. First used by Kwame Nkrumah, it was then adopted as the slogan of the Organization of African Unity (OAU). Furthermore, in 1960, in the aftermath of independence, various African countries were experimenting with the more or less ephemeral formation of confederations, such as Senegal and Mali, or Ghana and Guinea-Conakry. As such, envisioning the unity of the two future African states, Guinea-Bissau and Cape Verde, was a way to make an "important and original contribution to African unity," as Luís Cabral wrote. Hence, in these years, it was not hard for Cabral to make the political and diplomatic case for unity.

With this in mind, Cabral envisioned the creation of a movement which would bring together Guinean and Cape Verdean militants alike. Since there were a number of incipient nationalist organizations operating in these countries, he attempted to either create umbrella organizations to include all these formations, or to impose his PAIGC as such an organization. He had tested this technique before in 1959 when he founded the *Frente de Libertação da Guiné* (Guinean Liberation Front—FLG), which in practice had been an effort to enlist Rafael Barbosa's people into the ranks of the PAIGC. To this end, on 1 November 1960, Cabral organized a meeting of the ephemeral *Movimento de Libertação da Guiné e de Cabo Verde* (Movement for the Liberation of Guinea and Cape Verde—MLGCV). Founded in Conakry, this organization was not an affiliate of the PAIGC, but of the FLG. Members of the executive committee included, in addition to Cabral himself, Armando Ramos, Adriano Araújo, Richard Turpin, and Inácio da Silva.

In Senegal, the strategy of unity was not much different. From 12 to 14 July 1961, the PAIGC (this time as the MLGCV) called a meeting with various other nationalist groups, such as the FLGC of Henri Labéry

A UNITED FRONT

and other less important ones, such as the UDC and the UPG, which were satellites of the PAIGC. The *Movimento de Libertação da Guiné* (MLG) refused to take part in this meeting. At the end of the meeting, the *Frente Unida de Libertação* (United Liberation Front, FUL) was formed as an organization defining itself as a political structure open to all trade unions and mass organizations of Guinea and Cape Verde.

Whereas in Guinea, Cabral had only needed the favor of President Touré to illegalize organizations which were not sympathetic to the PAIGC, things were different in Senegal. There, people had the freedom to engage in political activities, and uniting all nationalists behind the same project was more difficult. Senghor himself did not support the PAIGC openly, preferring nationalist organizations that prioritized the search for peaceful solutions instead of the use of violence.

By this time, the PIDE had already infiltrated these groups, and the activities of Cabral were carefully monitored. According to the Portuguese consulate in Dakar, Cabral's intention was to impose the PAIGC on other forces, an easy task given their embryonic state of being. A number of them existed in name only and did not have any form of organized structure. The MLGCV, for example, was in practice formed by only three members, namely Henri Labéry, Vicente Có, and Lopes da Silva. The MLG had split and almost all the members had been dismissed. The UDC had essentially ceased to exist. And the RDG virtually disappeared when its leader Doudou Seydi was put in jail. Cabral's strategy in meetings with these nationalists, according to the consulate, was to foster open discussions in which these organizations were criticized, so that the members themselves proposed "the enlightening idea of organizing a new party."

While Cabral was seeking to politically unite the nationalist forces to fight colonialism, Portugal was naturally working towards the reverse, using almost the same strategy with a different outcome in mind. For the Portuguese, unity between Guineans and Cape Verdeans was a weak link to be exploited. In the years 1960–3, the Portuguese consulate in Dakar spent a great deal of time reporting on this issue, using information gleaned by the PIDE's informants. In a report to Lisbon, for example, an agent, seemingly preoccupied, demonstrated that the Cape Verdeans were opposed to "the plans of Cabral," and that they in fact preferred to maintain their links with Portugal. And if

Cabral adamantly tried to push forward his project, the document adds, there would certainly be a "war of extermination."

There was also vehement opposition to Cabral's case beyond Portugal. In fact, the majority of Cape Verdeans in these African cities were opposed to unity. The Cape Verdean national José Leitão da Graça was one of the most vehement and outspoken enemies of the unification of Guinea and Cape Verde. He had worked as a presenter and translator for Radio Ghana since 1957 and, according to the Portuguese, was involved in a campaign against Portuguese colonialism. In 1962, he and Cabral met in his house to discuss the pros and cons of unity. Cabral tried to convince him of the economic advantages of the project, which, for Leitão da Graça, did not make any sense. Cape Verdeans, he responded, had been agents of colonialism since the very beginning, and to propose a unification of the two territories was rather far-fetched. Cabral countered that the argument of rivalry between the two peoples was a thing of the past and that the party had been working to build awareness of this in the population. However, nothing deterred Leitão da Graça. As time passed, he became more and more opposed to the plans of Cabral and did everything he could to stop them. When he was dismissed from Radio Ghana, allegedly after the intervention of Cabral, he moved to Dakar and from there he tried to animate his UPICV—a political party founded by Cape Verdeans in Rhode Island, USA—to become the principal face of another campaign against the PAIGC, accusing Cabral's party of bribing people into joining them.

* * *

The year of 1960 has come to be known as the year of Africa. At least sixteen countries in Africa would become sovereign nations. Internal dynamics were certainly dictating the transfer of power from colonial empires to local elites, but influencing this process were also important developments in diplomacy and international law. Even before the end of World War II, the American President Franklin D. Roosevelt and the British Prime Minister Winston Churchill had signed the Atlantic Charter which, in one of its points, declared the right of peoples to choose their own form of government. This principle was later reiterated in San Francisco, in the United States, during a conference hosting all representatives of the free world for the creation of the UN in May 1945. Ratified by at least fifty states, the Charter enshrined in its Article 73 the system of international tutelage, advising the international powers or colonizing countries to facilitate progressive moves towards autonomy, or even independence, for the territories under their control.

This watershed moment was not a gift from the colonial powers to the soon-to-be independent nations. Far from it. Many organizations and representatives, some of them from countries that would later be called the "Third World," had been lobbying for the adoption of such a principle. Leading the delegation of the National Association for the Advancement of Colored People (NAACP), William Du Bois attended the San Francisco conference, as part the forty-six non-governmental organizations that made up the United States delegation. Between press conferences, dinners, and the distributing pamphlets, these individuals campaigned among the delegates of powerful nations for "the right of dependent people to govern themselves" to be included in the founding UN Charter. Vijaya Pandit, Jawaharlal Nehru's sister, was also instrumental in this project. In her suite at the Fairmont Hotel, delegates from countries such as Ethiopia, Vietnam, Egypt, Liberia, and Indonesia, often met to discuss strategies.

For Du Bois, it was particularly important to have contributed to the inclusion of the principle of sovereignty in the UN Charter. As his biographer David Lewis writes, he had achieved the inclusion of "black consciousness in the international law." Since the early 1900s, Du Bois had been arguing that the participation of African Americans in the American civil war was a betrayal of themselves, in the sense that they had not been compensated with any political rights afterwards. It was not coincidental that Du Bois had joined the Senegalese-born undersecretary of state for the French colonies, Blaise Diagne, in organizing the First Pan-African Congress in 1919. As High Commissioner for the African troops during WWI, Diagne had recruited more than 80,000 soldiers from Africa to the French army. The Congress took place on 19 February 1919 and brought together fifty-seven delegates, of whom twelve were representatives of nine African countries, sixteen represented the United States, and twenty-one the Caribbean. All these delegates were soldiers and met in Paris for the Peace Conference, which was used as an opportunity for delegates from soon-to-be independent countries to argue for self-determination. Du Bois and Diagne saw this meeting as a way to claim more rights for the people these veterans represented for their participation in the war of European nations.

However, the union between African Americans, such as Du Bois, and Africans from the French colonies, such as Diagne, was short lived. In the Second Congress, in 1921, which took place over three sessions (in London, Brussels, and Paris), Diagne sought to dissociate himself from Du Bois. By then, he had political responsibilities in the French government and Du Bois' positions were seen as too radical and communist. As the Congress chair, Diagne proclaimed that French blacks did not want independence, but rather wanted to their countries to develop a system of association with France. This was to be accomplished through political reforms of the colonial system. In fact, after the First World War, France had abolished forced labor, put in place tribunals, and consecrated the right of association and free union in its colonies. In the French parliament, dozens of representatives were originally from the African colonies.

As discussed earlier, the third edition of the Congress took place in London, with one of the sessions held in Lisbon, and no longer counted on the participation of the Francophone Africans. By the time of the Fourth Congress, which took place in 1927 in New York, the claims underpinning political compensation for African veterans were already fading. It was only eighteen years later, with the organization of the Fifth Congress in 1945 in Manchester, that pan-Africanism returned to the fore of the discussions. Accounting for this was that a new generation of Africans—who would later be called the fathers of independence—was politically coming of age. These included leaders such as Jomo Kenyatta from Kenya, Abafemi Awolowo from Nigeria, Wallace Johnson from Sierra Leone, Hastings Banda from Nyasaland (later Malawi), and, most prominent of them all, Kwame Nkrumah from Ghana, who dedicated a substantial part of his time as president to the project of African unity and the establishment of the Organization of African Unity (OAU). The fact that the Manchester Congress took place months after the UN Conference in San Francisco allowed the African delegates to use the Charter to support their demands for national sovereignty.

A UNITED FRONT

The adoption of Article 73 of the UN Charter was a move with unpredictable and unforeseen consequences. It is true that it came in response to the aspirations of a number of people who were striving for self-determination, but it also provided a rationale and a justification for the formation of nation-states. Africans, and particularly Lusophone Africans, could now rely on international law to bolster their aspirations for freedom. As Portugal was preparing to join the organization, it could not avoid recognizing such principles. For diplomatic Portugal, it seemed easy to demonstrate that the country was not a colonial power. Portugal repealed the Colonial Act in 1951, and through a semantic legal arrangement, "colonies" became "overseas provinces," and the "Portuguese Colonial Empire" was turned into the "Portuguese Overseas Empire". All the colonial legislation was subsumed into the Portuguese Constitution under Title VII "Of Portuguese Overseas." The rationale for such changes was to persuade the international community that Portugal was not a colonial empire, but a nation divided across different continents.

Portugal was only admitted into the UN in 1955, after almost ten years of unsuccessful attempts. The Soviet Union had used its power of veto in the Security Council at least ten times to prevent the admission of Portugal. As a member of the organization, the Salazar regime initially enjoyed a peaceful couple of years, but in 1960, the fifteenth General Assembly of the UN approved resolution 1514 on the concession of independence to colonized countries and peoples, and proclaimed the "the necessity of bringing to a speedy and unconditional end colonialism in all its forms and manifestations." Despite all of Portugal's diplomatic efforts and constitutional changes, for the UN, the country possessed and dominated autonomous territories and not overseas provinces.

By going against the orders of the UN, Portugal was positioning itself against the free world. Things were changing rapidly on this front. By the late 1940s and into the early 1950s, many events occurred which suggested to even the most skeptical that colonialism was becoming an anomaly. Take 1947 for example, when India became independent under the leadership of Jawaharlal Nehru. More significantly, in 1954, France was forced out of Indochina after being defeated militarily by the guerrillas. These events showed for the first time that mighty colonial armies could be defeated on military grounds. Still not convinced, and to avoid a repeat of Indochina, France deployed a significant military presence to Algeria to suppress the military insurrection of a few thousand insurgents which had begun in November 1954.

By mid-1955, former colonies were leading the international campaign for the end of colonialism. In April 1954, various Asian countries, such as Burma, Ceylon, India, Pakistan, and Indonesia, met at the Colombo Conference, preparing the way for the famous Bandung Conference (18–24 April 1956). Besides the delegations from Asian countries, a number of African countries also participated. These included Egypt, one of the main organizers, Ethiopia, Libya, Liberia, and Sudan (the only independent nations in Africa at that time), as well as the Gold Coast (later Ghana)—whose independence was scheduled for the following year—and Algeria, Tunisia and Morocco, as observers. Taken together, more than 1.35 billion people were represented by the countries present at Bandung. More significantly, these countries chose not to take sides in the polarized world that came about in the aftermath of WWII. As such, they formed a non-aligned movement which became a third force in the Cold War, depicted as being based upon respect for the sovereignty of its members and upon mutual assistance.

In an attempt to keep up with these transformative events, France accelerated the formation of a union between the metropole and its colonies through what was known as 'association'. But nothing could prevent the outbreak of war in Algeria, plunging France into a serious political crisis. The government was dissolved, and France called on former hero General Charles de Gaulle to lead the country out of the turmoil. In this context, parliament produced the "Loi Defferre"—also known as the Reform Act—which offered French colonies partial autonomy, as long as they agreed that France would still manage a number of important dossiers, such as defense, domestic security, monetary policy, justice, and diplomacy.

As previously discussed, shortly after being inaugurated, de Gaulle decided to personally share the good news and embarked on a tour of Africa from 19 August to 1 September 1958. In Guinea, however, Sékou Touré refused the proposal presented by the French president, opening up the prospect of decolonization not only for his own country, but also for other French colonies in Africa. For this reason Guinea became a kind of "revolutionary Mecca," offering refuge to a number of African nationalists and organizations, including not only the PAIGC and the MPLA, but also the PAI of the Senegalese Majhemout Diop, who opposed the appeasement policy of Senghor in relation to the French, as well as the Union of the Peoples of Cameroon of Ruben Um Nyobé and Félix Moumié.

The general feeling about events in Africa in those years was aptly captured by the British Prime Minister Harold Macmillan, in a speech delivered on 3 February 1960 in the South African parliament. With his famous declaration that "the winds of change" were blowing across the continent and his acknowledgement that the "growth of national consciousness" was a political fact, he made clear that his regime had no intention of standing in the way of African countries seeking independence. In the spirit of these times, on 21 January 1961, the Portuguese captain Henrique Galvão, a former colonial inspector and representative for Angola in the National Assembly, led a group of twenty-four rebels to hijack the Portuguese ship *Santa Maria*—on its way from Curaçao in the Caribbean to Port Everglades, Florida. After renaming the ship *Santa Liberdade* (Holy Liberty), Galvão informed the world, three days later, that the operation he was leading was part of the DRIL (*Directório Revolucionário Ibérico de Libertação*), comprising Portuguese and Spanish dissidents, and that the hijack was a revolutionary act against the Iberian dictatorships. The group also mentioned that its final destination was Angola, where they intended to proclaim an independent republic.

Galvão's action had an enormous impact on international public opinion. The French magazine *Paris Match* parachuted a journalist down to the ship to interview the hijackers. And although the ship later changed course to Brazil, since Brazilian authorities were keen to grant political asylum to the hijackers, this act was certainly the trigger for the beginning of nationalist activities in Angola. On 4 February 1961, a group of youths armed with machetes attacked Luanda's prisons with the aim of liberating political prisoners. In this action, coordinated by the priest Manuel das Neves, a number of white policemen were killed. In retaliation, armed settlers took revenge by raiding the slums of Luanda and indiscriminately shooting black people. Seeking to control and take advantage of these developments, MPLA leader Mário Pinto de Andrade organized a press conference in Conakry and claimed responsibility in the name of his party for beginning the anticolonial war. In the following month, on 15 March, the UPA of Holden Roberto attacked plantations in the northern part of the country and massacred more than 2,000 people, which again was followed by indiscriminate killings by groups of armed whites.

Confronted by these events, Portugal was forced to act swiftly to save its empire. Adriano Moreira, professor at the *Escola Superior Colonial*, Colonial College, was appointed minister of colonies. Moreira was the most renowned specialist in colonial law, and in 1954 he had presented as part of his tenure examination a dissertation called "The Prison Problem Overseas", having as examiners other experts in colonial law such as Marcelo Caetano and Joaquim Silva e Cunha. In this work, Moreira argued that Portuguese colonial law should codify various aspects of indigenous cultures and introduce moral precepts adapted to the local sensibilities. As such, Moreira was making the case for Portuguese colonialism to move in a different direction: from a colonization that at least formally attempted to assimilate Africans, to one which was concerned with differences between Africans and Europeans.

As minister of the colonies, Adriano Moreira was given the task of elaborating and coordinating the necessary policies and efforts to respond to the unrest in Angola. He was behind the idea of setting up a body of armed volunteers and advised the settlers not to abandon the places where they lived. On the political front, he championed sweeping reforms of the colonial law, such as the repeal of the *Estatuto do Indígenato*, which became law on 6 September 1961, through which every person born in the Portugal-dominated territories in Africa was given Portuguese citizenship. He also argued that the colonial crisis could not have been averted and that the solution should contemplate autonomy of the overseas provinces for a future community of Portuguese-speaking countries. For him, only the constitution of a Portuguese-speaking community could survive the end of the empire.

* * *

A UNITED FRONT

The first signs of the disintegration of the Portuguese empire were seen in Asia, on 18 December 1961, when a force of 45,000 soldiers of the Indian Union occupied the Portuguese territories of Goa, Daman and Diu. Nehru's forces met little resistance from the 3,500 ill-equipped Portuguese soldiers who defended the region. In his dramatic style, Salazar sent a telegram to the governor-general of these territories, Vassalo e Silva, urging him to fight to the end, sacrificing his troops and killing himself if necessary. For Salazar, there were two ways of losing a war: diplomatically or politically, which was irreversible, or militarily, which was not the end of the story, as it allowed for negotiation and settlements according to international law.

For Cabral's group, all of these events had proved that war was not only a legitimate means to end colonialism, but also, in the case of Portugal, the only path to national liberation. After the first nationalist uprisings in Angola, a delegation of the MPLA, composed of Lúcio Lara and Viriato da Cruz, met with Cabral and other PAIGC leaders to discuss the start of a military offensive against colonialism in Angola. In the meeting, Viriato da Cruz, after updating PAIGC members on the developments in Angola, asked the PAIGC to attack Portuguese positions in Guinea so as to force the dispersal of the Portuguese army into different areas. However, Cabral refused this proposal on the grounds that conditions for a direct confrontation with the Portuguese were not yet ripe.

Angola was providing an example of how things could go wrong when a military insurrection was not properly prepared. The attacks on the prisons had caught the MPLA by surprise, forcing the movement to strategically claim responsibility for these acts at a time when it was still largely unknown and not yet well established in the country. This was a lesson that Cabral took to heart. Although he would later also be surprised by unfolding events, forcing him to start the war as an act of despair, Cabral had far more time to prepare his men and to get them to take up positions on the ground.

Before he could launch the offensive against the Portuguese army, Cabral still had a herculean task ahead of him: turning the PAIGC from a mere political organization into a war machine. By this time, very few of the party's founders were still part of the movement. Many of those who had joined the party in Dakar and Conakry had also left, putting Cabral under enormous pressure to recruit more militants. Those who joined and took the party to the next level largely came from three groups.

The first group was formed by militants who lived in Guinea and had to an extent settled down there. They were heads of households, and were ultimately trading in their relatively comfortable positions in the colonial administration for active militancy in the PAIGC. One of those was Luís Cabral, brother of Amílcar, who was an employee in the powerful concessionaire *Casa Gouveia*. Luís had abandoned Bissau after Aristides Pereira told him that he had intercepted a phone call from Lisbon with orders for his detention. Pereira himself did not stay long in Bissau. He applied for a *licença graciosa*, a leave of absence, to visit Cape Verde. From there, he travelled to Portugal, from where he unsuccessfully tried to reach Conakry through Dakar. He was first forced to go to Paris in order to apply for a visa to Guinea-Conakry. Overall, it took him about a year to reach Conakry from Bissau.

The second group did not come to the party from Africa, and was mostly made up of students in Europe, particularly in Lisbon. In the party, they had the skills to make things work, especially at an administrative level. Their admission into the party was somewhat convoluted. It began when Jacques Beaumont, the leader of the French NGO CIMADE, contacted some African students, mostly from Angola, to offer them logistical support for a mass escape from Lisbon. This organization, which supported refugees, intended to give these young people the opportunity either to continue their education in the democratic countries of Europe or to join the national liberation movements, especially the FNLA. More than fifty young men and women residing in Lisbon were given passports, left Lisbon, and crossed Spain by train, before being stopped in San Sebastian by Franco's border police. Salazar was personally alerted and—admiring the diligence of the group, whose escape had not even been foreseen by the PIDE—demanded their immediate repatriation. CIMADE staged an international campaign and appealed for the intervention of various governments, particularly the American, with the alleged support of John F. Kennedy being instrumental in the subsequent release of the group.

The group was then authorized to continue their journey onto Paris where the young people parted ways. The Mozambicans took up Eduardo Mondlane's proposal and travelled to the United States

A UNITED FRONT

to pursue their studies. Most Angolans and Cape Verdeans were given the choice to travel to the Soviet Union to further their education, or join the liberation movement—which many of them knew very little or nothing about. As the second option was not what the students had had in mind, they staged another escape. One of the group leaders, Gentil Viana, contacted the famous French lawyer Jacques Vergès, a friend of Algerians in the FLN, who approached the Ghanaian ambassador to France—then the only African country with diplomatic representation in Paris—in order to send the group to Africa. New passports and visas were issued and, with the support of the FLN, the group travelled to the German city of Bonn by bus and from there to Accra, Ghana.

In Accra, the group split up again. Many of the Angolans were looking for the MPLA representatives in that city, while the Cape Verdeans, such as Pedro Pires and Osvaldo Lopes da Silva, waited for Cabral. On the verge of despair after their long wait, Pires and Silva were finally told that Cabral had arrived in the Ghanaian capital and had asked to meet them at the Black Star Hotel. Cabral, wrapped in a bath towel, received Pires and Silva in his hotel room, promising to give them tickets to Dakar, where they were to start work for the political bureau of the party.

The third group of people who joined the party was composed of natives of Guinea-Bissau, and mostly formed the backbone of the movement. They started to arrive in the early days of Cabral's stay in Conakry asking for *Senhor Engenheiro* (Mister Engineer), whom many had heard about but very few had had the opportunity to meet personally. They had migrated to Guinea-Conakry with the hope of pursuing their studies or even finding a job, even though most of them could hardly speak a word of French—the official language in the country—and were barely literate. The first thing of which Cabral attempted to convince them was that their dreams must wait, as the liberation of the country was the top priority.

Among these youths was Chico Té, who would later become one of the most important militants of the PAIGC, and who was one of the few who had been personally invited by Cabral himself to join the movement when they met in Bissau in September 1959. Bobo Keita, another one of the first soldiers of the PAIGC, had also met Cabral earlier in the 1950s, when the latter was coaching a local football team. At that time, Cabral had been careful not to discuss political issues, so it was a surprise for Keita to discover that the agronomist he had met in Bissau was leading the party in Conakry. Later he confessed his happiness at being under the command of his former coach.

The important thing to bear in mind about these youths who were fleeing from Bissau is the social group they belonged to. It was a huge concern for Cabral, who addressed this problem as he integrated them into the movement. Even those who came from Bissau had a peasant background and could cling to their traditions when needed. However, they learned very quickly how to operate the PAIGC military machine and soon became military commanders. In the party, they came to be the link between the national liberation movement and the population in general.

These militants began to arrive mainly from Bissau, either of their own volition or sent by Rafael Barbosa—as part of the recruitment campaign he had agreed with Cabral. To accommodate them, they set up the *Lar do Combatente*, initially located in the neighborhood of Minière in Conakry. In the beginning, the *Lar* was simply a sort of resting house, where the youths from Bissau would not have to work or be hassled, and where they were given free meals and beds. It was only after a while that Cabral started to spend more and more time with them, engaging them in informal discussions on various topics. According to Chico Té, who later reminisced about these times, Cabral used these interactions to try to detect in everyone the skills required to fight the Portuguese.

As the number of recruits increased—which consequently brought about health issues, especially allergies and skin problems—the *Lar do Combatente* was relocated to the outskirts of the city, in the neighborhood of Bonfi. There, it occupied a two-storey house, with a garden big enough to practice sports. In these early days, Cabral managed the house singlehandedly, preparing and giving the first lessons on subjects ranging from gymnastics to the use of weapons. But since Cabral did not have any military experience, the content of his teaching largely drew on his experience training teams for the agrarian census. The young men at the *Lar do Combatente* learned the basics of Guinéa's sociology. Cabral gave lectures on the ethnic composition of the territory, on the kind of relationship traditional chiefs had with the colonial administration, and on the agrarian practices of the different groups. He also spent a great deal of time speaking about the particular needs and concerns of the local populations and how to turn them into effective support for the liberation movement.

Despite Amílcar Cabral's Marxist leanings, he advised his men that the key to mobilization was not to appeal to big theories, but to speak to the everyday, material problems of the people. Peasants, Cabral would say, were humble people; they were mostly concerned with concrete solutions to their practical problems. They wanted schools for their children, roads on which they could transport their produce, lighter and better-compensated work, and, above all, they wanted to pay lower taxes. Cabral taught his mobilizers to demonstrate to the peasants that the party would fulfill all these promises as soon as the Portuguese left the country.

Cabral's classes also had a practical component, with the students rehearsing techniques for mobilization. António Bana told journalists many years later that Cabral used to summon them one by one to run through different scenarios that could unfold during a mobilization campaign. To set the scene: the mobilizers would arrive in Tabanka, a village in Guinea, where they would start by greeting the older people. They should not reveal their identity until sitting down to share a meal where, due to the poverty that affected most people in the countryside, they could expect to simply be served rice cooked in palm oil. This should be the cue to ask why it was that an elder, who had spent his entire life working, did not have enough money to buy chicken to offer a visitor? This provided the pretext to broach the topic of a national movement which intended to fight the Portuguese off the territory, they would explain, in order to improve the people's living conditions, particularly those of the workers. But in order for independence to be achieved, the peasants must send their children to Conakry, either to enter the military wing of the party or to be sent abroad to train to be the future of the country.

As is often the case, training conditions are seldom reproduced in practice. In reality, the mobilization of the peasants was far more complicated, raising many issues which Cabral could not have anticipated. Cabral was operating under the assumption that peasants would enter the party in their droves. But this did not turn out to be the case, forcing the mobilizers to improvise. As part of the first wave of mobilizers, Nino Vieira, who belonged to the group of trainees sent to the Military Academy of Nanjing in China, underwent a painful experience. He was denounced to the Portuguese by the very people he was attempting to mobilize, forcing him to take flight and run a great distance to save his life. Upon his return to Conakry, as he later recounted, he felt tired and despondent. But he was then interrogated by Cabral, who not only managed to convince him to return to the interior, but also to return and mobilize the same people who had just attempted to kill him.

Nevertheless, this early contact with the combatant masses of the movement forced Cabral to come to terms with his notion of nationalism. By the time the anticolonial war started, Guinea-Bissau was even more divided in terms of its ethnic structure. Creole, the main language used during the time of the military uprising, only later acquired importance. As such, Cabral came to the conclusion that it would be impossible to send his mobilizers to any region, as in a country where over twenty languages were spoken, it was likely that they would not be able to communicate with the local populations. As a result, the mobilization efforts gained a strong ethnic character, with campaigners ending up going to their regions of origin. This produced two outcomes that the party would later have to deal with: either mobilizers succumbed to the pressure of the seniority system—whereby, in ethnic groups such as the Balanta, age determines one's place in the social hierarchy—and therefore never acquired the necessary authority to execute their work, or they became so successful in their own regions that they imposed themselves as the new chiefs, side-lining the previous authorities and refusing to fight in other parts of the country.

* * *

While Cabral was preparing the armed forces of the PAIGC, he did not abandon the diplomatic work that was necessary to secure international support for the movement. On the diplomatic front, winning the support of African leaders was the most pressing issue in these years. Between 1960 and 1963, he travelled throughout the continent and met with a number of African political leaders. As he would recall later, the first attempts were frustrating. When he first met Malian President

A UNITED FRONT

Modibo Keita, Cabral asked him to grant permission for his men to move weapons through his territory. Keita politely declined and advised him to talk to Sékou Touré, as Guinea-Conakry not only shared a border with Guinea-Bissau, but was also equipped with a modern port. In Côte d'Ivoire, the country's president Félix Houphouët Boigny agreed to provide assistance to the PAIGC, although he too mentioned that Sékou Touré would be in a better position to do so. Cabral had arranged to return to Côte d'Ivoire at the same time as a scheduled visit from Sékou Touré, when the three men would meet together. However, when the time came, Cabral and Sékou Touré were no longer on good terms.

The most effective support, however, came from countries in northern Africa. Algeria, for example, trained some of the PAIGC's first guerrillas. Morocco, in turn, hosted various nationalist organizations from the Portuguese colonies such as the FRAIN and the PAIGC. And it was in the Moroccan capital of Rabat that the CONCP was founded to replace the FRAIN, during a meeting which was held from 18 to 21 April 1961. The meeting was attended by representatives of the MPLA, the UDENAMO, led by Marcelino dos Santos, as well as by a number of delegates from Goan organizations, including João Caracciolo Cabral, Aquino de Bragança and George Vaz, representing the Goan League, the Goan People's Party, and the National Campaign Committee for Goa, respectively. Representatives of China, the Soviet Union, and the Provisional Government of the Algerian Republic (GPRA) were also present as observers. The conference deliberated on the creation of a permanent secretariat, with headquarters in Casablanca.

Morocco was also the first country to offer weapons to the PAIGC. King Mohamed himself made the gift under the condition that his country would not take any responsibility for the transport of the materials. Accordingly, the PAIGC's men had to go to the military headquarters themselves to pick up the weapons and send them to Guinea-Conakry. Retrieving the materials from the Moroccan base was accomplished without any difficulty, but problems soon arose when the weaponry had to be sent to Touré's territory. The Guinean president supported the PAIGC's effort to liberate Guinea-Bissau, but in these early stages he frowned upon the idea of military materials flowing through his country. He was afraid that such an event could be used to disguise one of the many conspiracies that were frequently organized against him. For Cabral's part, he had not forgotten the lessons of 1961, when Czechoslovakia had given his party weaponry, imposing as a condition that these war materials had to be sent with the acknowledgment of the Guinean authorities and delivered directly to the Ministry of Defense. The PAIGC, however, never received the shipment. It was to avoid such a situation that this time Amílcar Cabral and his men decided to smuggle the material from Morocco straight into the party's bases in the interior of Guinea, without informing the local authorities.

Cabral's men could not wait much longer. Fighters trained in China and other places had been scattered throughout Guinea and were ready to begin confrontations against the Portuguese. The colonial army, in turn, had learnt from the beginning of the military insurrection in Angola—where armed rebels had attacked from the northern frontiers—and this time reinforced their positions on Guinea-Bissau's borders with Senegal and particularly with Guinea-Conakry. At the same time, the PIDE launched major raids in Bissau, which resulted in the capture of key members of the PAIGC, including the much-hunted Rafael Barbosa. As a result, the military wing of the PAIGC asked Cabral to give the order to attack, threatening desertion if the leader refused to do so. Up until that point, all that Cabral had been able to do was advise his men to stay put, hide in the bush, conduct minor military operations, and protect themselves as best they could, assuring them that any act of violence against them would be met with retaliation by the party against Portuguese settlers and their property. Following the ABCs of guerrilla warfare, Cabral encouraged his men to conduct fast actions against isolated Portuguese military bases, and to lure African soldiers in the Portuguese army with weapons and ammunition to desert.

In this environment, the ability to equip the units in the interior with weapons was of the utmost importance. As such, the party devised a scheme to smuggle them out of the territory of Guinea-Conakry. First of all, the weapons had to be taken from the headquarters in Rabat and left at the office of the CONCP, or even, going up four floors, stored in the apartment of Cabral's wife, Maria Helena, on Paul Hole Street. The second step required a great deal of imagination in order to move them through Touré's territory. To hide the biggest weapons, such as rifles, guns, and machine-guns, couches, cabinets and desks were used, while ammunition was put inside cigarette packs and boxes for typewriter ink. Furthermore, recorders were taken from Conakry to Rabat under the pretence of needing repairs, so that their contents could be replaced with ammunition and detonators. According to Luís Cabral, Cabral himself made a number of these trips, trying to walk steadily as he crossed through customs at the airport, with his body bent under the weight of his briefcases.

In Conakry, the war materials were then taken out of their casing and put inside boxes of canned food and medicines, before being sent to the port to be shipped to the interior of Guinea. Often the boxes were transported by road to Coloboi, a location close to Boké on the border between the two territories. There, the boxes were unloaded and taken to the interior, this time transported by the women who operated as the rear-guard of the movement, carrying the weapons on their own heads in order for them to finally arrive at the places where the fighters were concentrated.

The smuggling went well until the party had to increase the shipments in order to respond to demand. A decision was taken to use iron boxes labelled as containing medicines. As these operations began to be dangerous, Cabral reached an agreement with his colleagues that whenever a shipment was coming in, he should not be in Conakry. The rationale behind this cautious attitude was that being absent from the capital in such an event would allow him to mobilize his diplomatic contacts for help. In fact, the PAIGC did not have to wait long to see the wisdom of such an arrangement. The same day that one of the boxes of ammunition fell from a crane in the port, breaking open and leaving its content exposed, Sékou Touré ordered the immediate arrest of every single party leader in Conakry, namely Aristides Pereira, Luís Cabral, Vasco Cabral, Pedro Ramos, and Fidélis Almada Cabral.

Otto Schacht, one of the party leaders, managed to pass as a militant who was only in Conakry for a short stay, sparing him from arrest. Schacht, alongside Luís Cabral's wife Lucette, sought help in the embassies in Conakry, which interceded with the Guinean authorities and allowed them to keep in touch with the detainees. Amélia Araújo, another of the PAIGC's militants, who was also spared from the purge for being Angolan, was allowed to leave the country and travelled to Dakar, Senegal. Together with her husband, José Araújo, they managed to contact Cabral, who was in Rabat and initiated negotiations with Sékou Touré via telephone. The negotiations, however, did not produce the desired result. Touré had instructed his minister of defense, Fodéba Keïta, to inform the detainees that their release was dependent on the arrival of Cabral in Conakry. But Cabral made it clear that he would only travel to Conakry after the release of his men. It was only after Cabral contacted a number of heads of states, including the Cuban Fidel Castro and the Algerian Ben Bella, who intervened with Touré, that the PAIGC's militants were released.

In retrospect, according to Aristides Pereira, this event worked in favor of the party, demonstrating to Touré that the PAIGC had the structure and organization required to run such a clandestine operation inside his own territory. At the diplomatic level, the intervention of heads of states whom Touré held in high esteem showed Cabral's growing diplomatic weight. However, to save his men, Cabral used his most powerful argument: he was about to prove that the weapons smuggled into Guinea-Conakry were not destined for any coup d'état, but rather for the onset of the anticolonial war in the neighboring country. This is the context in which Cabral gave the order to attack the Portuguese garrison of Tite, in the center of Guinea. The anticolonial war had begun. Persuaded by this demonstration, Touré freed the members of the PAIGC.

6

MODES OF MAKING WAR

During the All-African Peoples' Conference in Accra in 1958, Frantz Fanon, representing the GPRA, met with the group of Angolan nationalists present at the event, namely Mário de Andrade, Lúcio Lara and Viriato da Cruz. Fanon asked the Angolans to recruit eleven youths to be trained in the camps of the Algerian National Liberation Front (FLN), so that they could open the first guerrilla cell (*foco*) upon their return to the country. As we have already seen, Cabral had been assigned the mission of traveling to Angola to transmit this message to the nationalist cells operating there at that time. However, when he arrived in Luanda, he failed to find any of the nationalists he was supposed to meet. Alerted to the nationalist activities, the PIDE had detained dozens of activists who were later taken to court under the accusation of terrorist activities. Two years later, the same group met with Fanon, who criticized the Angolan nationalists for their predominantly urban-based armed insurrection. Based on the experiences of the FLN, Fanon insisted that any armed vanguard depended on the support of the popular masses.

Fanon would not have needed to direct the same criticism at Cabral had he known the strategy the latter had devised in Guinea. After the massacre of 1959, Cabral was convinced that nothing would be achieved through urban protests and, according to the PAIGC historiography, invited cadres to abandon the cities and find shelter in the neighboring countries. What turned Cabral into one of the most important guerrilla leaders of the twentieth century was the way in which he used the lessons of other revolutionary experiences and applied them to the context of Guinea. The military techniques used in Guinea were not just about the human factors or the particularity of Guinea's geography, but about the symbiosis between man and land.

Until then, while Cabral's military strategy had been close to what Mao Zedong had proposed in China, he had not yet read any texts by Chairman Mao. However, his strategy, or at least how he came to speak of it, reproduced the teachings of the Chinese theoretician. Before moving to military action, the groups led by Mao had staged various protests and strikes in big cities. As these actions resulted in many casualties, Mao instructed his men to leave the cities in what has come to be known as the Long March. Settling in the northern part of the country, the Chinese guerrillas not only moved out of the legal environment which was hampering their action, but created their own base for political engagement. The areas controlled by the guerrilla movement became the cradle of the new order which would later sweep through the entire country.

So, more than Cabral wanted to admit, China served as the template for the military uprising in Guinea, even if only by osmosis. Cabral was certainly lectured on the Chinese experience when he visited the country for the first time in 1960, and, more importantly, some of the first groups of Guinean soldiers were trained at the Military Academy of Beijing. As such, Cabral's military strategy was saturated with Maoism.

Cabral may also have absorbed the Chinese experience which had seeped into many other guerrilla insurrections. In 1970, in answer to a question on the strategy of his movement in an interview for the quarterly magazine *Tricontinental*, he said that there was not much to invent with military uprisings and that it was enough to learn from the examples of all the peoples who had previously risen up against their oppressors, such as the Chinese, the Cubans, the Vietnamese, and the Algerians. All these movements, to a greater or lesser degree, had reproduced the principles laid out by Mao.

Out of the examples mentioned by Cabral, it was the Cuban experience of Fidel Castro and Che Guevara which had departed more from the Chinese "style" to the point that it had created a genre of its own. Mao's guerrilla warfare was essentially rural, and the strategy of the movement revolved around the grievances of the peasants. Of paramount importance was the question of land distribution. Peasants were therefore able to join the guerrilla movement to further their own interests. More importantly, Mao's emphasis was on working with and mobilizing the masses, to the extent that he did not encourage starting any uprising without the fulfillment of this pre-condition. The Cuban revolution slightly diverged from this model. In its essence, it was not anchored on peasant revolt, but was largely a movement of cadres and intellectuals, many of them coming from exile, whose immediate goal was to seize political power. Guevara has emphatically written that "it is not necessary to wait until all conditions for making revolution exist; the insurrection can create them." This model of subversion received some praise in the 1960s on account of its innovative character compared to Mao's theory. Che Guevara contributed to the diffusion of this methodology through the book he authored, *La Guerra de Guerrillas* (Guerrilla Warfare), published after the triumph of the Cuban Revolution in 1960, and translated into English and French the next year. In this manual, Guevara argued that a well-organized group of highly motivated insurgents could defeat a conventional army even if the "objective conditions" (which Maoism put so much emphasis on) to launch a popular movement were not yet in place. Key to this is that the military uprising itself becomes a catalyst which forces the population to adhere to the movement. The French philosopher, Régis Debray, who took part in the operation in which Guevara was arrested (and later executed), called this set of principles the "foco theory".

As such, the insurrection in Guinea derived its strategy from a mixture of the Chinese and Cuban theories. From the former, Cabral learnt the need for the emerging movement to rest on legitimate peasant concerns (even if the adherence of peasants to the party was not that straightforward). Important here was that Guinea was not a colonial settlement and the land question had never been an issue. From the latter, Cabral used the experience of a group of cadres (most of them coming from exile, like the Cape Verdeans) operating a nationalist movement. But this was the extent of the borrowing, and in all other aspects Cabral added specific substance to the existing theories.

Unlike the regions of northern China, Cuba, or Vietnam, Guinea did not provide optimal conditions for guerrilla warfare. The first handicap of Guinea comes from the geographic conditions of the country. It comprises only 36,125 square kilometers, which facilitates the action of a conventional army, as their combat units are more easily supported by the air force and troops on the ground. Secondly, Guinea does not have mountains, with its tallest point, Madina do Boé, no higher than 200 meters. Mountains were important factors in any guerrilla campaign, providing sanctuaries for the fighters, as in the famous case of Sierra Maestra in Cuba. However, Guinea has distinctive natural features of its own, which were well exploited by the guerrillas and became significant factors in their success.

A significant part of Guinea is made up of a complex hydrographic network. Rivers flood during the rainy season and the wet zone may occupy almost a third of the whole territory. The lush vegetation that grows in these places is a crucial factor which must be taken into account in conducting warfare. The Portuguese military was fully aware of this fact. In a book on the colonial war, the Portuguese military experts Aniceto Afonso and Carlos de Matos explained the impact of the environment on the preparation and execution of military operations. According to Afonso and de Matos, the meandering of the rivers and the dense vegetation forced military convoys to pay particular attention to their security, prolonging journeys and putting pressure on escort units. In the areas with dense underbrush vegetation, the situation was not much better for the Portuguese troops, leaving them without any protection and at the mercy of light artillery fire which could come from anywhere.

The success of the PAIGC's guerrillas depended on skillfully taking advantage of these natural conditions. As such, it was not by chance that the guerrillas invested a great deal of their military efforts into the south of the country, as it was there that the natural obstacles which hindered the Portuguese army were most present. More importantly, the south was a region dominated by the Balanta ethnic group, who had a keen knowledge of the area where the armed conflict was taking place. As a delegate to the Congress of the People of Guinea put it many years later, although the Portuguese had maps on which the rivers of the country were represented, only the Balanta knew their depth and the best places to cross them by heart.

MODES OF MAKING WAR

This turned the Balanta into the motor of the revolution, and Cabral's party, whether freely or due to the circumstances, had to reconcile the nature of a modern liberation movement—governed by sophisticated principles of sovereignty and national independence—with elements of the traditional fabric of Guinea. In the textbooks on the history of Guinea, the Balanta came to be described as the ethnic group which most vigorously resisted the Portuguese domination. To Amílcar Cabral, the participation of the Balanta in the colonial war was a continuation of the more traditional forms of resistance, which were sporadic or spontaneous, as Fanon would describe them, as opposed to the more modern form embodied in the liberation movement. The war of liberation was itself a renewed expression of the tribal protests which had been repressed since the surrender to the Portuguese in 1936. It is only by evoking this logic that we can understand the support of the Balanta for the national liberation movement.

Since the Balanta were one of the ethnic groups which had more fiercely resisted colonialism, it was them who had suffered most from the Portuguese presence. Unlike Angola and Mozambique, Guinea was never a settlement colony, meaning Portugal had barely invested in public works or infrastructure. Hence, the colonial state had not had much need to resort to forced labor. Most of Guinea was dominated by concessionaires, such as the *Casa Gouveia*, a branch of the Manufacturing Union Company (CUF), which purchased a significant part of the agricultural produce of the territory. As discussed in Chapter 3, the exploitation of the natives was based upon this concessions system, whereby they were forced to sell their produce at a fixed price. The Balanta were most affected by this system as they produced rice, which was not an export crop. Unlike groundnuts (mainly produced by the Fulani), which accounted for 95 per cent of exports in 1948, rice was essentially consumed internally and, since it was abundant, rarely yielded much profit. The Balanta were therefore left to exchange part of their produce for other foodstuffs or items such as fabric.

In this regard, the war for independence may also be seen as a convergence of the old grievances of the Balanta and the emergence of the national movement. As such, in many respects, the PAIGC simply became hostage to that which it was trying to eliminate: the traditional. The Balanta, according to various descriptions by travelers and colonial clerks, are an acephalous society. This means that, at least historically, communities, or *tabanka*—a village composed of an extended family—are autonomous and do not recognize the authority of a chief, of families, or even of clans. This is extended to whichever power attempts to rule over them.

This partly explained the difficulties faced by the Portuguese in attempting to subdue the Balanta. While in relation to the Fulani, for example—who were organized according to extremely hierarchical political structures—it may have been enough to dominate the chiefs for the whole group to follow, this did not apply to the Balanta. For them to pay taxes, for example, they had to be convinced from *morança* to *morança* (compound to compound).

In this society, the restrictive family group forms a "political and economic unit." Here, age becomes of the utmost importance, dividing the group into parts. One part consists of the older members, and the other, the younger, the former naturally dominating the latter as they control the sources of wealth and reproduction, such as animals and land. Men are only respected when they marry, but for a man to be eligible for marriage, he needs access to cattle from the previous generation to pay the dowry. The youngest therefore have no other option than to be at the service of the elders.

The Portuguese began to dismantle this structure when they arrived in the country. During the late colonial period, the state offered the young Balanta new paths to accumulate wealth. Instead of staying in their field cultivating rice and protecting the *tabanka* until they were bestowed with cattle by an elder, for example, they could simply migrate to the city to learn a trade which would give them a salary, or even to enlist in the colonial army. As the PAIGC was fighting in the south, in lands occupied by the Balanta, it absorbed the tribal logic of the age system. But the PAIGC involuntarily exacerbated the dismantling of what anthropologists call kinship structures. Like the Portuguese, they also offered an alternative way for the young to acquire fame and power, without having to wait for an elder to give them access to land and livestock.

But this absorption of Balanta culture went further. The Balanta also brought their guerrilla tactics to the national liberation movements,

MODES OF MAKING WAR

honed by centuries of war against stronger neighbors. With the expansion from the fourteenth century onwards of the Mande Empire, an authority which they refused to recognize, the Balanta were forced to seek refuge in the wateriest zones of dense vegetation, locally known as the *tarrafo*. There, their opponent was unable to maneuver its horses, which in any case could not be effectively used as they were vulnerable to the parasite *trypanosoma rhodesiense*, which is transmitted by the tsetse fly. In order to capture slaves, steal cattle, or simply to ward off the more numerous and better-equipped enemy, the Balanta developed warfare methods, or raids, which were not dissimilar to what later military doctrine would define as guerrilla techniques. Most important was to take advantage of the swamps and thick riverine forests of their natural environment, perfect hide-outs from which attacks could be launched. Alberto Gomes Pimentel, a Portuguese administrator, described some of these warfare techniques at the beginning of the century. They consisted,

> above all in not resisting the attacks, pretending they were fleeing, hiding in the *tarrafo*, in the margins of the rivers and lagoons, or spreading through the rice paddies, carefully separating themselves from the others so that they could not be hit by bullets. They only counter-attacked when the attackers, thinking they had won, started to retire with their spoils of war.

Notwithstanding the similarities between the revolutionary processes in China and Guinea, it was the example of Cuba which, at least organizationally, most influenced the PAIGC. Maoism needed a peasant organization, but this would perhaps require giving too much power to the tribal institutions. So rather than avoiding engaging with the peasantry altogether, Cabral instead devised ways to prevent ethnic predominance within the party. Reflecting on this question, or the extent to which the rebellion in Guinea was a peasant movement, Cabral later reminisced about the difficulties in winning the peasants over. "We know by experience all the problems we faced in bringing them to fight. In Guinea, apart from in certain zones and groups who received us favorably from the beginning, unlike the Chinese, we had to work ferociously to conquer them."

So while these different schools contributed to the movement in Guinea, traditional ethnic structures had to be taken into account.

Guinea was not China, where during the regime of Chiang Kai-Shek millions of peasants had languished, dispossessed of their land, therefore forming a mobilizable mass due to their disconnect from the traditional structures. And contrary to Angola and Mozambique, where the installation of the agricultural concessionaires took place through the dispossession of the natives from their lands, in Guinea, as we have already established, colonial domination was essentially based on fixed prices. As a result, in Guinea no real group emerged which could be called detribalized—individuals detached from their tribal structures and the alleged land of their ancestors.

Not being able to count on this detribalized population, Cabral conceded that tribal structures were a major factor in the participation of the various ethnic groups in the anticolonial struggle. The Balanta youths, unlike those from other groups, had more freedom to join the liberation movement, or to put it differently, to use the tribal logic itself to subvert relations of power within their own groups, as they already belonged to a decentralized society. It was different for the young people of other groups, such as the Fulani and the Mandinka. Both ethnicities formed hierarchical societies in which participation in the war generally depended on the approval of the "great men", which was conditional on the general interest of the group. The Fulani had always been allies of the Portuguese in the occupation of Guinea and in the subjugation of other ethnicities, and were generally more receptive to the colonial system, even though the lower groups were no less exploited by the higher ones than they were by the Portuguese. This was why this group made up a large part of the African troops, which, alongside the colonial army, fought the guerrillas. The case of the Mandinka was precisely the opposite. They were the biggest losers in the occupation and nurtured a deep resentment against the Fulani, accusing them of having colluded with the Portuguese occupiers to destroy what was left of their empire in the nineteenth century. With the beginning of the war in Guinea, a number of Fulani groups took the opportunity to persecute the Mandinka, accusing them this time of being behind the liberation movement. Because of this, the Mandinka were one of the groups who were most compelled to seek refuge elsewhere, fleeing particularly into neighboring countries. As a result, they were easily convinced to join the combatant masses of the PAIGC.

Teachers and students of the Liceu Gil Eanes posing for the year's picture, September 1939.

Amílcar Cabral on Lisboa Street, São Vicente, Cape Verde, 1949.

Amílcar Cabral, top right, with colleagues from the Instituto Superior de Agronomia.

Amílcar Cabral with friends in Estrela Park, Lisbon, during his time as a student in Lisbon, March 1948.

Amílcar Cabral with colleagues, in Angola, during the time when he worked for the colonial state and private companies with interests in Angola.

Amílcar Cabral with Nha Lucinda Andrade (mother of Lucette Cabral, Luís Cabral's wife).

Outside Amílcar Cabral's residency in Conakry, from right to left:
João Cruz Pinto, Aristides Pereira, Ana Maria Cabral, Amílcar Cabral,
Lilica Boal and Paula Fortes.

Cabral on his way to the Congress of Cassacá, February 1964.

Meeting of PAIGC's leadership, from left to right: Lourenço Gomes, Honório Chantre, Victor Saúde Maria, Abílio Duarte, Pedro Pires, Luís Cabral and Aristides Pereira.

Amílcar Cabral talking to journalists in Algiers, Algeria, alongside Marcelino dos Santos (to his right) and Joseph Turpin (to his left).

Cabral and PAIGC guerrillas meeting peasants in a village.

Youth during training for the PAIGC military forces.

Ceremony of the pledge of allegiance of PAIGC's military at an academy in the Soviet Union. Cabral is in the middle with a Soviet official and to the right is Inocêncio Cani, one of Cabral's assassins.

Visit of Cabral to Romania, arrival at the airport, 1972.

Members of the PAIGC's popular militias.

Nino Vieira making a speech during the first National Assembly, in Madina do Boé, 23–4 December 1973.

The PAIGC, at least during the war, not only tried to curb ethnic divisions, but energetically fought ethnicity-based tendencies. Members of the party leadership had little interest in the tribal question; the PAIGC was largely a party of cadres or militants, both civilian and military. Since the party's inception, its core leadership had been members of the clerical bureaucracy, predominantly the Cape Verdeans, who assumed in Guinea "the subaltern roles of supporters of colonialism," as Jean Ziegler put it. Amílcar Cabral, Luís Cabral, Aristides Pereira, and Abílio Duarte had all been clerks in institutions of the colonial state or in private entities such as the *Casa Gouveia* or *Banco Nacional Ultramarino*, before leaving their jobs and heading to Dakar or Conakry to join the party.

However, with the onset of the war, the Cape Verdeans were gradually ceding their place to another group, which Cabral called the "occasional proletariat petit bourgeoisie." Members of this class had in common the fact that they were "sons of the land", having been born in Guinea. Cabral met a number of these youths during his time working in Bissau as an agronomic engineer. They had little education, although they could speak Portuguese. They did not have any profession or permanent jobs. In most cases, they were learning trades, such as tailoring or mechanics. They were sometimes involved in petty crime, such as theft. Some of these youths went on to join the party in Conakry.

The success of Cabral's nationalism hinged on articulating the interests of these different social layers. This is what Cabral meant by the notion of war as a factor of culture. For Cabral, the anticolonial war forced people from different groups to fight together and be subjected to the same deprivations, as he would famously go on to write. This was also the context for understanding Cabral's controversial statement—made in a speech to the Tricontinental Conference in Havana in February 1967—on the need for the "suicide of the petty bourgeoisie," the meaning of which becomes clearer when compared with the concept of violence in the writings of Frantz Fanon.

Although *The Wretched of the Earth* has been interpreted as an apology for the violence of the colonized against the colonizer, this was not necessarily the idea behind its writing. Fanon was a psychiatrist, and most of his findings came from observing Algerian patients who suffered from mental illnesses. He found that colonialism was a form of violence which produced complexes and repressions that could only be overcome with the use of a greater violence, destroying the effects of the previous one. But this was not necessarily a physical kind of violence. Above all, it was a process through which colonizers and the colonized would free themselves from the structures contributing to the formation of their identities. While Fanon has for the most part been read literally, there is another dimension of this theory which should also be taken into account: violence was conceived of as a means to achieve a higher dimension of the human.

This is the context in which we can read Amílcar Cabral's theory of suicide, as a way of renouncing the structures that formed the petty bourgeoisie as a class. In the name of the national interest, which transcended their comfort-based class interests, they should relinquish power through the dynamic of the revolution itself and submit themselves to the "control of workers and peasants". This concept can be extended not just to the theory but also the practice of Cabral. While the suicide of the petty bourgeoisie depended on its own generosity and consciousness, according to Cabral, the submission of the peasants to the ideal of the party depended on the dynamic of the struggle. In other words, peasants were forced to abandon their traditions and beliefs and submit themselves to the rules of the party. This difference, as we will see later, was the basis for many of the problems arising between the liberation movement and the ethnic structures.

* * *

The war in Guinea started as an act "of rage and despair" on 23 January 1963, when the rebels attacked Portuguese positions in Tite. For the Portuguese, it was a major surprise, as they did not expect the revolutionary forces to strike in the interior, in the heart of the country. As such, the guerrillas were able to hold the initiative in the operations, forcing the Portuguese to withdraw to a defensive position. On 19 July 1963, six months after the beginning of the war, the Minister of Defense Gomes Araújo admitted publicly that the guerrillas of the PAIGC had spread to an area that covered 15 per cent of the national territory.

Despite the expansion of Cabral's forces, encounters with the Portuguese army were for the most part sporadic. The first major skirmish with the colonial army only took place a year later in 1964.

MODES OF MAKING WAR

The Portuguese command in Guinea decided to undertake a major military operation between January and March of that year, which would become the largest of all three stages of the war. Its objective was to regain absolute control of the rivers in the south, an area that had been taken by the guerrillas. The island of Como was the nerve center of this fluvial zone; the force that controlled it had guaranteed access to all the rivers and canals which started there. There, the PAIGC had set up its forces and installed some makeshift infrastructure, such as schools and hospitals, converting the area into a liberated zone.

The guerrilla militants were not the only enemy of the Portuguese army. For the first time, the Portuguese would be confronted with the reality of fighting under difficult geographic and climatic conditions. The archipelago occupied an area of 210 square kilometers, of which only a small part was formed of solid ground. The remaining area, about 170 square kilometers, or more than two thirds, was formed of *tarrafo*, land which would fill with water when the river flooded, and when the water subsided, would leave kilometers and kilometers of sludge and mud. Besides high temperatures, recently deployed Portuguese soldiers also had to deal with the unbearable humidity, which averaged at around 67 per cent throughout the year.

The Portuguese military operations started with the distribution of pamphlets appealing for the collaboration of the population. It was only after this that the military command gave the order for the dispatch of more than 1,200 men, composed of units of paratroopers, marines, and sappers—a military apparatus to fight a guerrilla force of no more than 300 men, according to the most generous estimate by the Portuguese command. Throughout the seventy-five days of the operation, the Portuguese had the support of the air force and torpedo boat destroyers which bombed the island day after day. Under such fire, very little could be done by Cabral's men. During the heavy bombing, the guerrillas hid themselves under the *tarrafo*, or in tunnels dug in the scant firm ground. Such military techniques could protect them against the napalm bombs, which targetted the tall trees. But they were not enough to protect against depth bombs, which, while with less power of destruction, had a forceful psychological effect: after the explosion, the noise was so deafening that most guerrilla men felt momentarily disoriented.

AMÍLCAR CABRAL

On the fortieth day of the assault, and at the height of despair, Nino Vieira, commander of the troops in Como, sent Cabral an agonizing letter which read as follows: "Comrades, be patient, but I have to ask for your help. I am in a very serious situation, and the number of troops is increasing every day […] all I can tell you is that we will lose our troops and population." Vieira would not receive the support he requested as his letter never arrived at its destination. The soldier who was given the mission to hand the letter to Cabral was captured by the PIDE.

On the Portuguese side, things were not much better. The colonial army was reduced to less than half of the forces deployed for the mission. But this was not because of casualties, as the PAIGC would later claim. A significant number of soldiers were put out of combat on account of the deficient sanitary conditions, the poor quality of the food, and, above all, the low-quality drinking water. The Portuguese military command would only admit to the combat deaths of a dozen soldiers, against the 650 claimed by the guerrillas. The PAIGC, on the other side, would lament the death of forty-eight comrades in the seventy-five-day campaign. On 20 March, the Portuguese troops, convinced that they had attained their goal of clearing the island of terrorists, finally received the order to withdraw.

However, by this time Cabral had already ordered his men to abandon the Como region. Behind the withdrawal was the fact that Como Island, notwithstanding its privileged geographic location, had very little that justified the sacrifices being made for its occupation. The PAIGC's forces would return there many times in the future, forcing the Portuguese troops to organize other clearing operations, but never again would they attempt to establish themselves there permanently.

By occupying Como Island, the forces of Amílcar Cabral had probably overestimated their own power. Or at least they had not counted on the determination of the Portuguese to keep them at bay. But the guerrillas had learnt an important lesson: to avoid direct confrontations of the conventional type, as the Portuguese troops were much better prepared and equipped for this. But the occupation of the island also showed a lack of interest in, or resolve to finish the war through military action. From then on, the guerrilla troops would above all exploit regions less accessible to the Portuguese, such as Cantanhez and Quitafine. Located at the border with Guinea-Conakry, these regions became sanctuaries for the guerrillas, since Portuguese troops could not disembark there as they were too far from any point of support. In this way, the armed conflict in Guinea entered the second phase of the guerrilla war, known as "stabilized resistance". In an interview given to the *Tricontinental*, Cabral stated that in the context of the war in Guinea, this phase mainly consisted of allowing the enemy to dominate certain regions, dispersing its forces and weakening other positions. This then allowed the guerrillas to occupy the positions where the enemy had become weak, so as to politically work with the populations in these areas and prevent them from allowing the return of colonial forces. Although this interpretation is weak precisely in what is usually Cabral's strength, mathematics—as Guinea was not a closed circuit and it was impossible to fill the gaps, simply bringing in more troops or recruiting Africans without necessarily opening new spaces—it condenses the essence of Guevara's "bite and escape," since the important thing in this phase was to constantly pester the enemy. However, one wonders whether this was an accurate description of what was going on in Guinea, or if Cabral was just saying what his audience was expecting to hear.

* * *

While the fighting in Como was taking place, Cabral summoned all available militants for a first extended meeting, in mid-February 1964, which, given its importance, turned into the first Congress of the PAIGC. The place chosen for the meeting was Cassacá—between Como and the border of Guinea-Conakry.

The military insurrection had started only three months before, and cracks were beginning to appear in the organization and leadership of the movement. The challenges the PAIGC had to address, as Vasco Cabral reminisced twenty years later, put the party "between victory and defeat." They were the product of the disconnect between the goals of the liberation movement, on the one hand, and certain cultural manifestations or tribal resiliencies, on the other. These problems began to endanger the relationship between the party and the population and even threatened the survival of the party itself.

As if Cabral were admitting to an error that he himself had committed around the time of his "re-Africanization of spirits," he later disavowed the so-called "Return to Sources." He argued that only the petty-bourgeoisie, or the *assimilados* at a certain stage in their development, needed to return to the source in order to discover the culture colonialism had separated them from: the more distant the "source", the more desperate the search. Unsurprisingly, he added, these calls for a return to the source began among the African diaspora in the New World and Europe. According to Cabral, Africans did not have the appetite for such a search. On the contrary: Africans were the source of their own culture and this culture was a way to resist colonial repression. At a later stage, with the emergence of the national liberation movement, the process through which its action would take place would become a factor of culture itself.

Cabral defined culture as being "at any moment in the life of a society (whether an open or closed one), the more or less conscious result of economic and political activities, the more or less dynamic expression of the relationships prevailing in that society." In this way, culture changes as soon as the historical material and spiritual conditions of a people change. This is the point which the action of the liberation movement had to take into account: it had to inscribe on the individual and collective consciousness the necessary procedure for cultural change. This process for Cabral implied "the practice of democracy, criticism and self-criticism, the growing participation of masses in the administration of their own lives, literacy, the setting up of schools and health centers, the formation of cadres extracted from peasants and workers' environments," among many other measures to bring about a "great acceleration of society's cultural process." In sum, war influenced the process of cultural change in many ways, even if only to suddenly force the "primitive population" into a confrontation with the use of "advanced war materials produced by the most modern science and technology."

Accordingly, Cabral strongly believed that war constituted a powerful means to combat "tribal mentality," since fighters, sooner or later, would have to confront belief and reason. Before the beginning of the war, there were very few fighters who did not fear the *irã*—supranatural beings that were believed to inhabit the forests. Few would enter into a forest at night; even fewer would not kill a relative if they knew from a witchdoctor that the latter were the cause for their misfortunes.

Initially, Cabral accepted these practices. Quite often he gave money to his men in order to buy *mezinhos*—amulets to hang on the waist, the inside of which were lined with pieces of cloth with Quranic surahs on them, to bring luck, or, as many believed, to make them invulnerable to the enemy's fire. Cabral expected these beliefs to become obsolete after the beginning of the war: the fighters would learn from their own experiences, seeing other people dying, and come to know that a trench was more valuable than a *mezinho* in a firefight; or they could be persuaded of the nonexistence of *irãs* if they needed to find shelter in the forest.

However, these practices did not vanish with the beginning of the war. Some of them flourished or were adapted to the new circumstances. The PAIGC needed to move away from being an organization formed by armed *maquisards*—with lost and isolated units in the forest and malnourished soldiers—to become an organization with the modern structure of a burgeoning state. The party needed to become an entity with a logic that was no longer tribal but strategic. It would get there through the creation of a political sphere with its own legitimacy, above that of the military, the civilians and tribal chiefs, and the populations.

For Cabral, it was urgent to set up the instruments through which the military could be controlled by the political. The priority was to bring the military wing of the party under the scrutiny of civilians once more. For this to be achieved, the first measure was the creation of strategic zones (the North, South and East Fronts being the most important) as well as of the War Council, an entity that was formed by a dual leadership from each front (a political commissar and a military chief for each of them).

Cassacá was also the beginning of Cabral's most cherished project, and the raison d'être for the war itself. The rationale for their creation was the need to fill the void left by the abandonment of Portuguese colonial administration. In the beginning, the party attempted to provide populations with the basic resources for their subsistence. As time went on these zones became central to the life of the party to the extent that a considerable part of the party's action was the protection of such zones. Behind this logic, particularly in regards to justice, was the idea that civilians should not only have control over the military, but also traditional authorities. Accordingly, the logic of the party should be above both the forces of weapons and tradition.

Cassacá was about breaking with the past and paving the way for a new future: as such, this Congress is less remembered for the reforms it introduced in the party organization than for the lucid ways in which questions regarding the morality of the party were discussed. Since the start of the confrontations Cabral began receiving reports that militants sent to fight in certain zones had become warlords. They refused to accept orders or comply with instructions from the party, instead torturing or murdering anyone who challenged them.

Given the circumstances, it was understandable that a number of military men had committed such grave errors. However, what Cabral and other party leaders did not expect was that the military would not show any remorse over their own failures. In fact, not only were they proud of them, but they were even trying to attract their compatriots' esteem and admiration. Many of them came to the Congress accompanied by their *griots*, their harems of adolescents and their bodyguards. Instead of representing party authority in their zones, these rogue military men had instead become tribal chiefs.

Cabral began by discussing the question carefully. Only towards the end of the Congress, when he raised more mundane topics, such as the deterioration of the population's living conditions due to the war and the actions the party were to take, did he address the issue at hand. He introduced the topic of criticism and self-criticism. On the table was the poor behavior of some militants. A number of people were summoned to testify, namely those adolescents who, after some initial hesitancy, confessed what they had been through with these militants. After the self-criticism, the party started the trials, which lasted through the night of the 15th and only finished at dawn next day. By this time, Cabral had already given the order for everyone to be stripped of their weaponry, with the exception of those who were part of the Northern Front, the guerrilla unit Cabral trusted more.

Over the thirty hours that followed, Cabral pursued the interrogations, calling the accused one by one. As time went on, Cabral had little doubt as to how to deal with these issues. As a guerrilla leader, he knew what he had to do: impose a severe punishment on these militants in order to prevent the deterioration of the relationship between the military and the population. As such, on 17 February, Cabral summoned all militants for the Congress' final remarks. He read out his conclusions and only then moved onto the verdict of the accused. Democratically, he chose to ask the people what the sentence should be. They chose to have the accused detained and later rehabilitated by the party. Those who had been accused but were not at the Congress were also sentenced; commissions were formed to put those militants on trial in their respective regions. Among those accused, some were rehabilitated by the party, but at least two were shot dead in front of the populations they had abused.

The PAIGC never had any qualms about the death sentences, and Cabral referred to these killings as an example of what could happen to those who deviated from the party norms. However, the Congress alone was not enough to bring together the two methods of warfare: the modern one, championed by Cabral and his followers, and the traditional one, which was ultimately how most Guineans had incorporated anticolonial war and its consequences—pain and death—into their own worldview.

Although Cassacá marks the moment when the PAIGC managed to absorb the military and traditional into the political, this Congress did not end all the problems produced by the convergence of these two ways of being: the modern and the traditional. Vasco Cabral wrote many years later that the trials in Cassacá never stopped being part of the daily life of the party and that they certainly deserved many other Cassacá Congresses.

7

THE CAPE VERDEAN QUESTION

Although the PAIGC claimed to be fighting for the liberation of Guinea and Cape Verde, the fact of the matter was the armed struggle was only taking place in Guinea. The few dozen Cape Verdeans who had joined the movement held positions in the leadership and administration. The Guineans were the ones who were paying, as it was said at the time, the *imposto de sangue* (blood tax). Not only were they the ones contributing to the party's military units, but as the combat was taking place in Guinea, the civilian population was also greatly affected. In turn, this imbalance negatively impacted on the national liberation movement. Pressure was therefore mounting within the party to change things by expanding the war into Cape Verde. Military theory played a role in this argument: opening a new military front in Cape Verde would further disperse the Portuguese troops, which would certainly result in an increase of the Portuguese war effort in terms of recruitment, logistics and so on. Furthermore, the need to expand military operations to Cape Verde also had a moral dimension: Cape Verde should contribute to its own liberation.

To discuss the issue of military action in Cape Verde, the party's directorate held a meeting in Dakar from 17–20 July 1963. Tiago Aleluia and Lourenço Gomes from Conakry, Aristides Pereira and Vasco Cabral from Accra, Victor Saúde Maria from Algiers, and Abílio Duarte, Bebiano d'Almeida, Lilica Boal, Pedro Pires, and José Araújo from Dakar were among the participants. Osvaldo Lopes da Silva and Silvino da Luz, who were not representing any particular group, were also at the meeting. The latter had just deserted from the colonial army, in which he'd been serving in Angola. The minutes of the meeting emphasize its informal character; only those residing in Dakar were invited, perhaps explaining the absence of Guineans, with the exception of Victor Saúde Maria. The meeting was described as a gathering of comrades to share ideas for the preparation of a military mission in Cape Verde.

The overall tone of the meeting was optimistic. It was simply taken for granted that it would be feasible to dispatch militants to the islands, although the geographic peculiarities of Cape Verde were also taken into consideration. Since the islands did not have physical borders, any militarized unit that landed there would have to completely fend for itself, without being able to rely on supplies from support groups. Moreover, since Cape Verde did not have the same historical background, Cabral thought that the terms of mobilization should be different. An appeal against colonialism would not work, as most Cape Verdeans did not consider themselves colonized: they considered themselves Portuguese. As a student in Lisbon, Cabral himself had written that "Cape Verde is, in fact, and to such an extent, a Portuguese product". So logically, the first task for those landing there would to be to convince the Cape Verdeans that they were being colonized by Portugal, even if it was simply for the reason that because they were originally from Africa, they had nothing to do with the Portuguese. Crudely, it was because they were not white. The case for the right of Cape Verdeans to self-determination, according to Cabral, essentially rested on the fact that they had created their own distinct personality.

The particular identity of Cape Verdeans, more than Cabral could perhaps admit, was not simply an idea conjured up by the natives of the islands. It was derived from the political status of Cape Verde in relation to the colonizing country, Portugal. For most of Cape Verde's existence, particularly since the end of slavery, Portuguese rulers had not known what to do with these islands. While Guinea, Angola, and Mozambique were unequivocally colonies of *indigenato*—where the law divided the natives between the vast majority of *indígenas* and an insignificant minority of the so-called civilized—Cape Verdeans as a whole population were considered civilized, and in legal terms, the archipelago was half-way between a colony and an "adjacency," like the Portuguese "adjacent" islands of Madeira and the Azores, whose status was effectively that of an island province of Portugal. For most people, it seemed more for logistical reasons than political ones that Cape Verde had never been given the same status as a Portuguese island in the Atlantic.

The question of "adjacency" inspired the most brilliant minds of Cape Verde, who produced a significant amount of literature on the subject. The proponents of this type of legal status formulated two arguments: the first was humanitarian and the second civilizational. Firstly, turning Cape Verde into a part of Portugal was considered the most effective way to protect the islands from the natural tragedies that they periodically faced. In other words, because the local government did not have resources, the islands could be more easily assisted by the central administration if they were a part of Portugal. Second, and more importantly, it was argued that Cape Verde should be a part of Portugal on account of the unusual "civilizational" level that Cape Verdeans had reached.

"Adjacency" was a political project whose concretization dragged on for more than a century. In 1822, a new law made every new-born in the Cape Verdean archipelago Portuguese. In 1836, the Marquis of Sá da Bandeira—who had signed the decree abolishing the slave trade in the Portuguese territories—suggested that the islands should be transformed into administrative districts. In the twentieth century, adjacency would find other advocates, such as Óscar Carmona, the president of the republic who, during a visit to Cape Verde in June 1939, described the archipelago as a natural extension of the Portuguese provinces in Europe. In the 1950s, Adriano Duarte da Silva, the representative for Cape Verde in the National Assembly, became one of the most fervent advocates of adjacency. For him, it was an aberration that Cape Verde depended on administrative procedures to effectively become part of Portugal, when adjacency should be granted to the islands on account of the fact that Cape Verdeans spoke Portuguese, practiced the Catholic religion, dressed like metropolitan whites and, in some areas such as education, performed even better than the inhabitants of some regions of continental Portugal.

But the fundamental difference between Cape Verdeans and natives of other territories dominated by Portugal was that the former were not subject to the *indigenato*—notwithstanding the cases of Cape Verdeans from the island of Santiago who had been recruited and sent to São Tomé e Príncipe as simple indentured workers, sharing the same conditions as the forced laborers from Angola. The *indigenato* was above all a tool for social engineering, determining the social expectations people could have in the colonies. Being "native" or "civilized" determined the salaries workers could expect, the area of the city where they could build their houses, and the schools their children could attend. Since Cape Verdeans were civilized, they came to have higher expectations than most other natives of the other Portuguese territories.

For Cabral, Cape Verdeans first and foremost had to join the ranks of the colonized, as acquiring the status of an "adjacency" or being granted Portuguese citizenship would only mask their real conditions. The armed struggle was a tool to achieve this level of consciousness, as Cabral had made clear in a letter written years before to Mário de Andrade, in which he disagreed with the notion that the existence of race, or of any group of people, conditioned the "behavior of a human aggregate." Instead, he argued that it is a "human group" that forms a "race" or "ethnic group," or any other social reality, to the extent that its members face similar problems and struggle for the same kind of common aspirations. In other words, Cabral did not see race and ethnic affiliation as a priori categories, but rather as the outcome of concrete conditions. This notion also underpinned his understanding of the role of the national movement as a factor of culture. War in Guinea was a factor of culture in that it molded the people itself, bringing together members of diverse ethnicities who were subjected to the same kind of hardships. In this materialistic view, those who were forced to live together under these circumstances were accepting new forms of identity. Cabral believed that the armed struggle in Cape Verde would accomplish the same goal. As such, Guineans and Cape Verdeans could be brought together through the armed conflict, resulting in a higher level of mutual identification and shared interests.

Cabral's understanding of history and culture prevailed, and his theories filtered into the preparations for the military operation. The conclusion of the meeting was that it should be possible to send the first troops to the islands within two years. But first they needed to recruit. Immediately after the meeting, Cabral's party started to enlist Cape Verdeans from the diaspora communities residing in African cities. Dakar was the city where the party's efforts were most productive, as it was not only the home of one of the largest communities of Cape Verdeans abroad, but it was also where the party had its most well-organized support committee. Cabral himself set the example: he recruited Cape Verdeans such as Herculano Andrade, the son of Nha Laurinda (who was herself the mother-in-law of his brother Luís, and whose house he stayed in when he visited the city), who brought his entire family—his wife, Henriette Vieira, who for many years would work as Cabral's secretary, and her sons, who would be sent to Cuba with scholarships. The accountant Lilica Boal was also given the task of recruiting Cape Verdeans. She reminisced many times later that she would sometimes leave the party office on Félix Faure street, using the car-rapid (informal public transportation) to search for Cape Verdeans across the city. In most cases, however, she got a cold reception.

According to initial estimates, the party hoped to recruit at least 1,000 Cape Verdeans in Dakar—a number deemed reasonable in a city of about 40,000 Cape Verdean nationals. However, these expectations had to be adjusted as the party found few people interested in being deployed to fight on the islands. Pedro Pires, who brought in some of the highest numbers of people, only managed to convince about sixty men. This number drastically decreased when the time came to send the recruits to Algiers for military training. Those who remained with the movement and arrived in the Algerian capital caused so many problems that the party's representative in that city was forced to arrange their return to Dakar. From this group, the few who stayed with the party were militants such as António Leite, Nicolau Pio and Afonso Gomes.

Recruitment was increased when Pedro Pires moved to France, after spending a short period of time in Moscow, where he studied politics and techniques of clandestine work. A member of the famous group of students who escaped Portugal in Jun 1961, Pires settled in Moselle, in the region of Lorraine, and tried to recruit the Cape Verdeans who worked there. When the PIDE became aware of Pires' activities, the Portuguese police contacted the French secret services, who summoned Pires and informed him that he was no longer welcome in France. Since France was an ally of Portugal, he could not continue his political activities within French territory. The PAIGC then decided to withdraw its thirty men and send them to Algiers.

The recruits from Europe and Africa were sent to Algiers in 1965, where they were assigned their responsibilities. Pedro Pires was appointed as commander of the group, with Honório Chantre as his deputy. Pedro da Cunha became the political commissar, while Silvino da Luz was given the duty of military coordination, which involved overseeing the collection of all necessary information for the mission, such as maps, as well as data on the Portuguese military units in Cape Verde.

The outlines of the mission began to take shape when the group arrived in Havana, where from 1966 onwards more training was planned. Here, the preparations consisted of techniques such as maritime landings, swimming, and survival techniques in high seas. Classes in guerrilla warfare were the core of the preparations, for the PAIGC's plan was to carry out in Cape Verde an operation similar to that of Che Guevara and Fidel Castro in Sierra Maestra. They could reach the center of the largest island, Santiago, by sea or with parachutes, taking over the highest mountains and forming there the first *foco* of insurrection. In later stages of the plan, and only after intensive political work with the population, the group would begin recruiting soldiers and taking positions on the island, but above all, would always avoid direct confrontation with the Portuguese military forces until the conditions were in place for the launch of the final phase—the invasion of the major urban centers.

However, for various inter-related reasons the training programme had to be interrupted. In October 1967, Cuba was shocked to hear of the disastrous operation that Che Guevara had been leading in Bolivia. The death of the Argentinian revolutionary was a major setback for his revolutionary theory: Guevara had been convinced that it could be applied anywhere, discounting the notion that the triumph in Cuba could have been the exception to the rule. The disastrous escapades in Bolivia had not only cost the lives of some of the instructors who had been assigned to accompany the PAIGC to Cape Verde, but also threw into disarray the theory of *focos* itself. More importantly, the virtual disappearance of Guevara some years earlier and his sudden reappearance in Bolivia provided the American secret services with confirmation that Cuba wanted to spread their revolutionary creed to other parts of the globe. From then on, Cubans were placed under even tighter surveillance.

In January 1968, at an event for the Cape Verdean pledge of allegiance, Cabral travelled to Cuba to meet with his men and discuss alternative ways of landing on the islands without the support of the Cubans. After the meeting, a decision was taken to transfer the entire group to the Soviet Union. The Soviets, however, more realistic than the Cubans, refused from the outset to support a mission that they considered suicidal. Nonetheless, they received the Cape Verdeans in their military institutes and helped them develop their skills in ballistics and artillery. With the Cape Verdeans still insisting on their mission after they had finished their training, the Soviets provided them with a boat, which would be commanded by Herculano Vieira, an ex-captain of the merchant navy who had just joined the group.

The group returned to Algiers, but as their mission drew closer, its cohesion began to falter. A number of militants wanted to abandon the assignment, but they were forced to stay in order to prevent any leaks of information. In the meantime, the PIDE seemed to be aware of the ongoing preparations, and various efforts were made to prevent the possibility of a military landing. For example, migrants returning to the islands from other places were more tightly scrutinized. All boats using the ports of the island were more rigorously monitored. The local police also carried out a number of random searches with the aim of detaining supposed militants of the PAIGC. Dozens of people in Santo Antão and other areas were detained and accused of collecting information on the viability of the mission and of possessing propaganda materials.

It is not far-fetched to suggest that Cabral himself may have inadvertently caused these detentions. In January 1968, Cabral was detained at the airport in Paris while attempting to enter the country with a passport issued by Guinea-Conakry, in the name of Ousman Keita. Although he did not have permission to enter France—he had been issued with a travel ban by the French government in 1964—he had visited the country many times under different identities. However, this time, alerted by the Portuguese police, the French not only prevented him from entering the country, but also took this opportunity to search his documents, which were photographed and the copies sent to Lisbon. As the PIDE then discovered, Cabral planned to send a number of Cape Verdeans to the island from different European countries who, under the cover of developing commercial activities, would conspire against the colonial regime. In a letter written immediately after his detention, Cabral tried to reassure Pedro Pires that the French police would not send the photographed documents to Lisbon. However, the detentions that followed, specifically of people that had recently arrived in Cape Verde, showed the extent to which Cabral's optimism was misplaced.

With all these setbacks, the party was forced to postpone the invasion. However, in general, these events were a win for the party. From this point forward, the PAIGC could count among its numbers more militants trained in artillery and other military techniques, even if a number of them refused to fight in Guinea, preferring to return to their previous lifestyles. These militants did not believe the party's argument that every bullet shot in Guinea contributed to the independence of Cape Verde. However, in Cape Verde the news of the cancellation of the operation was received with great concern. Pedro Monteiro, in his memoirs, used harsh words to convey his frustration. At that time, he had been a semi-clandestine militant on the island of Santiago, and he considered that this change of plans both gave the impression that the party had no strategy for Cape Verde, and also left the nationalists there totally unarmed against PIDE brutality.

After these detentions, plans for a possible military landing in Cape Verde were largely discarded. For the most part, Cape Verdeans were not interested in independence. And without the possibility of extending the war to the archipelago, the PAIGC was left to address increasing accusations over the privileged position of Cape Verdeans in the national liberation movement. This failure therefore only heightened tensions within the movement, the result of which would be tragic.

8

A STATE INSIDE THE COLONY

For most of the war for independence, the military situation in Guinea was a so-called "low-intensity conflict". This was partly due to the size of the colony itself, with the total area of the Guinean territory only being about 36,125 square kilometers. Each location within the territory where military confrontations were taking place was close enough to the rear-guard that it was more tempting for the guerrillas to simply retire to one of the sanctuaries than to defend any given position. Furthermore, for Cabral's men, it was also possible to enter the territory by sunset, strike a target, and leave the territory before sunrise. On the other hand, the size of the territory was also an advantage for the defending force, the Portuguese. The air force could easily deploy or withdraw troops to strike the guerrillas, since it was possible to reach any point in the country within a maximum of thirty minutes.

But the flexibility that Cabral's men enjoyed also allowed the Portuguese to deny on several occasions that the PAIGC had military units inside the country at all. In fact, in 1967, Cabral had ordered his men to abandon the military bases which the movement had maintained inside the territory. The extra mobility afforded by closing these sites was well known to the Portuguese, but it was also used to allege the non-existence of any party structures inside Guinea. A message intercepted by the Portuguese military intelligence, for example, and exhibited to foreign journalists, mentioned that Cabral had warned his men not to stay in the same location for more than two days, or else they would risk revealing their positions.

With such tactics, the PAIGC was downplaying the military component of the struggle. By attacking a position one day and abandoning it the next, Cabral's militants were not making any serious inroads in their attempts to liberate the country militarily. It was rare for them to occupy positions and defend them at all costs against the attacks of the colonial army.

But these measures were less a result of the weakness of the movement, as implied in the commentaries of Portuguese officials, and more about the need to curb the power of the military. For Cabral, military actions should be limited to protecting the movement's civilian activities. These activities, as the years went on, would become the *raison d'être* of the PAIGC.

In his manual on guerrilla warfare, Guevara not only emphasizes the importance of rear-guard zones as being "unattainable to the enemy", but also adds that no guerrilla movement could do without them. These sanctuaries should be used to supply the troops, to politically and militarily train new recruits, and, more importantly, to provide a space for the development of social actions within the population. But few guerrillas in Africa had taken the maintenance of these sanctuaries as seriously as the PAIGC. For Cabral, retaining these zones became the war's *raison d'être*, as if the goal of his movement was to build a state within the colony.

In February 1964, about a year after the beginning of the war, the PAIGC leadership met for the first Congress, the so-called Congress of Cassacá, as discussed in Chapter 6. Confronting numerous cases of abuse of power, Cabral had pushed forward the notion that the PAIGC was not a militarist party, but rather a party formed by armed militants. As a bloody confirmation of this truth, the party had made the difficult decision to physically eliminate those who had abused the population. From then on, the PAIGC would strive to limit the power of the military wherever possible, or at least to make it more transparent to civilians.

These concerns were translated into practical measures through the creation of dual power structures: military units were to be led by a political commissar alongside a military commander. Furthermore, military units were reorganized into units of the FARP (*Forças Armadas Revolucionárias do Povo*—People's Revolutionary Armed Forces)—created at this Congress—which became the military backbone of the party. FARP units were composed of mobile and flexible groups, called bi-groups, made up of thirty-eight fighters including the political commissar and the military commander. Bi-groups could operate in conjunction with other bi-groups or separately. As the FARP received express orders not to remain too long in any one location, the protection of the liberated zones was mostly undertaken by the local populations themselves. The bi-groups, in this way, had to be constantly on the move, never stopping for more than six weeks in Guinea, during which time they depended on a "network of militias in constant expansion" for their logistics and information, according to Basil Davidson.

To keep the struggle alive, Cabral not only depended on his organizational abilities, but also on his diplomatic skills. Since the party largely depended on international aid, Cabral was constantly engaged in intense diplomatic activity. This is illustrated by a report written by the journalist Suzanne Lipinska for the *Africasia* magazine. Lipinska interviewed Carmen Pereira, then one of the most prominent female militants in the party, who, introducing the journalist to the guerrillas and the population, stated that although she was white, "her color was not the symbol of oppression." According to Pereira, there were two kinds of white people: those who helped and those who did not. Even though France, Lipinska's country of origin, was an ally of Portugal, providing it with the *Alouette* helicopters, for example, it was also where a number of support committees were based, sending blood, medicines, and a range of health materials to the militants of the PAIGC.

Pereira was alluding to the diplomatic maze that Cabral and the PAIGC had to navigate. While most Western countries were allies of the Portuguese under the banner of NATO, many of them were also democracies, meaning the PAIGC was allowed to work there in order to raise humanitarian funds for the social work of the party. But to get the support it needed, the party had to invest a considerable amount of time and skills into information, communication, and outright propaganda. The narrative in most of the PAIGC's outreach work was that despite the pressure from the Portuguese, the party was carrying out social work with a considerable impact on the population under its protection. But more importantly, the PAIGC was also campaigning in France to raise the consciousness of its citizens. In the long run, this strategy would help secure the support of the international community for the independence of Guinea.

The PAIGC did not have to bear the entire burden of the propaganda effort. Since its beginnings, Cabral's party regularly met with opinion makers, photographers, filmmakers, and representatives of European parliaments. One of the first citizens of a Western country to visit a liberated zone was the French filmmaker Mario Marret, who directed the documentary *Lala Quema*, shot entirely in the south of the country. At that time, the guerrillas did not even have uniforms, so they had to "buy blue jeans, shirts and sandals for the fighters of the central base of the south." Marret returned in 1966 to shoot *Nossa Terra*, the same year that the PAIGC received the Italian filmmakers Piero Nelli and Eugenio Bentivoglio to shoot the documentary *Labanta Negro*, this time in the northern part of the country in Morés. In 1967, the Cuban José Massip visited the liberated zones to film *Madina do Boé*. The following year, the Britons John Sheppard, Richard Dodds, and Christian Wrangler from Granada TV visited these zones to shoot the episode *A Small Group of Terrorists Attacked*, for the series *World in Action*.

The life of the liberated zones was also captured in pictures by photographers such as Bruna Amico and Michel Honorin and depicted in reportage and books. All this material circulating in Western countries contributed to increased awareness of the war in Guinea. Basil Davidson wrote *The Liberation of Guiné* and its publication in 1969 coincided with the that of *The Struggle of Mozambique* by Eduardo Mondlane. In Italy, the book *Guinea-Bissau—una Rivoluzione Africana* was published, authored by Bruno Crimmi and Uliano Lucas, the former a journalist and friend of Cabral. In France, a number of reports and books by Gérard Chaliand were also available, such as *Lutte Armée en Afrique*, and the various articles and essays of Mário de Andrade for his magazine in Paris, *Présence Africaine*.

A number of politicians from European parliaments, especially from northern Europe, also travelled to Guinea to visit some of the liberated zones. One such example was the visit by a Swedish delegation led by Birgitta Dahl, a representative for the Social Democratic Party, and the coordinator of a commission for aid to developing countries. The invitation was made by Cabral himself and the travel was supported by the Tage Erlander Fund, which was managed by her own party to finance the travel of its youngest members who were interested in "studying the social economic conditions in developing countries." Upon her return to her country on 6 January 1971, Dahl published a lengthy report in the *Aftonbladet* (a newspaper published in Stockholm with an average circulation of 507,400 copies a day) with the following frontpage headline: "Representative of the *Riksdag* visits the most successful guerrilla in the world." The article, referenced in other Swedish newspapers, mentioned that the group had visited 162 schools and fifty-three health centers. In a communiqué from the Ministry of Foreign Affairs, the clerks of the Portuguese embassy in Stockholm wrote of their belief that this visit was linked to the Swedish government's increased contributions to various liberation movements, since, as they explained, Dahl also worked for SIDA, the department of the Swedish Ministry of Foreign Affairs in charge of aid to the poorest countries in the world.

Although the party was receiving a considerable amount of support in its propaganda efforts, Cabral's organization still faced serious problems with internal communications, despite the fact that Guinea's size, at least in the dry season, facilitated the rapid movement from one front to another. The Congress of Cassacá had upheld the belief that a major cause of the militants' mistakes was the isolation in which they found themselves. They were largely cut off from contact with other members of the party and significantly they were unable to receive updated party guidelines. The PAIGC consistently tried to fill this gap through many initiatives, including the publication of the newspaper *A Libertação*, which was typed and printed by Cabral himself.

However, as most of the Guinean combatants were illiterate, radio became both the most important means of communication and the most powerful weapon the party could use against the enemy. Also known as the *canhão de boca do partido*, or "mouth cannon of the PAIGC," it gave everyone a sense of connectedness. In the beginning of the war, the PAIGC had been given a small radio transmitter through which the messages of the party and some Cape Verdean songs were broadcast. More regular shows would only start in the beginning of 1965, when Amélia Araújo, nicknamed Maria Turra by the Portuguese (Turra colloquially translating to terrorist), became its main voice.

AMÍLCAR CABRAL

As the importance of radio in the party's internal propaganda grew, a few militants travelled to the Soviet Union in 1966 to participate in nine months of training in this area. At the end of the course, they were given a Soviet-made portable transmitter with a range which only allowed for broadcasting if it were in the interior of the country. As the risk of broadcasting being detected was very high, with the consequent risk of airstrikes, Cabral never authorized the use of this transmitter. It was only in 1967, thanks to the donation of a transmitter and a studio by Sweden, that *Rádio Libertação* (Radio Liberation) started to be heard throughout Guinea and Cape Verde

The beginning of *Rádio Libertação* broadcasts was recorded by the Portuguese themselves. According to a communiqué from the Ministry of Foreign Affairs, the PAIGC started broadcasting on 14 August 1967 at the frequency 5000 kc/s. The choice of this specific frequency was interpreted as a provocation, since the official Bissau broadcast operated on 5040 kc/s. So, according to the commander-in-chief of Guinea, it was likely that an individual searching for the state broadcaster would end up tuning into the guerrilla one. This was even more dangerous as *Radio Libertação*'s signal, according to the PIDE, could be received across the whole of Guinea. They arrived at this conclusion through tests conducted at 9am on 30 July 1967, which coincided with the broadcasting of an appeal exhorting listeners to gather in the Pidjiguiti Dock on 3 August to mark the anniversary of the "massacre." According to this report, Amélia Araújo expressed herself in correct Portuguese and the listening conditions were perfect.

Radio became the main link between the militants of the party, as well as a fundamental component of its propaganda campaign. It was through these broadcasts that many fighters, on their long and risky journeys through the country, received news, listening in to the frequent war communiqués on the military situation on other fronts. In addition to this, the forces on the front lines, as they passed through or returned to Conakry, constituted a privileged source of first-hand information on the situation where they had been deployed. Initially, Portuguese and Creole were the languages of the radio programs, but the range of listeners soon expanded when the radio started offering shows in other languages, such as Balanta, Beafada, Macanha and, subsequently, Fulani and Mandinka. The radio broadcast shows such as

A STATE INSIDE THE COLONY

Vamos Conhecer a Nossa Terra (Let's get to know our land), which was fifteen minutes long and focused on themes relating to the geography of the country. Years later, the show was extended to half an hour in order to include news on Portugal's other wars in Africa, especially in Angola, thanks to regular communications with staff at the MPLA's radio, *Viva Angola Combatente*, broadcast from Brazzaville to the Angolan territory. The radio programs were also targeted at the Portuguese: they constantly invited Portuguese soldiers to desert, and, whenever possible, deserters were interviewed before being returned with pomp and circumstance to the Red Cross in Dakar. To lower the morale of the colonial force, the names of Portuguese soldiers killed in combat were often read out, using the obituaries written in Portuguese newspapers themselves.

Producing the content for the shows was hard work, and was mostly carried out by Amélia Araújo, as well as her husband José Araújo, and fellow nationalist Dulce Almada. Cabral was one of the main contributors to *Rádio Libertação*: he was always interviewed on his return from a trip abroad, and he also wrote a weekly editorial. But more importantly, he also provided a great deal of moral support, often stopping by the radio facilities in the evening—either by himself or accompanied by his wife Ana Maria—to ask if there was anything he could do to help or simply to encourage the staff. Working conditions were difficult, so these visits were highly appreciated. During the rainy season, for example, the radio's staff had to work with the door of the truck open because of the heat, despite the mosquitoes. With almost every member of the radio's team also carrying out other tasks in the party administration, the recordings were made throughout the night, rarely finishing before the morning—just in time to "press the button to go on air."

Rádio Libertação had become one of the main elements of the PAIGC's strategy, as General António Spínola quickly understood when he arrived in Guinea as governor and military commander. In his concept of total war, in which the military and civilian categories are blurred, he identified the PAIGC's radio as one of his main targets. The official Bissau broadcast began to respond to the PAIGC's attacks and to take advantages of its Achilles' heel: the supposed unity between Cape Verdeans and Guineans. The radio started a campaign against the Cape Verdeans in all the languages of Guinea, appealing to nativism to pit the two groups against each other. Spínola promised to demote all Cape Verdeans from their leading positions in the administration, to be replaced with the "true sons of Guinea."

Aware of the damage that could be done by these messages, Cabral tried to respond:

> The colonists know that the political and moral unity, the combative unit of our people of Guinea and Cape Verde is the principal force of our people and our fight. In this way, they pretend to destroy it, attempting to create hatred which never existed before to stir the ambition and the opportunism among those that, although they do not take part in the fight, are nationalists and want the liberation of our country. But even there they are completely lost. First, because the true nationalists from Guinea are not racist nor opportunists and know, as militants of our party, who their leaders are and what the value is of the people of Guinea and Cape Verde. Secondly, they lie when they say they will expel the Cape Verdeans. They can't do it, since they need the Cape Verdeans who serve them, in the same way that they need the Guineans who serve them. And the colonists know very well the great service they would do to our party and our fight if they would expel the Cape Verdeans.

As we will see, Cabral's words, unfortunately, were wishful thinking. Spínola had touched a raw nerve.

Many other methods would be used in an attempt to silence the radio, or at least to make its transmission more difficult. The most basic technique was to produce interference by issuing a signal in the same frequency. But other more sophisticated techniques were also used. For example, after a thorough study of the legislation of the International Union of Telecommunications (UIT), the secretary of state for Foreign Affairs presented a complaint to this organization against the PAIGC. The argument was that the nationalist radio was interfering with the transmission of the official Bissau broadcast which had already been given the frequency of 5000 kc/s by the UIT, meaning this frequency could not be used to transmit any other signals. But the Portuguese government did not want to insist on this. Even if the claim was accepted as justified, the situation could only be resolved if the other party complied voluntarily.

Since information on the liberated zones is very rare and hard to find, often buried in personal archives—with the possible exception of references made to them in Cabral's speeches—many questions about their management and location remain unanswered. Mustafah Dhada's *Warriors at Work* provides a wealth of detail on the everyday life of the liberated zones. The conclusions that came out of the Cassacá Congress presented the party with a contradiction. While the creation of fixed administrative structures had been identified as a priority, the organization of the military into mobile and flexible units called bi-groups had been abandoned. In this way, the party had sacrificed its ability to defend specific points in the field. The PAIGC could not have maintained populations of several thousand people in the face of a bombing campaign, even if one considers the facts that these zones were defended by popular militias; that the fighters had developed sophisticated systems of defense, such as false paths, broken bridges and landmines; and that many of the liberated zones were found inside the forest.

But this does not mean that the PAIGC had not retained the so-called liberated zones inside the country. This, at least, was the thesis defended by a number journalists who covered the war in Guinea from the Portuguese side, such as Jim Hoagland from *The Washington Post*, and the South African Al Venter, author of *Portugal's War in Guinea*. The truth, however, is that the liberated zones did not always have the same strategic weight within the party and that their maintenance always hinged on the balance of forces between Cabral's men and the colonial army. It had been easy to keep those spaces in the early years of the war due to the withdrawal of the colonial administration from many districts. As many inhabitants had decided to stay, the PAIGC simply occupied the empty spaces that the local administration left behind. However, as the colonial army began its offensive—at the end of the consulship of General Arnaldo Schultz and the beginning of Spínola's mandate—it is unlikely that the FARP could still hold these positions by 1968, as the Portuguese airforce controlled the airspace and were bombing, or willing to bomb, more indiscriminately.

With this change of in the balance of forces, the PAIGC gave the populations the choice of staying in the newly liberated regions, despite airstrikes, or finding refuge in neighboring countries. During the first years of the war, as we have seen, the PAIGC had dominated a number of regions such as Como Island, where they had put in place basic facilities such as schools and hospitals. However, with the violence increasing, as the colonial army ceased to distinguish between military and civilian targets, thousands of people, especially those in the north, had no option but to leave their land and find shelter elsewhere. While the Balanta, even if against their will, could always resort to hiding in the forests, the northern populations, who did not have this option, were forced to abandon their villages. Some of them were relocated, as resettlement was one of the strategies of counter-insurgency which was broadly applied by the Portuguese army.

However, whenever the liberated zones could be held, Cabral tried to push their strategic role even further. It was not enough for them to be places of refuge for soldiers and the population: they must also be units of production. Being a scholar of agriculture, Cabral tried to make improvements to agricultural production in the liberated zones, many of which he had promoted during his time working for the colonial government. He encouraged the peasants in the south of the country to increase the size of their cultivated areas, but the results were not encouraging. With the FARP eating up manpower that would usually be focused on agriculture, Cabral instructed his men, in Maoist style, to help the peasants work the fields wherever possible. However, most refused to comply with the instructions of their leader. As such, rather than being a result of the agricultural policies of the PAIGC, the production surplus of 1969, which allowed the party to export rice, coconuts and kola nuts, was due to the popular appropriation of fertile land left behind by the Portuguese administration.

In order to distribute the dividends of agricultural production and assist the populations in the areas under their control, the PAIGC created the People's Warehouses. As with the liberated zones, the party published little information on these warehouses, meaning the location of many of these units cannot be determined. Out of the ten new establishments opened in 1968, according to Mustafah Dhada, it is only possible to locate four: one in the zone of Boké, one in the south of Quinara, one in the area of Tombali, and another in the east, close to Delaba. Of the others, very little is known.

Since the PAIGC did not want to increase demand for colonial currency, the warehouses operated under a barter system. Peasants were encouraged to exchange their crops for items that either they did not

A STATE INSIDE THE COLONY

produce, or that were imported or received by the party thanks to external help, such as dry fish, condensed milk, soap, shoes, tobacco, and sugar. Prohibiting the use of money in the warehouses was intended to encourage production (as one could only exchange if one produced), and to prevent the Portuguese from ruining the system—which could happen if they sent dozens of potential buyers to these places. The main issue with the warehouses was the replenishment of stock: supplying the warehouses was a complicated process, involving hundreds of carriers, among them women and soldiers, who left the border with Guinea-Conakry by night and headed to various locations in Guinea-Bissau.

It is true that the barter system protected the party from external sabotage, but it did little to defend it against corruption. Since the system did not involve money, accountability was difficult to ensure. Prices of products were flexible and easy to manipulate, allowing some militants to profit from these exchanges with the population. The party was aware that corruption was increasing in direct proportion to the increase in war weariness and fatigue. This took place at all levels. Inocêncio Cani, one of the top figures in the party—who would later shoot the fatal bullet that would kill Cabral—was judged by the party and sentenced for having stolen engines from PAIGC boats in 1971 to sell on the black market.

From 1968 onwards, the warehouses largely ceased to be operational, particularly once operational changes implemented by General Spínola began to take effect. His military strategy consisted of making the lives of the guerrillas and the population of the liberated zones even more difficult. He increased the use of airstrikes and of helicopters in search and destroy operations—aimed at eliminating the guerrillas. Meanwhile, his new programme "For a Better Guinea" attempted to win the support of the population, attracting a considerable number of people to fortified villages defended by the Portuguese military and by popular militias.

The PAIGC also made significant investments in education, partly to overcome the inadequacy of the colonial system. At the beginning of the conflict, 97.5 per cent of the population was illiterate and, according to Cabral himself, in the entire history of the colony only fourteen natives had earned a higher education degree. Except for the

145

medical doctor Francisco Baticã—who had migrated at an early age to Senegal—and himself, they were all the sons of Portuguese colonizers. It should also be added that it was not until 1958 that the first *Liceu* in Guinea was opened, forty-one years after the opening of the *Liceu* of Cape Verde.

The main goal of the schools created in the liberated zones was to supply cadres to the different party structures. When the FARP needed artillery men or nurses, for example, these schools provided the best students. This is perhaps the reason for the excessive politicization of the teaching in the party's schools. The students were trained to be militants of the PAIGC and had to be familiarized, from an early age, with the history of the party, the deeds of its leaders, as well as the history of other liberation movements. At the most advanced levels, they were instructed in the objectives of the national liberation struggle.

The party took responsibility for providing at least elementary education to all children in the liberated zones. In the academic year 1964–5, 4,000 children were enrolled and distributed across fifty very basic schools, with their only furniture consisting of wooden boards attached to trees. The main obstacle to the children's education was the lack of teachers; the few available had only finished primary school themselves. Obtaining teaching materials was another difficulty. The first ones, produced and donated by Germany, quickly ran out. Students therefore spent much of their time at the schools copying out entire manuals, which were produced by teachers of the party during improvement seminars in Conakry.

Tradition also played a role. A number of parents did not allow their offspring to go to school, which they justified in many ways: some parents stated that their sons were needed to work in the fields, while others wanted to prepare their daughters for marriage. But there were also security reasons: any concentration of people was easy for the Portuguese Air Force to detect. Schools were therefore an easy target.

Primary schools were part of a more complex educational system, which included boarding schools, located in the interior of Guinea, where independence fighters sent their children. There was also the highly sought-after *Escola Piloto*, Pilot School, in Conakry. Admission into this school was very competitive and one of the requirements was that the candidate should have spent at least two years in the interior of the country. The diploma from the *Escola Piloto* opened the door to the universities in Dakar and Conakry, and to the hundreds of scholarships offered to the party annually by countries in the Eastern Bloc.

The PAIGC also strived to provide health care to the people of the liberated zones. To promote the basic health services to its own militants and to the population under its control, the PAIGC created a network of makeshift hospitals. However, as in many other areas, this system developed according to the military situation. While the PAIGC claimed that it went from twenty-eight health posts in 1968 to 117 in 1971, in truth, this does not take into account the type of health care units. The party changed from using fixed to mobile units, putting nurses and health auxiliaries on the move constantly, either assisting the population in the zones under the influence of the PAIGC or instructing them in hygiene and preventive medicine. The most serious cases, such as combat injuries, were sent to the border with Senegal or to Guinea-Conakry, where there were better-equipped permanent units, served mainly by Cuban doctors, but also by the Angolan Augusto Boal and the Portuguese national Mário Pádua.

Another area in which the party invested a considerable amount of resource was the establishment of a judicial system. The objective of this system was to separate military and civilian affairs, preventing any overlap between the two. This policy had already been sketched out in Cassacá, but it would only be implemented once the need for it arose. As a priority, Amílcar Cabral wanted to prevent the military imposing their judicial system on civilians, instead providing civilians with their own instruments of justice. But the party would go even further: efforts were made to subject the military to the laws of the provisional tribunals in the regions where the crimes were committed. Only the most serious cases, according to the Law of Military Justice, would be solved by the War Tribunal. The system of justice provided for the condemnation of the accused to forced labor or to be sent to the prison in Conakry—known as *Montanha*—a measure that the party did not encourage since it decreased the workforce available for production and combat. The most serious cases, in accordance with the law, had to be punished by death.

AMÍLCAR CABRAL

As was shown by the Cassacá trials, the PAIGC did not have any qualms about ordering the death penalty for their members. Various reports providing details of these events were received by the PIDE. Between May and June 1967, in Madina do Boé, a court formed by Fidelis Almada Cabral, Vasco Cabral, and Aristides Pereira condemned Honório Sanches Vaz and Miguel Embaná to death by shooting for being involved in a conspiracy to kill Amílcar Cabral. According to the PIDE's report, the plot had been uncovered by Ansumane Mané, "Mandinka de Bafatá", and involved João Bernardo Vieira. Although Vieira had been summoned, he did not show up in court. The report also added that Cabral had thought of removing him from the command of the south zone, but had not done so since he was afraid of retaliations from the natives of Guinea.

All of this social infrastructure—education, health, and the judicial system—was ultimately the means by which the party intended to put Guinea on the path of progress and how the party negated, or downplayed, local traditions and forms of ethnic knowledge. In a telling description in his memoirs, Lúis Cabral discussed the boundaries that the party had established for itself between the old and the new, the traditional and the modern, superstition and science. During a public discussion with the elders, the *homens grandes*, of Morés, as he tried to convince them to allow their children—especially their daughters—to go to school, Amílcar Cabral did the following: in the middle of his argument, like a lawyer in a courtroom, he flicked his cigarette lighter, brought the flame close to one of the old men and asked him if he could explain the phenomenon. Faced with the inability of the men, whose education was limited to the "Quran of the *tabanka*," to do so, Cabral attempted to demonstrate the importance of education to explain such phenomena. It was against what he called "ancestral ignorance" that Cabral tried to build the new Guinea.

9

WINNING IN POLITICS WITHOUT LOSING THE WAR

The first person to simultaneously act both as commander-in-chief and governor in Guinea was General Arnaldo Schultz, who had previously occupied the post of minister for home affairs in the *Estado Novo*. The appointment of a single person to both positions was intended to facilitate the decision-making process involved in fighting the guerrillas. A veteran who had cut his teeth in the war in Angola, Schultz, who was appointed in May 1964, promised to clear the territory of the "terrorists" in less than six months. During his tenure, he escalated the war to unprecedented levels of violence. But he failed to improve the military situation in favor of the Portuguese, for his strategy put great emphasis on the militarist factor. He had estimated that to achieve his goals he need only increase the size of the military contingent operating in Guinea. By the end of his mandate in May 1968, more than 30,000 Portuguese soldiers were present in Guinea, far greater than the number necessary either to defend the small territory or to protect a white population of no more than 3,000 people.

Schultz's arrival in Guinea coincided with an increase in the military capacity of the Portuguese army, with its resources mainly allocated to indiscriminate bomb attacks on the PAIGC's positions by military helicopters. This new phase of the conflict hit the party hard. However, the PAIGC found ways to adapt to the new circumstances. As previously discussed, Cabral had ordered the transformation of large units into bi-groups. It was a question of recognizing the superiority of the Portuguese army and the impossibility of confronting it conventionally. During these years, from 1964 to 1968, the party increased its political and above all its diplomatic work, and by the time General Schultz left Guinea he had been defeated.

In May 1968, the *Estado Novo* appointed Brigadier António de Spínola—promoted to general soon afterwards—to replace Arnaldo Schultz as governor and commander of the troops in Guinea. This appointment took place at a time of dramatic change in Lisbon. Four months after Spínola took office, Salazar, the long-serving president of the council, fell from his chair. He was diagnosed with a brain hemorrhage which significantly impacted his ability to work. After serving the *Estado Novo* for thirty-six years as the president of the council, Salazar was replaced by law professor Marcelo Caetano, whose nomination aroused new hopes of a possible resolution to the Portuguese colonial question. Many people believed that Caetano was in favor of a federal solution to the colonial situation. In 1962, in a solicited opinion to the Minister of the Colonies Adriano Moreira, he advised that the formation of a federal state between Portugal and her colonies was the most viable solution for the colonial crisis. This was, for him, the only possible cosmetic operation—implying change, but keeping everything the same—through which the three problems of the colonial crisis could be addressed: the international pressure, the need to protect the interests of Portugal in the colonies, and the protection of the lives and assets of the Portuguese in Africa.

However, the regime—particularly the conservatives in Salazar's party, who made up its strongest faction—was not yet ready to contemplate this option. Marcelo Caetano wrote many years after his appointment to the post of president of the council that this was preceded by a conversation with President of the Republic Américo Tomás. In this conversation, the latter made clear that he expected that Caetano would not "change anything in the politics of the defense of the overseas territories, and that he should resist any temptation to experiment with the federative solution." But as Caetano would later reminisce, he had already discovered the "error" he had committed by his defense of federalism, since although federalism was an "acceptable solution for international public opinion, it constituted a small step into independence." This lesson was learned as a result of France's attempt to create a federation with its colonies.

Nevertheless, Caetano would go on to implement changes in colonial policies that over time would contribute to the end of the Portuguese empire. The first one was simply a question of semantics. Caetano lacked Salazar's political charisma, which to a certain extent had convinced most Portuguese that their country had the right to colonize Africa. The new president of the council, as Franco Nogueira would later write, would undermine the fundamental truths which had supported the empire by resorting to practical rather than metaphysical reasons: "the armed forces should stay in Africa to protect the Portuguese", and as for Africans, he explained, "independence should not be a panacea for the problems faced by the African continent."

In other words, the change in policy from Salazar to Caetano was that the defense of the overseas dominions was thenceforth anchored more in the need to maintain the two largest and richest territories of Angola and Mozambique—where the Portuguese had real economic interests—than in any mystique attached to the supposed indivisibility of the empire. The Portuguese were trying to move past the domino theory, by which the loss of one of its territories—even the poorer, minuscule, and insanitary Guinea—would inexorably open the way for the independence of other colonies. By the late 1960s, Guinea had ceased to have any economic importance for the colonial empire, as the chemical company CUF had been forced to suspend its activities in the country. But Africa as a whole had to be defended at any cost.

Spínola shared the same worldview as Caetano, both of them operating pragmatically when it came to matters of colonial policy. In an interview with the Portuguese journalist Dutra Faria in 1969, for example, Spínola intimated that the loss of Guinea would only have a minimal effect on the Portuguese economy. The companies that bought groundnuts and coconuts there could buy the same products in Angola or Mozambique at "perhaps even better prices, which in a way compensates for the costs of transportation." He also added that it was not a problem to transfer the few whites who lived in Guinea to another place in the empire. However, for him, the defense of the colonies was rooted in three points. 1) It was proof of the coherence of Portuguese overseas policies: "Either we keep, at all costs, everything in Africa that belongs to Portugal, or, if we give a single finger, sooner or later, we will have to give, because of international pressure, the hand, the arm, and the rest". 2) In the context of the Cold War, maintaining the colonies was Portugal's modest contribution to the efforts to prevent the expansion of the Soviet Union in Africa: "If Portugal leaves Guinea, the strategic archipelago of Cape Verde (fundamental for the defense of the South Atlantic by the West) would be exposed to the appetites of the Soviet Union". 3) Portugal was protecting the well-being of Africans: "The day the Portuguese leave Guinea the guerrilla war would become a civil war and for the "crime" of being loyal to the Portuguese, entire ethnic groups, such as the Fulani, the Felupes and the Manjacos, would be exterminated ..."

These three pillars underpinned Spínola's actions in Guinea. To clear the guerrillas from the territory, or at least to bring military actions to a halt, he did not change much in relation to his predecessor, Arnaldo Schultz. However, his strategy would combine the military and the social. At its core was the axiom, repeated many times to journalists, that counterinsurgency, even though it could be lost from a purely military standpoint, could only be won politically.

* * *

For both Cabral and the Portuguese, launching a guerrilla war was not difficult, as it was enough to adapt the experiences of other people. In terms of counterinsurgency, there was not much to invent, with the Portuguese simply able to draw on the experiences of other counterinsurgencies. But like the guerrillas, they also had to adapt these lessons to the particular geographical and sociological conditions of the region. When Spínola took the post in Guinea, there was already a considerable body of accepted works on how to conduct counterinsurgency wars. The main model, with many variations in different contexts, consisted of creating a link of gratitude between the army and the population—what Sergei Chakotin called the "rape of the masses" or the psychology of totalitarian political propaganda, referring to the techniques used by the Nazi army to lure the population to the occupied zones. According to Chakotin, these techniques were rooted in applying to humans what his compatriot, Ivan Pavlov, discovered in the study of animals. Pavlov developed the theory that certain patterns of behavior could be induced by conditioned reflexes, if these were properly trained. For Chakotin, the Nazi army produced the same results in humans, inducing particular types of behavior by meeting certain needs of the population.

When the anti-colonial war began, counterinsurgency was still only an incipient military discipline. It was only in the 1950s that British General Gerald Templar, facing a Marxist-inspired revolt in Malaysia, had formulated the principle that in this kind of war the military component should not account for more than 25 per cent of the total effort. The rest should be the political, the economic and intelligence. These lessons provided the outline of the counterinsurgency strategy that the French used during the Algerian war and was also the kernel of Portuguese policies. Even before the beginning of war in the Portuguese territories, the Portuguese army had sent a group of officials to Algeria as observers.

The officials assembled by Spínola in Bissau were well versed in these doctrines of counterinsurgency. After his arrival in Guinea, Spínola sent some PIDE agents and less competent staff back to Lisbon—those who did not understand the importance of intelligence in the new methodology, or simply did not fit the new scheme. He then surrounded himself with people he liked, such as the PIDE inspector Fragoso Allas, and a number of young ambitious officials who would become known as the boys of Spínola, or the boys of Guinea: Carlos Fabião, Otelo Saraiva de Carvalho, Manuel Monge de Lima, Nunes Barata, José Blanco, Jorge Moreira da Costa, and Carlos Azeredo, among others. They were experts in counterinsurgency, trained in Lisbon, with placements in various European countries and the United States. They had in common the desire to change the course of the war at any cost.

Helped by these young officials, Spínola developed his own principles for how to face the guerrillas. He first redefined the role of the armed forces, telling journalist Urbano Carrasco of the Portuguese newspaper *Diário Popular* that the army should go beyond just military missions, which essentially amounted to the defense of the population. They should also carry out other important functions such as "social action, particularly in the domains of sanitary assistance, basic education, the construction of new hamlets, the preparation of land for cultivation, etc." Spínola also devoted particular attention to the psychological aspects of war: "the war in Guinea is imminently psychological in that it can only be won if we win people's souls, and this is not about coercion, but about persuasion."

As the guerrillas tried to get the population on their side, the purpose of counterinsurgency should be to prevent that. Cabral had found out which groups would more easily support the guerrillas, so Spínola tried to understand which ethnic groups would be on the side of Portugal. The whole country was then mapped out based on these divisions. In the maps for military operations, blue zones represented the areas whose populations were on the side of the Portuguese, for example those who inhabited the eastern part of the territory, such as the Fulani. Red represented the zones in which the populations were on the side of the guerrillas; in these areas, there was no distinction between civilian and military targets, and the air force had authorization to strike them whenever necessary. Finally, there was a third area, yellow, which represented the places where, depending on the military situation, it was possible to advance to a blue zone or recede to a red one. Strategic hamlets, or resettlement areas, were built in blue zones, where people from the most scarcely populated regions were sent. Spínola elaborates: "the population reacts differently to the order to leave, depending on the degree of attachment to the land where they were born and other variable factors of local nature." However, "as soon as they start to feel the benefits that come from this order, their natural reaction is canceled out, and they come, voluntarily, to the poles of progress".

As the strategic hamlets were intended to allow the population to be withdrawn from certain areas, the guerrillas found themselves exposed, facilitating the search-and-destroy operations of the Portuguese army, which were undertaken by military helicopters carrying special forces and marines. These units moved in small groups, carrying out rapid strikes to destroy the guerrilla units. Their goals were, as highlighted in one of the reports of the commanding general, "to make the life [of the guerrillas] impossible, until they lose the will to fight."

In the general strategy to fight the guerrillas, the Portuguese paid particular attention to the Africanization of the troops. Counterinsurgency manuals advise the need to involve the natives in the war effort, and this principle was to a certain extent practiced by the British in Malaysia, the French in Algeria, and later by the Americans in Vietnam. However, the Portuguese, more than any other colonial power, preferred to recruit local troops for their own wars whenever they could. As we have previously shown, the involvement of Africans was decisive for the conquest of Guinea, particularly Cape Verdean troops. The colonial war produced a number of African heroes who fought on the side of the Portuguese, such as Abdul Injai.

The mobilization of African troops is an important chapter in the history of colonialism in Africa. As many Portuguese people have written, Africans were the soldiers best equipped to cope with the harsh conditions of the continent. According to Francisco Aragão,

> in those hostile climates, which soon crippled the European, the indigenous soldier resists every difficulty. Happily, without fatigue and tanned—he laughs at the sun that does not burn him—looking confidently to the entangled and impenetrable jungle, he goes, the brave and traditional walker who knows everything, treading the interminable kilometers of African land, without despondency or dismay.

To the Portuguese army, this arrangement was crafted out of necessity. Towards the end of the war, the costs of it came to 40 per cent of the Portuguese budget. Hence, training African troops, better prepared for the specificities of the terrain and with greater resistance to malaria and other tropical diseases, considerably reduced the costs of maintenance. The Portuguese were able to recruit African soldiers in part by exploiting ethnic grievances. The Fulani and the Mandinka had a historical dispute, stemming from the collaboration of the former with the French and Portuguese colonialists in the destruction of the Mandé empire in the nineteenth century. This rivalry was further exacerbated by the fact that the Portuguese did not recognize the Mandinka traditional chiefs and, even worse, assigned Fulani chiefs as heads of Mandinka *tabankas*. Besides the Balanta, a significant section of the PAIGC troops, as well as the president of Guinea-Conakry, Sékou Touré, were Mandinka, meaning the Portuguese did not have to put much effort into recruiting indigenous soldiers: many of the Fulani who enlisted were volunteers.

On the socio-economic front, Spínola's administration produced a carefully constructed economic plan, called *Por uma Guiné Melhor* (For a Better Guinea), whose principal goal was to address the need to improve social life in the territory. In the third *Plano de Fomento* (Development Plan, 1967–73), the budget for Guinea had increased considerably, to cover the construction of infrastructure, roads, bridges, and ports, as well as structures for the supply of electricity in Bissau. But the major public investments, according to the governor himself, were made in health care and education, especially in elementary, secondary, and vocational education.

Furthermore, Spínola's administration did not simply try to establish—as the French had in Algeria and the Americans in Vietnam—a power which demanded obedience from the dominated people, devoid of any "cultural content." Spínola went further. He understood that the national movement was using culture as a tool for mobilization, and he intended to prevent it. During his tenure, he would try to reinforce the tribal identity of the Guineans. But for that, he had to alter some of the main tenets of Portuguese colonial ideology at that time.

In terms of the ethnic question, Spínola's action touched on the most delicate subjects with which Portuguese colonialism had to deal. In the first chapter, I discussed how Portuguese colonial thinkers in the 1920s and the 1930s were working out how to integrate the African possessions into the Portuguese national territory. But this had coincided with the proliferation of demands for self-determination, which forced colonial empires such as Britain and France to reassess their ambitions. As such, these empires were beginning to understand that the best way to manage the Africans under their control was not to assimilate them—particularly in the French case—but to trap them within their own institutions of tribal power. Lord Frederick Lugard, a former governor of Hong Kong—later transferred to Nigeria—championed these principles. In his opinion, Africans should develop within their own tribal structures and be governed by their native authorities, who would determine the laws and the rules to access land within what was considered tradition. In the long run, this fragmentation would naturally work against the formation of a national consciousness.

Portuguese colonialism was different in that the *Estado Novo* had integrated the colonies into the national arena, but had left out the vast majority of Africans who were not considered citizens. It is not a coincidence that Adriano Moreira, the colonial thinker who had so painstakingly justified the *Estatuto do Indigenato*, also repealed it, granting, at least formally, Portuguese citizenship to all colonized Africans in 1961. Although this solved the issue of integration, it did not address the actual causes of anti-colonial protest and significantly differed from the actions of the British and the French in Africa.

With this in mind, Spínola tried to do something different in Guinea: he attempted to more dramatically reverse the assimilationist approach which had characterized Portuguese colonialism, creating consultative institutions of tribal power called *Congressos dos Povos da Guiné* (Congresses of Guinean People). Behind this move was the notion that Africans should never "adopt forms of European life," and that efforts to assimilate Africans neglected to acknowledge that tribal structures were the outcome of particular economic systems. In fact, as Manuel Belchior wrote, "Africans, for practicing an itinerant agriculture, were always at the mercy of famine". As such, Belchior maintains, only tribal cohesion—through systems of redistribution—protected them from hardships. This structure was disrupted by assimilation, he continues, which resulted in people feeling alienated from their own tribes (the so-called "evolved" or "evolués"). Ugandan scholar Mahmood Mamdani discusses the ways in which the colonial state in Africa tried to deal with such an uprooting of Africans from their traditions. The colonial state, Mamdani states, redefined itself as the guarantor of tribal cohesion by, on the one hand, protecting Africans against any form of alienation, and, on the other, by seeing "not the evolués, but rather the chief of the tribalized" as interlocutors with the colonial system, as representatives of the tribal world with the power to influence the popular masses.

This was the thinking behind the *Congressos*. The first Congress was held in 1970, when leaders of the Fulani and the Mandinka convened with the aim of reconciling the two groups. The origins of the animosity between the Fulani and the Mandinka has already been discussed: the Fulani as a group were somewhat "favored" by Portuguese colonialism in comparison to other ethnicities. Some of their chiefs received subsidies for trips to Mecca and for the construction of mosques. With the beginning of the colonial war, the Fulani persecuted the Mandinka, accusing them of being on the side of the nationalists. A number of them were forced to seek refuge in the neighboring countries. For the

Portuguese, therefore, it was important to bring the Mandinka to their side without alienating the Fulani. Out of this first Congress came the suggestion that the Mandinka should be allowed to elect their own leaders for the first time in their land, the region of Farim-Oio, instead of having Fulani chiefs imposed on them.

For the second Congress, the forum was enlarged to accommodate all ethnic groups. The work of the Congress was divided into two phases. The first consisted of the local tribal forums, which chose the delegates for the second phase—the interethnic summit. Although the Congress did not have deliberative power, it was an important instrument to ingrain tribal consciousness and create greater distance between the various ethnicities. The idea behind the Congress was that personhood was attached to ethnicity.

In the short term, the general strategy of Spínola—not to win the war, but at least not to lose it—produced positive results. The guerrillas were being deprived of the support of the population and from a military perspective the Portuguese were finally making some inroads. In many areas controlled by the PAIGC, the guerrillas were incapable of keeping the population in the regions under their control. The visible outcome of this was an exodus of 60,000 refugees to Senegal, a significant number of whom left after the arrival of Spínola. Having no qualms about indiscriminately killing civilians, Spínola's men were given the green light to destroy the facilities managed by the movement, such as schools and hospitals, the people's warehouses, granaries, and rice paddies. As a result, Cabral's party was—for the first time since the beginning of the war—on the defensive.

Crucial to Spínola's strategy was to redefine the areas dominated by each side. The Portuguese voluntarily abandoned their most isolated positions, such as the headquarters of Madina do Boé, whose occupation by the guerrillas had been hailed internationally as a victory for the movement. As these isolated units raised serious concerns in terms of supply, especially during the rainy season, the Portuguese preferred to concentrate their forces in large population centers, such as in Bissau, Bafatá, Gabu, or in the fortified villages. Portuguese forces also attempted to mimic the guerrillas, abandoning the rigid structures of the conventional army and breaking up its military forces into smaller units. If the guerrillas, in 1971, could claim the control of 50 per cent of the territory, this did not mean that they in fact dominated this area. It simply meant that, having more empty spaces, they could, like the Portuguese, move through this territory.

As expected, the violent Portuguese military offensive, combined with a vigorous program of social action, triggered a series of divisions within Cabral's party. When Spínola arrived in Guinea, the war had already been dragging on for five years and there was no end in sight. Negotiations for a peace agreement were out of the question. And by the early 1970s, fatigue was setting in within the PAIGC's forces. Desertions had become routine, and more and more militants were openly questioning the war effort. The further the militants were from the headquarters the harsher the criticism towards the party, and particularly towards Cabral. In the liberated zones, the preoccupation with survival and the various forms of control over the militants limited the space for open critique of the party. But in Conakry, in the rear-guard, the less put-upon Guinean fighters were more easily drawn into anti-Cape Verdean campaigns, sponsored by Spínola, which criticized the division of labor in the party. As Spínola himself put it: "Guineans represented the guerrilla mass of the combatants in the front, and the Cape Verdeans the cadres in the rear-guard. This friction is at the heart of the split among those who effectively suffer the harshness of the war and those, who, in the rear-guard, enjoy the benefits of foreign material support."

PAIGC bursary students abroad were those who most fiercely criticized the party. Having lost contact with the everyday life of the liberation movement, they challenged not only the decisions taken by the movement, but also Cabral's leadership. In the Soviet Union alone the party had more than 400 students enrolled in academic programmes as diverse as mechanics, agronomy, accountancy, and administration. These students organized themselves in groups of agitation whose leaders hatched plots and led rebellious acts. From these groups came some of those who would later conspire in the murder of Amílcar Cabral.

By the end of the war, everything served to fuel the discontent. And Amílcar Cabral, with his frequent absences, had become one of the primary targets of the criticism. It was true that the leader of the PAIGC did not provide many explanations for his constant trips abroad—where he went and for how long he travelled, or any other details regarding his itinerary—something that had saved his life at least once. By this time, nobody could fail to notice his absences. This is clear from the level and intensity of the diplomatic work conducted towards the end of Cabral's tenure as the party leader. In 1966, he made three trips abroad; in 1972 he went abroad 31 times. There are many factors behind the increase, and not just, as the enemies of Cabral would have it, that he preferred to spend more time abroad. Only by making these constant trips could he raise the funds needed to meet the increasing war expenditure: a great deal of what the guerrillas consumed, weaponry and sometimes even fuel, came as the result of these contacts. And not even alternating the trips abroad with periods of stoic and demanding routine in Conakry—getting up early in the morning to participate in physical exercises with the students at the *Escola Piloto* and spending the rest of the day working—was enough to quell the intrigue.

* * *

To damage the international cohesion of the nationalist movement, Spínola staged the liberation of political prisoners in Bissau. In 1969, Spínola was given authorization by Marcelo Caetano to grant amnesty to ninety-two PAIGC prisoners who had been kept in the cells of the *Polícia de Segurança Pública* (Portuguese National Police—PSP). The liberation took place symbolically on 3 August, the day the party commemorated the tenth anniversary of the massacres of Pidjiguiti. Rafael Barbosa was among the prisoners who were released. Barbosa had been hailed as a hero by the party in many international campaigns. He had been described in an issue of *PAIGC-Actualités* as having resisted all pressures and threats from the colonial authorities, and was considered an example for the youngest generations. The condition for the liberation of the prisoners was an oath of allegiance to Spínola and Portuguese colonialism. Spínola's stunt drew abundant coverage in the international press, and was taken up by a number of foreign newspapers, such as *The Times* of London, which quoted excerpts of the speech given by Rafael Barbosa in its 5 August 1969 edition: "Thank you, Your Excellency, for the fine attitude that you have taken upon your shoulders, in liberating these dozens of men who, deceived by the promises of those who, paid by foreign countries, launched them into rebellion [...] I promise that I will be as Portuguese as Your Excellency".

WINNING IN POLITICS WITHOUT LOSING THE WAR

The release of Rafael Barbosa was part of Spínola's *Por uma Guiné Melhor* strategy, as he would later explain:

> [I]t is the concern of the government of the province to satisfy the legitimate desires of access to the benefits of civilization and culture. Therefore, some of those who had been enthralled by the propaganda and intimidation of the enemy, recognizing now the error into which they fell, or by verifying the inconsistency of the promises they heard, have shown the will to collaborate in the construction of a successful Guinea for the future, under the Portuguese flag. And the proof of an undeniable Portuguesism, once reintegrated, is something that makes us trust in them, and, simultaneously, in the validity of this policy.

The case of Rafael Barbosa is worth examining. He had escaped the first round of detentions of PAIGC militants which took place in 1961. After a period in hiding, he was finally captured on the night of 13 March 1962, in the company of other members of the PAIGC—namely Mamadou Touré and Albino Sanca—in the house that had served as the party's headquarters in Bissau, in the neighborhood of Alto Crim. The PIDE also seized a range of propaganda material, such as emblems, instructions, subversive pamphlets, printouts, and correspondence. In one of the first interrogations to which he was submitted, Barbosa confessed that he undertook the role of "secretary of control" in the party, as the main representative of the movement inside Guinea, and the second in the entire movement—right below Amílcar Cabral. According to the PIDE's report, Barbosa was responsible for recruiting potential members to the party, bringing weapons and war material into Bissau, and also served as the link between the various elements of the party across many different centers, such as Bissará, Teixeira Pinto, Farim, and São Domingo.

It is likely that it was through Rafael Barbosa and other elements of Zone Zero—the codename for Bissau—that the PIDE managed to infiltrate the PAIGC. As he had collaborated with the police, he was given some liberties, being permitted to walk through the city without surveillance and even to sleep at home. This allowed him, as the PIDE would later find out, to act as a sort of double agent. Just as he collaborated with the PIDE, he also sent messages to his party, and, with the help of members from his cell, he tried to escape a couple of times.

Rafael Barbosa was not the only high-ranking member of the PAIGC who had deserted (or at least passed to the side of the Portuguese). At the end of the 1960s, desertions, both individual and group, were taking place so frequently that Cabral, forced to intervene, proposed the death penalty for collective desertions from the movement. It was not out of sheer cruelty that Cabral made such a proposition: the PAIGC was running out of solutions to deal with the fact that a number of militants, tired of the war, had preferred to go back home in order to benefit from the amnesty Spínola had promised. However, there were also a significant number of people who had been pardoned by Spínola and who, taking advantage of the party's leniency, eventually sought readmission into the liberation movement. Hence, the release of the prisoners in Bissau and the amnesty given to all militants of the party produced a certain flux between Bissau and Conakry. But these shifting allegiances also left the party unsure whether to accept all the militants who returned from Bissau without any reservations or to condemn to death everyone suspected of treason.

The infiltration into the ranks of the PAIGC was not random but was part of a consistent and ambitious plan to penetrate the headquarters of the movement and the military fronts. Accordingly, Spínola and his closest officials in military intelligence devised a plan to win over the PAIGC fighters in the Northern Front, in Catchungo. From the Portuguese side, these contacts were established by majors Joaquim Pereira, Raul dos Passos Ramos, and Osório Magalhães. On the side of the guerrillas, the main interlocutor was André Gomes, a revered combatant who had led the group of thirteen fighters who in 1968 had broken the security line of Bissau and fired artillery at the airport. The conversations between the two groups reached such a level of intimacy that the majors often went to meet the guerrilla group unarmed. Often the Portuguese officials offered them tobacco, alcoholic beverages, and money. The Portuguese were trying to negotiate a ceasefire with the members of the Northern Front and to incorporate the whole group into the Portuguese army. In exchange, this rebel group would be given a generous salary of 60,000 *contos* (Portuguese *escudos*), to which the Overseas Ministry had already agreed.

Informed by these events, Cabral dispatched to the front Luís Correia, the head of the intelligence service in the party, and a man he could trust. In association with the commanders of the region, Correia planned an operation to capture General Spínola himself, who had already met some of the fighters on that front and had promised to return to officially incorporate them into the Portuguese forces.

On the scheduled day, 20 April 1970, the three majors from the Portuguese army, Pereira, Ramos, and Magalhães, went to meet the fighters without General Spínola. They were shot dead soon after they left their car. The authors of the killing hacked up the bodies with machetes. In a speech at the fourteenth anniversary of the founding party, in September 1970, Cabral claimed responsibility for the killings and summed them up as follows: "after a number of contacts, ridiculous letters, offers, gifts and promises of all kinds, the colonists suffered another shameful defeat: our heroic combatants killed the majors and other officials and soldiers who thought they could buy us."

When reading the available information about the events of that day, it is hard to comprehend what really went wrong. Did the guerrilla fighters feign their interest in negotiating with the Portuguese so as to lure, arrest or even kill General Spínola, as Luís Cabral suggests in his book? Or did they only realize they were betraying the party when Cabral sent his intelligence officer? It has also been suggested that the Portuguese majors were killed by another group belonging to the party and not the one with whom they had been negotiating.

The killing had a serious impact on General Spínola himself. He was an old-fashioned military man, who thought that unarmed soldiers should not be killed. He also harbored genuine and fatherly concerns for the men under his command. In this sense, it is understandable that Spínola might have felt partially guilty for the turn of the events: he had, after all, authorized the negotiations. However, he had not imagined that Cabral's men (with or without explicit orders from Cabral), would have the courage to actually kill unarmed soldiers, who, according to him, were on a peace mission.

Although Spínola was still interested in a peaceful solution to the conflict, his patience was wearing thin. After the killing of the majors he was looking for revenge, and he welcomed any proposal for how to destroy Cabral's movement. Here, he was also following the counter-insurgency principle which states that the guerrilla movement is like a centipede: it can only be killed by a fatal blow to its head. As such,

Spínola started to be receptive to the idea that the PAIGC should be decapitated and began planning the arrest and even killing of Cabral himself. This is how the plan to invade the headquarters in Conakry came into being.

* * *

The original plan for what was then called *Operação Mar Verde* (Operation Green Sea) was the liberation of eighteen Portuguese prisoners and the destruction of the PAIGC's boats. One of these prisoners was António Lobato, captured in 1963 while piloting a T-6 plane which had hit another aircraft during an ill-calculated maneuver, "causing irreparable damages to both planes." But the author of the plot, Captain Alpoim Calvão, convinced General Spínola to add two more objectives: the deposition of Sékou Touré, by sending in a group of dissidents trained and armed by Portugal—who, once in power, would expel the PAIGC—and the arrest or physical elimination of Amílcar Cabral. Out of these two goals, General Spínola was more in favor of arresting Cabral, as he emphasized in a report of 1989, signed nineteen years after the events. The arrest and immediate transport of the nationalist leader to Bissau "was key in my handling of the management of the political-military process in Guinea, whose goal was a ceasefire on terms I found honorable to Portugal." This option, according to the report, promised to provide an end to the war in a "spectacular" way.

Alpoim Galvão was tasked with overseeing the operation. He travelled to South Africa to buy limpet mines, which were transported in his own hand baggage on commercial flights, and relying on smugglers, negotiated the import of guns from the Soviet Union, particularly the infamous Kalashnikov. He personally contacted various groups of political refugees from Guinea-Conakry, scattered across European cities. With the help of two other officials of the Portuguese army, Rebordão de Brito and Marcelino da Mata, he provided the dissidents with forty-five days of training on the island of Soga, in the archipelago of the Bijagós.

A military formation of 215 Portuguese soldiers (the majority were Guineans of the *Compania de Comandos Africanos*) and 150 Conakry-Guineans, among them political dissidents and former soldiers of the colonial army, left for Conakry on 21 November 1970 at 10 pm. They wore uniforms which resembled those used by the forces of Sékou Touré, but with light green bands attached to their shirtsleeves to distinguish themselves from the military forces of Guinea-Conakry. The military formation was transported in two LFG ships of the Alfange type, equipped with 20mm canons, and escorted by four Class Argos patrol tanks, armed with 40mm canons. The crew was exclusively made up of Portuguese nationals.

Conakry's power plant was the first target hit by the invading forces. The darkness that fell upon the city was the signal to the other units that the invasion was underway. Subsequently, the groups led by Rebordão de Brito succeeded in their part of the mission, sinking three PAIGC boats and setting the other four on fire. During the attacks on the docks, a PAIGC mariner was killed, and one of the commanders, Irénio Nascimento, managed to escape and run to Camp Samori to alert the forces of Sékou Touré. The group tasked with arresting or killing Amílcar Cabral encountered serious resistance, as later described by the Yugoslav doctor Dimir Streten. He worked in the hospital close to the party headquarters, and his daughter was killed by the bombs launched by the Portuguese forces.

The Portuguese were aware that the success of the mission depended on destroying the planes of the Republic of Guinea's Air Force, particularly the MIG 21. However, contrary to what the Portuguese had assumed, these military aircraft were not in a condition to fight. The Soviets had been late in supplying them with ammunition, and the country had no sufficiently trained pilots to operate them. In charge of the mission to take down the aircrafts was José Januário, who, like many other members of the *Compania de Comandos Africanos*, had been coerced into taking part in the operation. Once in the airport, Januário aborted the mission and convinced the men under his command to surrender. Calvão sent another group to fulfill the same mission, but they only found an Air Afrique Caravelle jet and four Focker 27 bimotors. None of them were combat planes.

As this part of the operation had failed, Galvão feared that the Portuguese boats were exposed to airstrikes, so on the morning of 22 November, he ordered the retreat of his groups. The mission had been partially fulfilled, since the Portuguese prisoners had been released and the PAIGC fleet destroyed. But those had been the objectives of

Calvão, which were obviously of a military nature. The political goals, those that Spínola had added—the arrest or killing of Cabral and the deposing of Touré—had been abandoned in favor of a safe withdrawal, with only very few causalities for the Portuguese contingent. Calvão later reminisced that he only cared about "bringing back the prisoners, the FLNG people had to fend for themselves."

The group of Guinean dissidents managed to force their way into the Villa Silly, the presidential palace, but Touré was no longer there. They then moved on to other positions, reinforcing units such as the one that had taken the military headquarters of Camayenne, a position that was defended until the afternoon of 22 November. The tide of the invasion was only turned in favor of Touré early in the afternoon of 22 November, when the Guinean president finally gave up the keys to the armory of weapons—which he kept on his person—and asked for the intervention of a Cuban force of 200 soldiers.

The invasion of the independent sovereign state of Guinea was a diplomatic debacle for the Portuguese forces. A number of people who participated in it and later spoke or wrote about it have pointed to a lack of information as the reason for its failure. Cabral, for instance, was not even in Conakry that night. But in defense of the PIDE, this information had not been incorrect at the time the invasion was being planned. In fact, Cabral had left Algiers on 18 November, and headed to Tripoli, Libya, where he was to stay a couple of days before heading to Conakry. Not only did his unexpected change of plans confound the police, but his own men also fell into the trap. When the press correspondents in Algiers found out about the events in Conakry, they rushed to the PAIGC headquarters to ask after the whereabouts of Cabral, and they were told that Cabral was in the Guinean capital. Only three days after the events did it emerge that Cabral had changed his mind at the last moment and, instead of going to Conakry, had gone to Sofia in Bulgaria, where he gave his first interview since the attacks to the Italian communist daily *L'Unitá*.

While diplomatically and politically the invasion was a failure, Calvão's mission was so successful from a military point of view that some people have speculated that Sékou Touré himself had collaborated in the rescue of Portuguese soldiers in exchange for the handover of opponents of his regime (a position hard to maintain, however, as it is unlikely that any party would run so much risk for so little reward). However, the highly impetuous actions of the Portuguese gave Sékou Touré—known for inventing plots to get rid of people from his own government—a justification to launch one of the worst acts of cruelty ever carried out in Guinea-Conakry. Sékou Touré set up a Supreme Revolutionary Court, arresting more than 5,000 people for interrogation. Sixty-two were subsequently sentenced to death and another sixty-eight given life sentences. Dozens of people were hanged, including incumbent ministers. Touré also had no qualms about ordering the killing of the wives and children of real and imagined opponents. Foreign nationals, members of the clergy, and the surrendering members of the African Commandos—the group led by Lieutenant Januário Lopes—were among the condemned. Upon his return to Conakry, Cabral was greeted by the bodies of the deceased hanging from the bridge which gives access to the city.

The invasion of Conakry was the final blow to the international prestige of Portugal, even though, in the first days after the events, its involvement could not be officially ascertained. Although the radio of Conakry had initiated a verbal offensive against the forces of Spínola from the early hours of 22 November, suspicions that Portugal had been involved only began to fully take shape on 27 November when Francisco Gomes Nangue, a soldier in the Company of African Commandos, was found in the sea off the coast of Liberia and saved by a British ship. Taken to Monrovia, he revealed that his company had participated in the attacks. His testimony convinced the Liberians to support Conakry in an act of repudiation against Portugal—an example followed by many other African countries, despite them not being on best terms with the regime of Sékou Touré—in the OAU assembly in January 1971.

Weakened by the failure of the *Operação Mar Verde*, Spínola continued to look for a solution to the conflict. In 1971, Léopold Senghor, the president of Senegal, suggested a meeting with Spínola to discuss the possibility of negotiations between Cabral and the governor of Guinea. But due to the reluctance of the regime of Marcelo Caetano to negotiate with the guerrillas, the encounter only took place the following year, on 18 May 1972, at the *Club Mediterranée* tourist complex in Cap Skirring, in the southern Senegal region of Casamance.

According to Carlos Fabião, one of the Portuguese army officers who took part in the meetings, Senghor proposed a ceasefire so as to allow the formation of a dual administration, composed of members of both the guerrilla movement and the Portuguese side, which would govern the territory according to a ten-year statute of autonomy. This proposition—the constitution of a community between Portugal and its colonies—was something that Spínola had previously believed in, but had been forced to renounce due to the circumstances he found himself confronting. In 1972, the president of the council, Caetano, stated that he favored a military defeat over negotiations with the guerrillas, since this would provide space for diplomatic action under international law. As Caetano would explain in his book *Depoimento*: "armies exist to win. And they must win, but it is not necessary that they win. If the Portuguese army is vanquished in Guinea after using up its capacities, this leaves us with our political and legal capacities intact to defend the rest of the overseas territories." Spínola, frustrated with this attitude, confided: "I do not want to hide my fear that perhaps we have lost the last chance of a dialogue between the governor of Guinea and Amílcar Cabral in a position of clear superiority."

In 1973, Spínola was discharged at his own request and returned to Lisbon, where he would be promoted to a four-star general, and appointed deputy chairman of the Armed Forces. Later, he would play a central role in the April revolution of 1974. I will discuss the relationship between the failure in Guinea and the April revolution later.

* * *

The actions of Spínola in Guinea are an important corrective to much of the writing on Cabral and the war in Guinea. Spínola not only attempted to counter the guerrillas in the military arena, but he also fought them on the psychological and political terrain. He successfully organized the desertion of a number of guerrilla fighters, even if in doing so he lost some of his own men. He failed to decapitate their leadership, but he did deal a serious blow to the confidence of the guerrillas. Spínola's policies and military strategies must, therefore, be taken into account if we are to fully understand the circumstances and intricacies of the war in Guinea in general, and the killing of Cabral in particular.

10

TOWARDS INDEPENDENCE

There was one thing that both Cabral and Spínola could agree on: a military effort on its own would not be enough to win the war. As we have seen, Cabral's military strategy rested on this principle. While military action inflicted irreparable damage on the Portuguese forces, damaged their morale, helped to protect the population, and allowed for the continuation of social work, it could not bring about a final victory. Without a political decision—implying negotiation—the conflict could in theory drag on for decades.

Guerrilla manuals take particular care to discuss the phase of equilibrium which follows the shock of the first actions. Che Guevara, in his popular style, called it "bite and escape", but other texts describe this stage in more formulaic terms, such as "stabilized resistance". This is the period in which conditions are prepared for the launch of the final phase of the movement, in which large swathes of the population are involved, and which constitutes a dissuasive factor on the side of the defending forces.

Guinea's anti-colonial war, according to this schema, would never reach its final phase, despite Cabral's frequent statements to the contrary. Once, when asked about the phase his country was in according to Guevara's framework, Cabral began by saying that he was against the "systematization of phenomena," since, in practice, "phenomena do not take place according to pre-established schemes." However, he added, "we say, *without affirming*, that this scheme is adaptable to our conditions". He concluded that the situation in Guinea would very soon be ready, "thanks to the advance of the *war of movement*, to begin, given the conditions in which we find ourselves, the *general offensive* to finish the Portuguese domination in our land" (emphasis added). The Cubans in particular favored attacking Bissau and finishing the war, as they had themselves defeated the Batista regime with the invasion of Havana in 1959.

Cabral's response not only revealed his ignorance of the theories of guerrilla warfare and his attitude in relation to the "military," but also his lack of interest in advancing in a direction that was exclusively military, as was expected by some international audiences, especially those that had been formed out of revolutions, such as in Cuba. Cabral knew the risks of this direction. First of all, leadership of the movement would have to be handed to the military, which would put him in a subaltern position. Secondly, the party would also have to obtain heavier war materials, such as helicopters, which, given the geographic conditions of Guinea, were considered the most efficient means of transport to distribute supplies, to support isolated positions and to evacuate the injured and dead. Thirdly, anti-aircraft materials would have to be acquired in order to challenge the Portuguese air supremacy.

Above all, it was necessary to intensify the military actions, which meant recruiting more fighters to the party's ranks and, as a result, establishing sophisticated means of surveillance to avoid internal subversion. For the South African activist Stephanie Urdang, for example, this was one of the main concerns in the liberated zones, since as well as the hardships, fatigue, bad food, and constant loss of family members and friends, the guerrillas also had to deal with infiltration by volunteer recruits.

For all these reasons, Cabral was convinced that the liberation of Guinea should not be achieved by increasing the military effort, but through the intensification of political action inside and diplomatic action outside the country. Influencing this decision was Cabral's personality itself. He was the principal strategist in the party. He signed almost all the documents it produced, wrote the communiqués, gave the press conferences, and took part in almost every diplomatic mission—he defined his agenda in line with his innate abilities. His personal inclinations made him more comfortable on the diplomatic front: he was a frank and cordial person, who always found a way to connect with others and did not find it difficult to strike up conversation with people from different walks of life. He was intelligent and adroit with words, expressing himself perfectly in Portuguese and correctly in French, although not very well in English; he was an apt thinker and responded carefully to questions, which gave his speech a kind of flexibility. With his words he could please both the most radical of communist audiences and the most moderate of democratic countries. As such, it is natural that he was more personally invested in the diplomatic field.

Powerfully representing the key tenets of his international action, Cabral used his theory of the two circles at a 1967 Conference of Nationalist Organizations of the Portuguese Colonies (CONCP) in Dar-es-Salaam, Tanzania. He asked the audience to imagine the Portuguese encircling the guerrilla fighters in all the positions occupied in the territory. But this circle was mutual, since the guerrilla fighters also encircled the Portuguese. As the Portuguese also relied on the exterior to get support for their military efforts, there was another circle around the PAIGC's fighters. Diplomatic action in favor of the PAIGC was meant to break the exterior circle imposed over the guerrillas. International campaigns in countries which were allies of Portugal were centered around the need to make people aware of the consequences of supporting the colonial power. In Cabral's terms, this was a way to encircle Portugal's positions, by engaging with the UN and other influential organizations such as the Vatican and the US Congress.

The UN had been founded in 1945 as a forum of free countries, integrating the powers that possessed colonies and protectorates, and the very few independent former colonies. By opposing colonialism, the 1955 Bandung Conference had helped create the conditions for the expansion of sovereignty throughout the world. It also gave these recently born nations new ethics based on what was called "positive neutrality"—that is, non-alignment in the Cold War struggle between the United States and the Soviet Union. This philosophy would underpin the participation of these new countries in the General Assembly of the UN, where they came to be known as the Afro-Asiatic group.

AMÍLCAR CABRAL

It was due to the emergence of the Afro-Asiatic group in the UN—at least at the level of the General Assembly—alongside the Soviets, that Portugal started to experience its first major setbacks in the organization. Delegates representing these countries took an active role in drafting Resolution 1514, approved in December 1960, which condemned Portuguese colonialism and urged Portugal to decolonize. They also lobbied for Cabral to be invited to speak as a petitioner at the UN Special Commission on 12 December 1962, which had been established in order to gather oral and written information on the true situation in the Portuguese colonies.

In the report that Cabral read to the members of the Commission, he appeared overly confident that the UN could contribute to the independence of Guinea. He inferred, for example, that the independence of Guinea depended less on the efforts of Cape Verdeans and Guineans and more on the help of the UN in putting pressure on Portugal to comply with Resolution 1514. Since the UN was the "guarantor of and responsible for international laws," Cabral may have believed that the organization need only recommend that the Portuguese government negotiate with the nationalist movement for this to occur.

Throughout the following years, the UN issued various appeals and resolutions urging Portugal to decolonize. But it was not enough, as in reality the organization had limited power and could not interfere in the internal affairs of the member states. At any rate, Portugal was not violating any principle of the UN, for the amendment to the Portuguese constitution had turned colonies into overseas provinces. Following this principle, Portugal had been able to survive in the organization, notwithstanding the pressure from the Afro-Asiatic group.

Cabral also had to learn the language of UN diplomacy in order to make his case for the independence of Guinea and Cape Verde. In his appearance before the organization in 1963, Cabral had tried to demonstrate—in a similar argument to the one he had employed in the pamphlet *Facts*—that Portugal was incapable of colonizing and that its attitude in the UN was in contravention to UN Resolution 1514. Seven years later, in 1970, Cabral presented a different argument to the UN to make his case. He asserted that the sovereignty of a given people is made up of territory, population, and administration; based on these factors, Guinea should be considered a state. Cabral's nationalist movement controlled various parts of the populated territory, where they had developed social infrastructure such as schools and hospitals despite Portuguese air attacks. In these parts of the country, Portugal could only claim control through a bombing campaign using napalm and herbicides. Any government, he added, that had to resort to such methods to defend its sovereignty did not have the right to represent Cape Verde and Guinea. Over the many years Cabral had been making his case for independence, Guinea had become a country "whose situation is that of an independent state, part of whose national territory, notably the urban centres, is militarily occupied by a foreign power."

* * *

Diplomatically, Cabral had always been a pragmatist; he tried as much as possible not to identify with any ideology. The world he was trying to navigate was complex and demanded flexibility of language. Ultimately, the liberation movement shared the same theoretical backbone as communist revolutions, inspired by Marx, Lenin, or Mao. This meant that the PAIGC received most of its support from the Soviet Union, East Germany, Czechoslovakia, Bulgaria, and Yugoslavia, including not only war material, but also sanitation products, food, and training in the form of scholarships. When travelling to these countries, Cabral had no qualms about using language which would identify him with communism. But he was also aware that support from these countries was not enough to gain Guinea's independence, as they were isolated on the international arena, diplomatically weak, and incapable of exerting any sort of pressure over Portugal.

On the other hand, the policy of Western countries was less bound by ideology and more concerned with human rights. Since the political system in these countries allowed freedom of speech, it meant that their societies and citizens did not have to align with their government's policies and were able to voice their discontent. Cabral's diplomatic efforts in these countries was meant to influence public opinion through the press in order to put pressure on their governments. In the West, therefore, the conflict in Guinea was largely framed as a humanitarian problem. As such, the PAIGC was able to obtain logistical support from committees in countries such as Great Britain, the Netherlands, and France, whose governments assisted Portugal militarily. Food and blood for hospitals came from these countries. Not only did this assistance come from far-left organizations, as a report written by the Portuguese Ministry of Foreign Affairs put it, but also from apolitical organizations such as the World Council of Churches, which in September 1970 donated USD 20,000 to Cabral's party.

But the aforementioned assistance came from NGOs or groups of citizens, in contravention of their governments' positions. In terms of non-communist countries, only the Swedish government openly supported the PAIGC. During the war, this Nordic country sent hospital equipment, a radio transmitter, vehicles, and consumables. Although the global level of help has never been made public, the Swedish government was open about its increased support to the guerrilla movement from 1970–1.

* * *

To a large extent, Cabral's movement was therefore torn between its necessary affiliation with the Eastern Bloc and the need to attract Western countries to its cause. As such, Cabral put a great deal of effort into changing the perception that he was a communist. To make this case, few diplomatic actions were as important and consequential as the private audience granted by the Pope to the representatives of Lusophone liberation movements, such as Amílcar Cabral, Agostinho Neto, and Marcelino dos Santos.

The aversion of the Catholic Church to communism is well known. Various encyclicals and papal interventions, such as the *Qui Pluribus* of 1846 and the *Nostis et Nobiscum* of 1849, had condemned newly emerging communist ideologies. In the twentieth century, other popes, such as Pius XI, extended the hatred of communism to its surrogates like Christian democracy, which he considered to be full of contradictions, maintaining that people could not practice politics and fear God at the same time. After WWII, on account of the formation of the Eastern Bloc, the Catholic position became more extreme. Things started to change in the 1960s with the *Concilio Vaticano II* (Second Vatican Council), when the Catholic Church was becoming more conciliatory. Continuing the work of his predecessor Pope John XXIII, Paul VI reimagined the role of the Church in the world, encouraging Catholics to leave the quietness of their chapels to participate in the debates that were shaping politics.

TOWARDS INDEPENDENCE

It is hard to know what was behind the Pope's decision to receive the African nationalists. The meeting had been planned by the Italian activist Marcella Glissanti, who had been introduced to Cabral in Paris in 1968 by Alioune Diop, the director of the magazine *Présence Africaine*. Diop had also been instrumental in her decision to create the Italian Association of Friends of *Présence Africaine* in Rome. This association proceeded to found the International Library *Paesi Nouvi*, a publishing house, which focussed on making works on what was then considered the African renaissance available to the Italian public. The bookstore, situated in the center of Rome, close to the parliament, soon became the hub of African cultural and political life in Italy, hosting a number of exhibitions and discussions on various themes related to Africa.

The Lusophone nationalist leaders were in Rome for the Conference of Solidarity with the People of Portuguese Colonies, held from June 27 to 29. It was organized by the three trade unions behind the Italian Communist Party, and included representatives from 171 national and international organizations. Glissanti decided to address a letter to the Pope, in which she introduced the three African leaders as opponents of the "African politics of Portugal," and mentioned their desire to greet the Catholic leader, in respect of the Christian upbringing they had all shared. The Vatican, in a letter dated 30 June, replied favorably to Glissanti's request and the meeting was scheduled for the next day. Pope Paul VI received the nationalists in the canonical room, where Popes usually receive ambassadors. Accompanied by two cardinals, Paul VI addressed the nationalists for ten minutes in French, offering each of them a copy of his most recent encyclical *Populatum Progressio*, and bade them farewell with the words "I pray for you."

Cabral took advantage of this encounter to start a propaganda campaign aimed at Catholics, especially Portuguese people who, while against the violence of the armed struggle, could nonetheless be responsive to the humanitarian problems in Guinea. Right after the meeting with the Pope, Glissanti hosted a press conference at her bookstore, with a significant turnout of Italian journalists and foreign correspondents. In his speech to the conference, Cabral stated that he was hopeful that the gesture of Paul VI towards the Lusophone nationalist movements could raise moral questions among Portuguese Catholics, who had given "concrete support to the Portuguese colonial war." For him, the Pope was giving a "concrete basis," beyond the encyclicals, "to stop supporting the colonial war."

The Pope's growing closeness to the national movements in Lusophone Africa was a diplomatic victory with profound negative consequences for the Portuguese presence in Africa. This, coming on top of many other events, was seen by Caetano as confirmation of the Pope's dislike of the *Estado Novo*. Although Portugal had one of the largest Catholic communities in Europe—through the *Concordata* signed in 1940 between the Vatican and the *Estado Novo* Portugal was practically a Catholic state—Paul VI had taken a number of positions which had raised tensions between Portugal and the Catholic Church. In 1964, Paul VI visited India, which had an unresolved diplomatic issue with Portugal on account of the annexation of Goa, Daman and Diu. In May 1970, he visited the Sanctuary of Fátima in Portugal without stopping in Lisbon. In March 1970, Portuguese ecclesiastic authorities sent vehement protests to the Vatican after the appointment of a black priest, the Angolan André Muaca, as the auxiliary bishop of Luanda. For the Portuguese, by distinguishing a black prelate, the Vatican was hierarchizing the black priesthood, and consequently "destroying the work of integration in Africa."

Between resentment and despair, the regime of Marcelo Caetano tried to repair the damage caused by this audience with the Pope. Firstly, the *Estado Novo* took an "energetic attitude," formally lodging a complaint with the State Secretary of the Vatican to express the "great sorrow" caused by the audience the Pope had given to the "most extremist anti-Portuguese terrorists of proven Marxist affiliation." While waiting for a formal response, Lisbon recalled its ambassador in the Vatican. The Vatican official newspaper, *Osservatore Romano*, tried to defuse the diplomatic crisis by arguing that the Pope could not turn down people who were asking for "the comfort of his blessing." With Portugal threatening to cut ties with the Vatican, *Osservatore* Romano went even further, denying that any audience between the Pope and a leader of the national movements in the Portuguese colonies had taken place, instead depicting the encounter as being a strictly religious affair as part of the weekly general audience. The *Osservatore* was suggesting that the nationalists had mixed with other churchgoers, consequently forcing the Pope to bless them. This version was later repeated by the

TOWARDS INDEPENDENCE

Cardinal Casaroli: "the three leaders were in the general audience, and then they went to talk to the Pope and asked for his blessing; Paul VI did not know who they were."

This explanation was good enough for Marcelo Caetano, who, in his weekly address on Portuguese TV, *Conversas em Família* (Family Talk), explained: "the audience discreetly granted [...] did not have any political meaning." The Pope had not spoken to the nationalists as "leaders of terrorism," but as Catholics or Christians, as they had presented themselves when requesting an audience. The Pope had used the opportunity to urge them that even in looking for something they considered their right, they should use "peaceful means." As "no words were said that could constitute an offense to Portugal, minor attention to its dignity, judgment to its politics, [or] interference in its internal affairs," the Portuguese government considered everything "clarified." With this gesture, the diplomatic relations between Portugal and the Vatican were normalized.

Since the Americans shared the same aversion to communism as the Vatican, American diplomacy was equally difficult for Cabral to navigate. Cabral's work in the US had two objectives: as well as attempting to cut Portugal off from its lines of support, he was also trying to change the perception of the PAIGC in the eyes of the American people, so as to shake off the exclusive dependency on the socialist countries. Although the PAIGC received humanitarian aid from American organizations, such as the American Auto Workers, which had made an important donation of medical supplies, there had never been any contact with official entities.

In 1970, at the invitation of Syracuse University, Cabral travelled to the US to attend the Eduardo Mondlane Memorial, in remembrance of the Mozambican nationalist—leader of FRELIMO—who had been killed the previous year. During this trip, Cabral visited the American Congress, attending a hearing with congressmen that took place in room 2255 of the Rayburn House Office Building. The African American congressman Charles Diggs, a supporter of the Lusophone nationalist cause in the US, may have been behind the invitation. The first African American to be elected to Congress from Michigan, Charles Diggs would be Cabral's man in the American administration. Later, in 1973, Diggs visited the liberated zones in Guinea and wrote

President Nixon a memorandum asking him to recognize the independence of Guinea, which had been proclaimed in September that year in Madina do Boé. By inviting Cabral to an audience with the Congress Subcommittee on Africa and the Subcommittee on Foreign Affairs, Diggs intended, above all, to illustrate the consequences of American military assistance to Portugal. Appointed as chairman of the Subcommittee on Africa and of the Committee on Foreign Affairs in 1969, Diggs argued that nationalist organizations fighting for liberation in Africa were not intrinsically communist. They were forced to seek the support of communist countries as a consequence of the United States closing the door to them.

To help Cabral make this point, Diggs began the hearing by reading a press communiqué, distributed by the Portuguese Embassy in the United States, the content of which was a speech given by Marcelo Caetano to the National Assembly. As Caetano had accused the PAIGC of being a communist organization, Diggs wanted to give Cabral the opportunity to refute the accusation. Quoting Caetano, Diggs asked Cabral if it was true that the independence of Cape Verde and Guinea would pose a "risk to the free world." Cabral started by saying that from the Portuguese point of view, Diggs was himself a communist, since it was the term used by Caetano to describe anyone who helped the liberation movements. Cabral also added that the support which his movement received from the Soviet Union did not dictate the strategic position of Cape Verde, since the PAIGC was bound by the principle that "a people fighting for independence should be independent in thought and action. If tomorrow, for any reason, any country, for giving support to us, tried to dominate us, we would fight again against this country, as we are fighting today against the Portuguese domination."

During the session, which lasted about one hour, Diggs also asked about the extent to which the Portuguese army was using American war materials in Guinea, which was prohibited. The US supplied the Portuguese armed forces with military aid, through the Military Assistance Program under the Lajes agreement, but these could not be used by Portugal in any of the fronts of the colonial war, due to an embargo decreed by the Kennedy administration in 1961. The violation of this clause had caused tension in relations between the two countries which involved the cancellation of licenses and requests for the return of military equipment.

TOWARDS INDEPENDENCE

Cabral showed pictures of Guineans with injuries clearly produced by napalm which, as Cabral tried to argue (but could not prove), were the result of airstrikes with bombs produced in the US. Some representatives in the room were moved by the revelations and reacted positively. Jonathan Bingham, from the state of New York, said at the end of the meeting that he supported the guerrillas' cause: "I have for quite a while, in my work in the UN [as member of the American delegation in this institution] raised concerns in relation to our politics of continuing to supply Portugal with military weapons and other assistance."

Portugal followed the hearing attentively. American representatives who supported Portugal's positions were given questions to embarrass Cabral. Since the hearing was open to the public, Portugal sent a couple of officials from its embassy in Washington to report on Cabral's performance. Bernardo Teixeira de Albergaria was among the fifty people who attended the hearing, the majority of whom, "among whites and blacks," were members of the African Research Group—"a research group dedicated to the analysis of the penetration of North American imperialism in Africa." Reporting to the Portuguese foreign ministry at the *Palácio das Necessidades*, Albergaria explained that Cabral was accompanied by two other persons, Óscar Teixeira and Gil Fernandes—whom he wrongly identified as Americans—and that Cabral, although he was not comfortable speaking in English and had spoken very slowly, only turned once or twice to the interpreter to ask him in French the meaning of a word in English, and only sporadically did not understand the questions he was asked. The rapporteur also added that since the hearing was not mandatory, the room was not full and Cabral could not hide his surprise when he failed to see congressmen such as Robert N.C. Nix, a member of the Congressional Black Caucus from Pennsylvania, and Benjamin S. Rosenthal from New York—both Democrats and from whom he had expected more support. To conclude, Albergaria reported to Lisbon that Edward J. Derwinski, a Republican representative from the state of Illinois and one of the supporters of the Portuguese position in the American Congress, failed to "grill Cabral on the question of ideology."

In his attempt to compromise Cabral, Derwinski referred to a speech Cabral had given in the Soviet Union in 1970, on the occasion of the centenary of Lenin's birth, in which Cabral criticized the "ideologues of the imperialist influence who try to minimize the role Lenin played, denying the importance of his ideas to the movements of liberation in Asia, Africa and Latin America." Derwinski was trying to get a confession from Cabral on his ideological affiliation. The congressman had more luck in his question on the involvement of the Cubans in the war in Guinea, forcing Cabral to lie.

By then, the Cubans were an important factor in Guinea's war against the Portuguese. Che Guevara met Cabral on 12 January 1965, during his trip to Africa, and they forged a lasting link. However, effective military and humanitarian aid only came after Cabral's first trip to Cuba to take part in the Tricontinental Conference in Havana, in January 1966. Fidel Castro was impressed with Cabral's speech and took him on a personal trip to the Escambray Mountains. During this trip, Castro committed to assisting the national liberation movement in Africa with supplies, namely tobacco, cotton, sugar, uniforms, trucks, and ammunition. Castro also sent drivers and mechanics to operate and maintain the trucks. But more importantly, Castro sent a group of Cuban doctors, who, during the war, were the only doctors to operate in the interior of Guinea.

The PAIGC also could also count a few dozen Cuban combatants on their side. Cabral, according to Piero Gleijeses, did everything he could to limit their participation and always vehemently denied that there were Cuban fighters in Guinea, until the Portuguese army detained the Cuban official Pedro Rodríguez Peralta in November 1968. But when asked about it, Cabral claimed that Peralta was in Guinea visiting his colleagues, also Cuban doctors, adding that he was not a Lafayette (a reference to the French general who participated in the American War of Independence on the side of the nationalists) and that the guerrillas did not have Cubans fighting with them.

If Cabral could use his contacts to be invited to a hearing in the American Congress, Portuguese diplomacy could also mobilize its influence. According to a note signed by the Portuguese ambassador Vasco Garin, *The New York Times* and *The Washington Post* did not publish anything either on Cabral's audience in Congress or on his conference at the University of Syracuse. This was, according to the ambassador, because his contact at *The New York Times* "asked his friends in the news agencies to avoid circulating news on Cabral as much as possible." Garin was so convinced of the success of his efforts that he added, in the final lines of the wire, that soon after Cabral's meeting with the congressmen, he received a phone call from George Landau, director of Iberian Affairs in the State Department, in which he was told: "we have survived."

But this was not entirely true. *The New York Times*, in fact, published a short piece on Cabral's journey to New York. A number of journalists, including one from this newspaper, went to see Cabral at his hotel, The Tudor, on 42nd Street, where the nationalist leader elaborated extensively on the North American military equipment used by the Portuguese army. The declarations of the African nationalist were given to the Portuguese Embassy for comment, to no avail.

These two diplomatic actions, namely the audience with the Pope and the hearing at the American Congress, were crucial in Cabral's strategy for the independence of Guinea. Cabral's plan was that once independence was proclaimed, his party would have support not only from the usual suspects—the Eastern Bloc and African countries—but also from Western countries, the most powerful in the world.

With this in mind, in 1972 Cabral started his last diplomatic offensive aimed at securing support in the event of the proclamation of independence in Guinea. First, he visited a number of Asian countries, including China, North Korea, and Japan. In October, he visited Sweden as a guest of the Social Democratic Party, to attend its Eleventh Congress. He then travelled to the US again, where he received a doctorate *honoris causa* from Lincoln University, in the presence of Charles Diggs and other important black figures, such as the poet and activist Leroy Jones. He gave a speech on the situation in Guinea to the Fourth Commission of the UN and met with Salim Ahmed Salim, president of the General Assembly of the UN. In December, he travelled to the Soviet Union to take part in the celebrations of the fiftieth anniversary of the Union. On this occasion, he was also given an honorary doctorate by the Institute of African Studies of the Soviet Academy of Sciences. It was on this trip to the Soviet Union that he was finally promised a delivery of Soviet-made *Strela* surface-to-air missiles, with which the guerrillas would finally challenge the superiority of the colonial air force.

According to *Jeune Afrique*, Cabral planned to proclaim the independence of Guinea before March 1973. With this timing, he expected to have the support of representatives of the states that would gather in Oslo to discuss the situation of the Portuguese colonies in Africa. He also expected that the General Assembly of the OAU, scheduled for May, and the conference of the Non-Aligned Movement which would take place in September, would recognize independence. With the support of the African states, Cabral expected he could count upon the recognition of the UN General Assembly which would take place in October.

To be credible to the international community, the independence of Guinea had to be proclaimed in the interior of the country, as proof that the guerrilla fighters had control of the allegedly liberated zones. In fact, a number of things had changed in the military situation of Guinea. The failure of *Operação Mar Verde*, the demoralization of the Portuguese troops in Africa, and the disintegration of Caetano's regime in Lisbon contributed to the belief in the armed forces that the military situation in Africa could only change through a coup d'état.

In February 1972, Cabral attended the 163rd session of the Security Council in Addis Ababa, Ethiopia. Speaking at the event, Cabral expressed himself in a "convincing manner," contrary to other leaders, "who failed to stir any interest," according to a British official at the United Nations. Cabral used this opportunity to invite the Security Council to send a commission to the interior of Guinea to ascertain whether the PAIGC controlled these parts of the territory. From 18 March to 9 April 1972, the UN General Assembly dispatched a team of experts to Guinea's liberated zones, comprised of Horácio Sevilha Borja, Folke Lefgren, and Belkhiria Kamel from Ecuador, Sweden, and Tunisia, respectively, and accompanied by two other officials from the organization, namely the Senegalese Cheikh Gaye and the Japanese photographer Yutaka Nagata.

The Portuguese army tried to block the work of the Commission in the territory and prove that Cabral's party did not control the liberated zones by launching a major military attack. As the agenda of the mission was secret, the air force indiscriminately bombed the places where the probability of hosting the Commission was higher, such as the bordering zones of Bolama and Quitafine, and from 2 April onwards, the regions of Catió, in the sectors of Cubacaré and Tombali. Later, Cabral said that although the objective of the Portuguese was to intimidate the members of the Special Mission, and to dissuade the population from collaborating with the envoys, the bombings ended up working in favor of the guerrillas. For security reasons, the observers stayed six days longer than scheduled in the Guinean territory, which for Cabral, notwithstanding the numerical superiority of the Portuguese army, was a political and military victory.

* * *

To ensure independence would be supported by the international community, Cabral wanted to demonstrate his party's democratic credentials, through the election of the first National Assembly in the liberated zones. The National Assembly should proclaim Guinea's independence, but its constitution also intended to achieve a number of other goals. By electing the National Assembly through secret ballots and universal suffrage, the PAIGC wanted to demonstrate that it was not aligned with the methods of communist leadership, which did not include popular consultation. The party was also trying to prove its absolute and effective control over some areas of the country.

The election process started in 1969 after work to register the population in the liberated zones had begun. In many of these areas, regional committees carried out civil registrations in order to provide an estimate of the number of people married and divorced, and to have records of births and deaths. However, the party only conducted the first population census in 1971, which proved more complicated and difficult than previously expected. First of all, a number of regions were constantly under fire from the Portuguese army. Secondly, the constant movement of the population and the high number of refugees in the neighboring countries made the figures recorded in the census untrustworthy. Nonetheless, the PAIGC estimated that around 800,000 people lived in the liberated zones, which gave the incorrect impression that there were more inhabitants of the zones controlled by the national liberation movement than in the urban centers.

The Supreme Council of the Struggle (CSL) met from 9–16 August 1971 to announce the holding of the election the following year. An informative campaign on the electoral act was carried out from the end of August until April 1972, after which a special commission travelled the country to form electoral commissions in each sector. The CSL also published an electoral law, stating that any Guinean could run for office regardless of sex, religion or social condition, as long as the candidate was above 18 years of age, was a professional in any domain and had never collaborated with the Portuguese since at least the beginning of the war. According to the Electoral Law, the party should appoint representatives for Bissau, Bolama, Bafatá, and the Bissagos Islands, due to the impossibility of conducting elections in these regions as the guerrillas had no access to them.

Confirmation that the PAIGC was involved in organizing an electoral process was provided by the most unlikely source: the PIDE. According to a memo, produced in Bissau and dispatched to the Portuguese Ministry of Foreign Affairs, Cabral's party was proceeding with the "census of the population under the control of the terrorists, namely in the southern and northeastern zones, also organizing elections for the Regional Council, the local organs of regional power."

The Swedish scholar Lars Rudebeck was one of the few foreigners to follow the electoral process and to write a book about it. According to Rudebeck, although by law the central electoral commission was supposed to discuss the drawing up of a list of candidates alongside the commissions in each sector, in reality, the party ended up imposing certain candidates without the consent of the people. This shows that for the PAIGC, a well-organized process was not the ultimate goal of the election. The party was less interested in the pedagogical nature of the elections than in the international prestige it could gain from them.

The final phase of the election process, the casting of ballots, started in the first days of August and continued until 14 November 1972. During this period, the cadres of the electoral commission travelled through the country to collect the votes to elect the 273 militants proposed by the party, from the 336 that composed the regional councils—out of which 63 were directly appointed by the party.

To this effect, 100,000 ballots were printed in each of two different colors, white for yes and gray for no, to be deposited in the ballot box according to the intended choice of the voter. According to the report on the elections, 83,000 ballots of each type were distributed, corresponding to the number of people registered in the census that took place from January to August 1972. According to the figures of the general elections, 75,163 people voted yes to the PAIGC's proposed slate, while 2,352 voted no. This means that a total of 77,515 people participated in the

TOWARDS INDEPENDENCE

election, 93.4 per cent of those registered in the 1972 census—although party propaganda claimed a turnout of 99.9 per cent.

With these elections, the Popular Assembly was finally constituted, whose first "historical mission," as Cabral would put it, consisted of proclaiming the national state, approving the constitution and creating the executive branch. However, Cabral would not live to see his country become independent—the moment to which he had dedicated ten years of his life.

* * *

In the ten years that Cabral led the revolution in Guinea, his approach to the colonial question changed considerably. In the very beginning, he may have thought that armed struggle could lead to independence. But he was not a military man and he feared that such a course would give too much power to the armed wing and be detrimental to the country's interests. Only towards the end of the war, by the early 1970s, did Cabral find the necessary words to gain international support for independence: basing his argument on the social experiment his party was conducting in the liberated zones, he argued that Guinea was no longer a colony but an occupied territory. In the end, however, Guinea's independence would not be achieved without a final push of military might.

11

THE KILLING OF CABRAL

A month before the murder of Cabral, Lilica Boal, a Cape Verdean teacher at the *Escola Piloto* in Conakry, received the sad news that a beloved uncle had died. To console her, Cabral used words which foreshadowed his own fate: "now, we are so close to getting there." He was killed on the night of 20 January 1973, within touching distance of his goal to which he had dedicated so much of his life.

Cabral was an unorthodox thinker and a revolutionary. He favored finding peaceful and diplomatic solutions to the colonial question over a complete reliance the military. He approached the prospect of his own death in a similar fashion. He was aware, through his familiarity with guerrilla literature, that the death of the leaders weakened these types of movement. But instead of properly protecting himself against the plots that were unfolding around him, he tried instead to devalue his own life. In October 1971, interviewed by Simon Malley, the director of *Afrique/Asie*, he used, perhaps for the first time, an expression which he would go on to repeat many times over: "if I die tomorrow, nothing will change in the ineluctable evolution of the fight of my people and their victory," since "we will have dozens, hundreds of Cabrals in our people. Our nation will find a militant to continue the work."

At a personal level, however, in the last years of his life Cabral began to worry about the possibility of being betrayed. In May 1972, for example, at the symposium in memory of one of the founders of the

OAU and first president of Ghana, Nkwame Nkrumah, Cabral was enthusiastically applauded—and later on praised by one of the biographers of Nkrumah—when he said that the African president had not died of throat cancer, but instead of "betrayal cancer." It was poverty, according to Cabral, that inflamed ambition and put Africans in the position to betray others.

Beginning in the mid 1960s, elements within the party had begun to see Cabral as a problem, as evidenced by the large number of plots against him. In 1967, a trial was convened by Fidelis Cabral, Vasco Cabral, and Aristides Pereira, and the militants Honório Sanches and Vaz and Miguel Embaná were accused of plotting to kill the leader and sentenced to death. The PIDE also sponsored a number of potential killers to assassinate Cabral. In 1969, a militant called Jonjon was found in the secretariat of the party with a grenade with which he intended to kill Cabral. In 1970, the PIDE organized an operation called *Amílcar Cabral* whose goal was the murder of Cabral. A Cape Verdean called Lachol, a resident in Dakar, had conceived the plan and had recruited a number of other Cape Verdeans in Freetown, Sierra Leone to execute it—namely Isidoro Manuel Lima, Augusto Divo de Macedo and José Nascimento da Silva. As all of these individuals had shown a willingness to kill Cabral, the operation, according to the PIDE's information, would be carried out by whichever assassin, in whichever location and using revolvers or pistols, "had the best opportunity." Although the plan was not realistic, according to the author of the document, the opportunity to kill Cabral in such a way should be considered. In February 1971, the delegation in Mindelo, São Vicente, placed a bounty of 1,000,000 *escudos* on Cabral's head. The plan welcomed volunteers for this operation, with payment only to be made upon completion of the job. But according to the PIDE, the "individuals interested in committing the crimes" insisted on receiving the money in advance, as only this way did they believe that they would actually be paid. Later, offering the modest sum of 10,000 *escudos* to each, the PIDE contacted six crew members of the boat *Margeretha* who had shown their willingness to "dynamite the ammunition deposit of the PAIGC, in Conakry, and liquidate Amílcar Cabral."

These plans were for the most part amateurish and did not worry Cabral. They were devised in places such as Lisbon, Dakar, and Bissau, by people who did not have the resources, or even the opportunity, to get close to Cabral. But he was hounded by the prospect of being the target of a plot carried out by his own men in Conakry. The PIDE had infiltrated the liberation movement and added a handful of militants with responsibilities to its payroll. To deal head-on with this possibility, Cabral drafted a memorandum and distributed it to his party's militants in March 1972, in which he revealed that the "Portuguese criminals" had succeeded in infiltrating the organization in order to kill the main leaders of the party by bribing cadres with responsibility within it. In the first phase of its operation, the PIDE would attempt to insert "African agents" into the party, who would arrive from Bissau under the pretense of wanting to join the liberation movement. A number of these individuals were former members of the party, some only recently freed from prisons and "trained by the PIDE in the technique of political subversion" to internally destabilize the organization. Once inside, they would then attempt to reconnoiter the various structures of the party, to uncover discontented militants and to take advantage of all the opportunities to sow dissent within the organization. These actions would be built, according to Cabral's assessment, on religious, racial, and ethnic differences, "so that an environment of intolerance should be nurtured in the party so as to hit it in its backbone: its unity."

After the first phase of the plan was completed, the plotters would move to the next: the creation of a clandestine network of high-ranking militants from various sectors of the party, especially the armed forces. A parallel leadership should be created and should seek support in the neighboring countries, primarily in the Republic of Guinea. This "leadership" would strive to be accepted as the legitimate one. Furthermore, this work would go hand in hand with acts of sabotage against the authority and prestige of Cabral, preparing his departure, "or, if necessary, his physical liquidation." In the final phase, these infiltrators would remove all the leaders faithful to the party's guidelines or, if this goal could not be achieved, the plotters should kill Cabral. Only after this was accomplished should the group start negotiating with the Portuguese government, represented by General António de Spínola, with the aim of obtaining the internal autonomy of Guinea—so-called "self-determination under the Portuguese flag." Finally, they would form a government for the Guinean state.

After the slaying of Cabral, Aquino de Bragança, the only journalist who was admitted to the investigations ordered by Sékou Touré to probe the cause of the assassination, wrote a number of articles for his magazine *Afrique/Asie*. His conclusions on the conspiracies against the nationalist leader helped to cement the official truth and to influence a number of people who would later write about these events. Bragança accused the PIDE/DGS of plotting the death of Cabral, recruiting a number of "adventurers, prisoners, old, tired, resentful and discontent militants," and inserting them into the ranks of the party in Conakry. He based these allegations on the confessions extracted from the conspirators through torture, on the declarations of various party members—particularly the Cape Verdeans—and, of course, on the portentous document drafted by Amílcar Cabral on the "coup d'état of the Guineans." The biggest mistake of the party, according to Bragança, was having lowered its guard and having allowed these people to occupy "essential positions of responsibility."

This narrative was convenient when the PAIGC was in a situation of crisis after the killing of its leader and militants desperately needed the motivation to move forward. It placed the burden of guilt on the antagonisms between Cape Verdeans and Guineans, and emphasized a conspiracy plotted by elements that had come from outside, after long periods of time spent in the Portuguese prisons, where they had been instructed by the agents of the PIDE/DGS to infiltrate the PAIGC. It is a version which coincides with the document written by Cabral. This group included, for example, Aristides Barbosa, detained by the PIDE on 18 July 1962 and later sent to the Tarrafal prison in Cape Verde, and freed on 3 August 1969 as part of the group of ninety-three prisoners pardoned by Spínola. Barbosa then fled from Bissau to reintegrate with the guerrillas. There was also Momu Touré, one of the historic cadres of the party, detained on 3 March 1962, alongside Rafael Barbosa, and also freed on 3 August 1969.

Bragança was more concerned with constructing a narrative than explaining what had really happened, and omitted the less convenient facts from his account. It is true that the militants who had been detained in Tarrafal had been in contact with the PIDE. This was the case with João Tomás, who had collaborated with the Portuguese police since 1969. However, the majority of those who took part in

THE KILLING OF CABRAL

the plot to kill Cabral had not had many opportunities to collude with the PIDE. This was the case with Inocêncio Cani, for example, the direct actor in the killing of Cabral, and one of the brains behind the operations.

Cani was not in good standing within the party. From 1967–9 he was in the Soviet Union for training on *Karla* boats, and it was probably during this time that the plot began to take shape. When he returned to Conakry in 1969, he was appointed Commander of the Navy, and member of the CEL. Two years later, however, accused of selling a boat engine on the black market, he was sentenced in a war tribunal. He was pardoned on 19 September 1972 and demoted to commander of a single navy ship. Another navy man, Inácio Soares da Gama, was in a similar position. He had been detained in 1971, and when the assassination took place, he was awaiting trial. In other words, more than the PIDE, what ended up linking the plotters was the fact that they were in trouble with the party. Cabral was correct to believe that betrayal was always motivated by the accumulation of errors: "little errors, that later on become big errors." Inocêncio Cani, Aristides Barbosa, João Tomás, Mamadou D'jai, Koba Nagonia, and many others were in debt to the party after having been involved in cases of corruption, or, even more seriously, betrayal. This was the case of Nagonia, Cabral's bodyguard, who had been accused in a previous investigation of having provided Cabral's agenda to his associates.

But the mistakes committed by the conspirators should not be separated from the general environment of suspicion and hatred between the Cape Verdeans and the Guineans. In July 1972, for example, the PIDE knew that there were "serious divergences" between Cape Verdeans and Guineans following an altercation between Amílcar Cabral and Momu Touré. Touré, shortly after arriving in Bissau, had received from the general secretary "a group of terrorists" to initiate a military campaign in the interior of Guinea. Touré disobeyed Cabral on the grounds that only the Guineans were sent to the bush while the Cape Verdeans occupied the highest positions in the party's hierarchy without exposing themselves on the front. This document also adds that Touré and forty other Guineans had been detained and accused of attempting to form a PAIGC without the Cape Verdeans. However accurate this document is, the fact remains that all the conspirators in the assassination of Cabral had been detained in the jail of the party, the *Montanha*, at least from April to September 1971.

Once out of jail the conspirators developed a parallel life to the party, choosing areas of the docks as meeting points, since almost all of them were members of the navy. Cabral was aware that the navy was one of the main hubs of destabilization, but only later did he take action to dismantle it. On 17 January 1973, a few days before his death, Cabral called Osvaldo Lopes da Silva and asked him to take charge of the Navy. Lopes da Silva, as he would later tell the journalist José Vicente Lopes later, refused this mission, asserting that the navy was "rotten" and if he removed the men there (Inocêncio Cani and company), he would be in trouble.

Lopes da Silva, however, agreed to assess the moves of the party's militants in Conakry in order to discover who was visiting from the various divisions on the front. By asking the cooks how many people were fed daily, Lopes da Silva arrived at the number of 600—minus the children of the *Escola Piloto* and the militants in transit—helping him to understand the scale of the plot against the Cape Verdeans. Of these 600 individuals, only a small portion (less than fifty, the number of Cape Verdeans) were not aware of the conspiracy. All the Guineans, even those who did not take an active role in it, knew that there was a plot against the Cape Verdeans, and there were those who tried to alert Cabral, such as Awa Cassamá, a Fulani known for her rare beauty and a mother of two young adults serving in the FARP. Knowing the weakness of Cabral for women, she was approached by the conspirators to "lure Cabral into a trap." She not only refused to take part but tried to alert Cabral to the danger. But before she was able to do so, she was killed.

Although Cabral knew that a conspiracy to kill him was underway, it was with surprise and awe that on the evening of 20 January 1973 he found himself face to face with the group of armed men who were waiting for him in front of his house. Accompanied by his wife, Ana Maria, Cabral was returning home from a reception held by the ambassador of Poland. The assailants took advantage of the fact that nobody was in the headquarters—except Aristides Pereira who, as usual, worked until late at night. The rest of the party members had gone to the neighborhood of Ratoma for a meeting with the leader of FRELIMO, Joaquim Chissano, who was visiting Conakry.

THE KILLING OF CABRAL

Cabral was parking the car when suddenly a jeep appeared before him, projecting its headlights onto his face. Various armed men, among them Inocêncio Cani, jumped out of the jeep. They manhandled the nationalist leader and—according to Ana Maria, the only survivor of the event—a brief argument ensued when the assailants tried to tie Cabral up. As Cabral resisted, he was shot at point-blank range. Laying on the floor and bleeding profusely, he tried to negotiate: "let's go inside, let's call the directorate, I am ready to discuss no matter what." The response was a blast of automatic rifle fire to his head, shot by Inocêncio Cani, which killed Cabral instantly.

According to the plan, the death of Cabral was the signal for the *coup d'état* against the Cape Verdeans to begin. Almost simultaneously, Mamadou D'jai, leading another group, broke into the party's headquarters where Aristides Pereira had barricaded himself on hearing the shooting outside. Caught by the rebels, he was tied up and sent off in one of the Navy ships, supposedly bound for Bissau, where he would be handed to Spínola. A third group, led by João Tomás Cabral, took the PAIGC prison and freed Momu Touré and Aristides Barbosa. Once they had completed the first part of the plan, the group split into two: the first half, led by Touré, headed to the presidential palace to meet Sékou Touré, and the second went to provide back-up for the mission to arrest all the *brumedjos* (Cape Verdeans).

The shooting was heard in Ratoma, where the meeting with FRELIMO was taking place, but nobody paid attention since shootings were a frequent occurrence, particularly in the evening. When the talk finished, José Araújo took Joaquim Chissano to his hotel in a car also carrying others such as his wife, Amélia Araújo, and Vasco Cabral. He stopped by the headquarters to drop off Amélia Araújo and Vasco Cabral and, although he found the movements there unusual, proceeded to take Chissano to the hotel.

Vasco Cabral knew that something unusual was taking place and left Amélia Araújo there to go home and pick up his machine gun. She was joined soon after by Alcides Évora, also known as Batcha, whose work in the party was centered around consular issues and other bureaucracy related to the trips of militants. But when Vasco Cabral came out to join Amélia Araújo, she and Alcides Évora had been forced to follow a group of conspirators who had found them there. They were saved by Vasco Cabral who, after hearing Batcha's screams, had taken the conspirators by surprise, shooting at them, injuring one and forcing the other to flee.

Hours later, this group of Cape Verdeans were picked up by a patrol of the Conakry-Guinean army, which would had received orders from the president to arrest all members of the PAIGC. The Cape Verdeans were taken to the Palace of the People where they were separated according to gender. Men were taken to be interrogated, while the women and children, ten in total—among them Amélia Araújo, Dulce Almada, Henriette Vieira, Lilica Boal, and others who worked at the *Escola Piloto*—waited two days until they were given shelter at the Vietnamese Embassy.

None of the Cape Verdeans involved in these tragic events had any problem pointing fingers at General Spínola, the governor and commander of the colonial troops in Guinea at the time. Spínola had been one of the principal architects of *Operação Mar Verde*, which had had as one of its objectives the physical elimination of Cabral. Furthermore, as the Cape Verdeans still relate today, Spínola did not like Cape Verdeans, and he had sponsored ferocious verbal attacks against them, through Radio Bissau and street protests. After freeing Rafael Barbosa in 1969, Spínola had not only helped him to re-found the FUL, but he also promised him the independence of Guinea, as long as it was without the Cape Verdeans. That was at least what Spínola had said to President Senghor in their meeting in Cap Skirring on 18 May 1972.

But this is not what Spínola refers to in his version of the assassination of Cabral. As Spínola later wrote, Senghor had proposed to him "the immediate beginning of a phase of ten-year internal autonomy, followed by a referendum, which probably would bring about independence in the context of a Luso-African, or Luso-African-Brazilian community." Spínola also added that Senghor had discussed this solution with Cabral, who was "extremely receptive." However, when Spínola met with Marcelo Caetano to discuss Senghor's proposition, Caetano ordered Spínola to stop any negotiations with the guerrillas. Accordingly, he was forced to cover for "the position of the central government, creating in the Guinean sector of the PAIGC a climate of uncertainty regarding the impediments to the meeting with Cabral." It is also possible that Spínola had used Caetano's veto to place the blame for the failure of negotiations on Cabral, causing even more discontent inside the PAIGC, as he explained: "the Guinean faction of the PAIGC attributed to Cabral the responsibility for the cancellation of the meeting, sharpening the internal dissidences adroitly exploited by Sékou Touré, leading to the death of Amílcar Cabral."

As soon as news started to spread about the death of Cabral, the Portuguese tried to dispel any suspicions about Spínola's involvement. The daily newspaper *A Capital* was the first news outlet to seek out Spínola to comment on the events. Spínola, while refusing to provide additional information, stated, however, that Guinea had received the news with calm, everything was quiet in Bissau, and that it was "premature to make conjectures on the repercussions that the assassination of Amílcar Cabral could have on the struggle." Portugal only reacted officially three days later, on 25 January. The state secretary for information read a communiqué on radio and television, denying the possibility that the crime could have been of "Portuguese origin," since, in the first place, "it was not part of the Portuguese methods." Secondly, there was nothing to be gained with such an action. Thirdly, it was not possible that "Portuguese agents could have penetrated into the headquarters of the party in Conakry and chosen the most intimate stronghold to execute this grave and condemnable act." This was written as if there had never been any *Mar Verde* operation or infiltration into the ranks of the liberation movement.

The Portuguese tactics regarding accusations of its involvement in the killing of Cabral were only refined later. It was not enough to deny the accusations to prove their innocence; they also had to find other culprits. On 22 January, an editorial in *Diário de Notícias* asked a question which still resonates today: "Who killed Cabral?" Members of the Fulani group, "toward whom Cabral had always been hostile? Rival agents in the fights between the Russian and the Chinese, or simply somebody who was interested in his disappearance, in the hope of seeing one day the partition of the Portuguese province of Guinea."

Ever since Guinea-Conakry and Senegal had become independent, the Portuguese authorities had not hidden their fear of losing their colony of Guinea-Bissau, nested between these two new African sovereign states. This was likely the legacy of the Ultimatum of 10 January 1890, when Portugal had given up the Casamance Basin in exchange for British support for the so-called Pink Map (*Mapa Cor-de-Rosa*). As a result of this, Portugal claimed the vast territories in southern Africa from Angola to Mozambique. When Senegal became independent in 1960, the Portuguese government was the first country to send an ambassador there. Senghor, still trying to establish the short-lived federation with Mali, was deeply touched by such a gesture. However, it was never made clear whether this move was in anticipation of a possible Senegalese attempt to annex Guinea into its territory.

Portuguese diplomatic authorities soon became convinced that Senghor did not have any expansionist ambitions. However, this was not the case with Guinea-Conakry. Guinean President Sékou Touré, from the Mandinka ethnic group, claimed descent on his mother's side from Almamy Samory—ancestry which has been disputed—an African warlord of the nineteenth century and founder of a short-lived kingdom (1882–98) which had extended into areas of today's Republic of Guinea, Mali, and Ghana. Samory's army, however, was vanquished by French troops. Despite not being the largest ethnic group in the country (the Fulani were the majority), the Mandinka held power in Guinea. Sékou Touré, at various times in his presidency, evoked the memory of his supposed ancestor to build national consensus, which culminated in the "non" to the French project of creating a Franco-African community.

Sékou Touré never abandoned the dream of restoring the glory of Samory, either through the formation of a so-called *Grande Guinée* (Greater Guinea), or simply by exercising power and influence over every country containing people of his ethnic group. This goal was more easily attainable in the case of Guinea-Bissau if Cabral were not in the picture, which would leave room to exert influence over a directorate formed by people of his own ethnicity. However, Touré did not have the means to bring such an empire to life. He was afraid of the military and preferred to avoid any actions that could increase their power.

Perhaps convinced that suspicions hanging over Cabral's death could implicate him, or perhaps just trying to remove any potentially incriminating signs, Touré decided to act swiftly but with determination. He was informed of Cabral's assassination by Oscar Oramas, the Cuban ambassador and Cabral's friend, who had received a phone call only minutes after the shooting at the PAIGC headquarters. He spoke with

THE KILLING OF CABRAL

Otto Schacht, the head of security, who summoned him to the place of Cabral's death. Armed and escorted, Oramas headed to the party's headquarters, where he found the remains of Cabral "bloody, facedown on the ground, a meter from the gate of his house." He abandoned the crime scene minutes later when he heard other shootings from a group of rebels pursuing Cape Verdeans.

Oramas had then gone to the house of Bakary Ghibo, an official in the Guinean government, who supposedly put him in touch with Sékou Touré. Although he found it strange that Touré had asked him twice if he was sure that Cabral was dead, Oramas was content that the president had promised to put his forces on the ground and isolate the zone of Minière, so that the conspirators could be detained. Other actions were also taken, such as closing the borders and using aerial support, which, with the help of the Russians, managed to locate at sea the boat that was presumably taking Aristides Pereira to Bissau.

Hours later at around 2 am, Óscar Oramas received a phone call from Touré, the president himself, summoning him to the presidential palace to attend a meeting with members of his government, the ambassador of Algeria, Messaoudi Zeituni, and a group of the rebels, namely Momu Touré, the spokesperson, Aristides Barbosa, João Tomás Cabral, and Soares da Gama. According to Oramas, Touré had called this meeting to give to the rebels the opportunity to explain the factors which had driven them to commit the assassination. At the end of the meeting, to the surprise and disagreement of Oramas, Touré had given the order to detain not only every member of the rebel group, but also the Cape Verdeans—who had not been involved—so that a thorough inquiry could be conducted.

It is thanks to the French citizen Jean-Paul Alatas that some insight has been provided on what actually happened when the detainees were sent to the dungeon. Alatas had been an adviser to Touré before falling from grace and being imprisoned in 1970, having been accused of complicity in the *Mar Verde* operation. In his book *Prison d'Áfrique*, he describes the arrival of the Guineans in the prison. The prisoners had heard the shootings, but they would only become aware of what was going on when the gates to the cells were open to let in Cabral's assassins: "three dozen people, barefoot and dressed in fatigues, laughing and celebrating, heads up, seeming very happy about what they had done," for they were still convinced that Touré would end up backing the coup.

On 21 January 1973, the day after Cabral's death, Touré announced in a broadcast that the leader of the PAIGC had been "cowardly assassinated, in front of his own house, by the poisoned hands of imperialism and anachronistic colonialism." The culprits, he went on, all of them in prison, were "professionals of subversion, prepared and bribed by the special services of anachronistic colonialism." According to Touré, the goal of this crime was "to liquidate with one strike the great prestige that he [Cabral] had acquired in the struggle and for the struggle," and to hit the Republic of Guinea, destroying its democratic and popular regime. Touré announced the establishment of an International Commission of Inquiry, formed of high-ranking members of the PDG and some foreigners, such as Joaquim Chissano from FRELIMO, and the Cuban and Algerian ambassadors Óscar Oramas and Messaoudi Zitouni, respectively. Days later, this commission was extended to include the participation of ambassadors from other countries, including Senegal, Sierra Leone, Egypt, and Zaire.

The commission began work immediately and called the accused for interrogations that lasted over twelve hours non-stop, in the presence of Alcides Évora, the only member of the PAIGC appointed by the Guinean secret services to serve as an interpreter. The testimonies were recorded. According to the report of the sessions, in the beginning all the suspects denied the accusation that they were acting on behalf of the Portuguese, with the exception of Valentino Mangana, the first to confess to their involvement. According to Mangana, Portugal was ready to concede independence to the "blacks of Guinea," as long as the PAIGC was extinct, or at least, as long as the Cape Verdeans were excluded from this nationalist movement. This was the condition sine qua non for Portugal to grant independence to Guinea so as to keep the island of Cape Verde as a strategic and important base. Mangana also told the commission that blacks wanted to remove the brumedjos from the party and only those who participated in the coup could be part of the government.

These confessions, extracted with torture, provided Sékou Touré with what he needed: culprits. During a meeting of the PDG on 23 February, he communicated to his fellow party members that

THE KILLING OF CABRAL

Inocêncio Cani had confessed to being the author of the plot. On the same day, in a broadcast message, Touré announced that 465 militants of the PAIGC had been interrogated, all of them residing in Conakry. With the exception of fifty-one, they all had been released. Those who were not released had been found guilty of being "entirely aware of the plot, or taking part in its execution." Of these, forty-three were simply suspects, where nine were considered active participants. He also announced that the prisoners would be handed over to the PAIGC so that they could be tried internally and punished in line with the rules of the movement.

The PAIGC, profoundly affected by the events, had to create some order in the house. The CEL met from 7–9 February and appointed Aristides Pereira as the acting general secretary. Pereira was not present in the meeting as he was still recovering from the injuries inflicted by his kidnappers. The party formed a commission of inquiry, whose members were Fidelis Almada Cabral, the head of military justice Lourenço Gomes, Otto Schacht, António Buscardini, José Araújo, and Vasco Cabral. This commission received the suspects, delivered by the Guinean authorities at four points along the border, Kandjafra, Boé, Fulamory, and Kaurane, to be tried in the interior of the country, in the liberated zones.

The party, going through a crucial moment in its history, failed to establish the truth of the conspiracy. All of the accused were subsequently killed. Some were simply shot; others were only shot after being tortured, such as Inocêncio Cani, who according to Fernando Baginha, had his fingernails and toenails pulled out. A number of militants, taking advantage of the situation, tried to resolve old quarrels. The consequence was that a number of people who were not involved in the death of Cabral ended up being killed. It was as if the party, through this climate of revenge and reprisals, could restore the sense of unity that had been lost through Cabral's death. But ultimately, Cabral had been the only guarantee of the unity between the Cape Verdeans and Guineans.

Sékou Touré gave Cabral the funeral of a head of a state. Cabral's body was laid to rest in the Mausoleum of Camayenne, on the outskirts of Conakry, where the remains of legendary heroes of the resistance to the French occupants, such as Alpha Yaya and Samory

Touré, lay. The service, lasting for over two and a half hours, took place at the Stade du 28 Septembre. The 20,000 places were filled not only by nationals, but also by 680 representatives of foreign delegations, from Africa and beyond.

The crowd stood when the funerary urn entered the stadium, escorted by the Guinean Republican Guard to the sound of the Funeral March, transported on artillery carriages and covered with flowers offered by the international delegations. When the funerary urn was placed in the center of the stadium, the PAIGC anthem was played, followed by a parade of the various Guinean organizations, including pupils from the centers of revolutionary education—the *Escola Piloto* and the *Escola Politécnica* (Technical School)—the popular militias and, finally, military units of the PAIGC, in fatigues, a number of them coming straight from the front to pay their last respects to the nationalist leader. To close the funeral, a procession was formed, and the remains of Cabral were laid to rest in Camayenne. Sékou Touré received the international delegations to offer their condolences.

In Bissau and Praia, a number of people went out onto the streets to mourn the loss of Cabral. Iva Pinhel Évora, before leaving for Conakry to attend the service, requested that a Mass be held in Bissau to pray for the soul of Cabral, attended by family members and friends. The priest, according to Helena, a niece of Cabral, was expelled from Guinea the next day, since he had express orders to not refer to the name of the nationalist. In Praia, a number of militants of the PAIGC took to the streets dressed in black, as a way to publicly show the loss of the African nationalist.

Cabral's remains would make a last trip, after independence, to Bissau, with Guinea under the presidency of Cabral's brother Luís. In the ceremony of farewell from Guinea-Conakry, Sékou Touré, not hiding his emotions, said: "Cabral, you are not leaving a foreign land. You are leaving a part of your country for another part of your country." The urn of Cabral is still at Amura Fortress in Bissau, in a courtyard shaded by mango trees. The remains, ironically, rest on the same monument inaugurated in 1948 to celebrate the heroes of the occupation and pacification, Portuguese and, naturally, Cape Verdean.

Cabral, a revolutionary of Cape Verdean origin, was killed at the hands of his own men from Guinea. Cabral had not taken the resentment between Cape Verdeans and Guineans seriously, but at a deeper level, this shows that Cabral was incorrect in his explanation of the social process in Guinea. He was convinced that a process of cultural osmosis would make the Cape Verdeans and Guineans into a community; in reality, Guineans took advantage of the anti-colonial war to advance their own agenda of power. But it also shows that Cape Verdeans and Guineans, pushed apart by colonialism, were culturally irreconcilable.

EPILOGUE

(DIS-)CONTINUING AMÍLCAR CABRAL

When Cabral found out that his comrades may be plotting against him, he tried to downplay the advantages that could come from his physical elimination. It would not be beneficial to anyone, he seemed to reason, since by the time of his death, the PAIGC would already have produced other Cabrals: people who would hold onto power and lead the country to independence. But this was not what took place, for the death of Cabral amounted to far more than his physical elimination. The attempt to eliminate the Cape Verdean elements in the party was also the repudiation of its unity, which had been one of its main theoretical underpinnings.

Cabral founded the party in his image. The idea of unity made more sense to him—since he was born in Guinea to Cape Verdean parents and his second wife Ana Maria was a native of Guinea—than to many other party members. He controlled every aspect of the life of the party: he produced its ideology and he trained his own men to begin the process of mobilization. He was the face of diplomacy, the spokesperson, and the only one authorized to give interviews to foreign journalists. He was also the person who gave the most significant military orders. Such a concentration of power, at least in the beginning, did not seem to create conflicts within the party. Later, a number of militants, according to Onésimo Silveira, were quoted as saying: "we don't have to think, Cabral thinks for us." Looking back on Cabral's life, Aristides Pereira described the cult of personality that had been built up around the nationalist leader: "I remembered that Christ was also irreplaceable, but committed disciples and those faithful to his doctrine carried on the work he had delineated…"

With the death of Cabral, the party was lost. From then on, militants in the party entered into a sort of guessing-game to try to establish what Cabral would have done or said if he were alive. This attitude can be seen by the fact that excerpts of Cabral's speeches after independence appeared daily in the newspaper *Nô Pintcha*. Vasco Cabral was the author. The need for this was more urgent in the days and months which followed Cabral's murder. Conjuring up what the leader would say or do became an important part of the process of making decisions within the party.

Part of this thinking was encapsulated in the expression "*Continuar Cabral*": how to "continue Cabral" was a central question in the aftermath of his death. Fortunately, the party did not have to carry out much soul-searching in this regard. By creating the conditions for his men to proclaim the independence of Guinea—his final diplomatic mission before being killed—Cabral had, in a way, prepared his own succession.

Unlike Mao in China or Che Guevara in Cuba—two of Cabral's own guerrilla inspirations—Cabral predicted the war ending with a political and diplomatic victory, one that would not result in the defeat of the Portuguese army. With the proclamation of independence on 24 September 1973, the party undermined the basis of Portugal's justification for staying in Guinea.

However, this goal would not have been achieved had the PAIGC not put in place the necessary military conditions for the proclamation of independence. In this aspect too, Cabral would once again—posthumously this time—rescue his party. In one of his last visits to the Soviet Union, he had finally been given the famous *Strela* land-air missiles. With the nationalists' use of this powerful weapon, Portugal would finally lose their uncontested domination of the skies.

With confidence in the new military equipment, the party took the decision in a council of war to execute major operations in the three battle fronts: north, south and east. The results came fast and were surprisingly positive. In the first week of April, PAIGC artillery took down a fighter-bomber Fiat G-91, a Harvard reconnaissance plane, and two Donier 27s. The downing of these aircraft, according to Al Venter,

EPILOGUE

was equal to everything the Portuguese Air Force had lost before the arrival of the land–air missiles. From then on, without the effective aerial support for their terrestrial operations, the Portuguese armed forces would be hopelessly isolated.

The guerrilla forces, who were better equipped, besieged two of the most important Portuguese military bases: Guidage, in the north, and Guilege in the south. In Guidage, despite numerical inferiority (700 men against 1,300), the guerrilla fighters forced the Portuguese to withdraw. The Portuguese, however, succeeded in keeping Guilege, thanks to the launching of *Operação Ametista Real*, involving paratroopers and African commandos who landed in the rear-guard of the nationalist forces. But even if the guerrilla fighters had not taken positions, and had withdrawn, they would still have put the colonial army on the verge of a military defeat, so great was the damaged inflicted both on the composition of the military and on morale. It was these battles that convinced certain groups within the Portuguese army that if they could not win the war, they would have to put in place the political conditions to rescue the army from the quagmire it had found itself in.

It was in an atmosphere of military triumph that the party convened the Second Congress from 18–22 July, in Madina do Boé, to discuss Cabral's succession. There were two options on the table. The first consisted of electing a Cape Verdean cadre to ensure that the party continued along lines consistent with Cabral's thinking: working for the unity of both countries. The second was to elect a Guinean. Nino Vieira, the legendary commander, was the name most talked about. But this idea did not enjoy the support of the majority, since, naturally, it would represent a tacit acceptance of the reasons which had brought about the revolt of the Guineans against the Cape Verdeans. Aristides Pereira, the acting general secretary, and recently arrived from the Soviet Union, was eventually chosen as Cabral's successor.

On account of the climate of mistrust between Cape Verdeans and Guineans, the Congress of Madina do Boé was no less tense than that of Cassacá. A number of delegates arrived armed and the Northern Front sent a battalion to guarantee the security of the event. Ultimately, the assassination of Cabral had confirmed the existence of tensions between Cape Verdeans and Guineans, and increased feelings of mutual suspicion.

The way to confront this problem was to put forward internal mechanisms to institutionalize a separation between Cape Verdeans and Guineans within the structure of the party. This was the context in which the Congress ended up recognizing the creation of the CNCV (*Conselho Nacional de Cabo Verde*—National Congress for Cape Verde).

The idea of the CNCV was first proposed by Dulce Almada in 1962, when, in Rabat, she presented a dossier on Cape Verde to the UN committee on the territories administered by Portugal. However, this project had never been put into practice. Only later would Cabral reconsider it in his last communication of 1 January 1973, which was later published in *Jeune Afrique* as "*Le Testement Politique de Cabral*" (The Political Testament of Cabral). Attempting to deal with the criticisms inside the party, this project counters some of Cabral's previous positions. In the first years of the war, Cabral thought that "the fight for the unity between Cape Verde and Guinea was not a true problem. By nature, by its history, by its geography, by the economic tendency, even by blood, Guinea and Cape Verde are only one." But later, Cabral would allow himself to be convinced that a more pragmatic unity was more useful, taking into consideration the fact that Cape Verde and Guinea were in different stages of emancipation. But it was the Congress of Madina do Boé that put this proposal into effect, situating the two countries on different timelines in their journeys towards emancipation. In other words, the two countries would have separate processes of independence.

The Congress also deliberated over the composition of the CNCV, which was coordinated by Pedro Pires, and on the structures of the new "state," whose independence should be proclaimed on 24 September 1973 in the same location. The political leadership of Guinea was also established at this time. Luís Cabral was elected president of the State's Council (president of the republic), having as prime minister Francisco Mendes. Nino Vieira, the war hero, was the president of the Popular National Assembly and Commissar of the Armed Forces. Pedro Pires, who had tasks in the CNCV, was appointed Deputy Commissar of the Armed Forces, and José Araújo was chosen to be the state's general secretary.

When the PAIGC, in a declaration read by Nino Vieira, proclaimed independence, more than forty states (African, Asian, and Eastern

EPILOGUE

European) recognized it immediately. The General Assembly of the UN approved a resolution (with ninety-three votes in favor and seven against) in which the organization welcomed "the independence of the people of Guinea, in creating a sovereign state of Guinea-Bissau," and condemned Portugal for waging a war of aggression against the Guinean population.

Guinea's proclamation of independence became one of the main triggers of the events leading up to the Carnation Revolution, which toppled the last government of the *Estado Novo*. Out of all the theaters of the colonial war, it was in Guinea that the Portuguese army was under most pressure from the guerrilla fighters, and it was also in Guinea that the problems facing the Armed Forces were most clearly revealed: difficulties in equipping the troops; the breakdown of combat morale which translated into high numbers of desertions; and, above all, a general atmosphere of insubordination.

The MFA (Movimento das Forças Armadas—Armed Forces Movement) was the product of precisely this deterioration in the Portuguese army. Although fewer officers were predisposed to go to the combat fronts by the end of the war, the announcement that militia officers who completed a brief training program could be commissioned at the same rank as military academy graduates was the straw that broke the camel's back, leading to the formation of the MFA. The organization was created in a meeting in the officer's canteen in Bissau; almost all of its members had fought in the battles in Guinea.

In the beginning the MFA was apolitical, but it was soon radicalized by the climate of tiredness in the Portuguese army and by the disintegration of the *Estado Novo* from the end of 1973 and beginning of 1974, which largely explains the success of the loosely conceived Carnation Revolution. Salgueiro Maia, at the head of a unit of the cavalry school, marched to downtown Lisbon, occupied the areas in which the different ministries of the Portuguese state were situated, and forced Caetano to recognize his deposition. The people quickly and enthusiastically adhered to the movement, and carnations were distributed on the street. For the soldiers involved in this campaign, the revolution was a leap of faith, founded on the assumption that neither the navy, deployed on the outskirts of Lisbon, nor the air force would attack the Chaimite armoured vehicles which blocked access to the city. Salgueiro Maia, hugging, kissing, and shaking people's hands, convinced the units of the *Guarda Nacional Republicana* (National Republican Guard—GNR) and PSP not to resist to the coup. So great was the degradation of the regime that very few people would risk their lives to save it.

At the *Convento do Carmo*, on receiving the young captain who came to inform him that a "revolution" led by the MFA was underway, Marcelo Caetano still wielded enough power to impose a condition: he would only be deposed by a high-ranking member of the military. By telephone, he called General Spínola, who became the head of the revolution, and took on the position of the president of the *Junta de Salvação Nacional* (National Salvation Junta). This agreement became the bridge between the *Estado Novo* and the Carnation Revolution. Or at least, it was the restatement of an old agreement. For many years, the *Estado Novo* had survived thanks to a tacit agreement between many national groupings, namely the military, the Catholics and the fascists, controlled by Salazar. And after Salazar had restored civilian power in 1933, the military left the political arena with the guarantee that the presidency of the republic would always be occupied by a general. That was the case until 1974, and even after. António de Spínola was also one of the most distinguished officials of the Portuguese army. In 1968, he was mentioned as a possible candidate to replace President Américo Tomás. He would use Guinea—with his charismatic methods of leading the military and civilians and with his blows pf propaganda and self-promotion—to cement his "presidential" image. *Portugal and the Future*, a book that he published in February 1974, two months before the revolution, is the self-portrait of a man who was convinced he had the right words for the country in a very difficult time.

The Carnation Revolution of 25 April was seen with much contentment among the guerrillas in Guinea. It offered the chance to negotiate with a new government, which was from the outset more favorable to the recognition of the independence of Guinea. But contentment soon turned to apprehension when they learned that Spínola was the head of the new regime. Spínola had been the most ruthless adversary of the PAIGC: he had organized anti-Cape Verdean campaigns, instigated plots in the party, and led the invasion of a sovereign country, Guinea-Conakry, to detain or kill Amílcar Cabral. And for the vast majority of the party's members, Spínola was the finger behind the trigger of Inocêncio Cani.

So it did not come as a surprise to the guerrillas when they discovered that António de Spínola had organized a referendum in which the populations of the colonized territories would be called upon to approve the constitution of a *Comunidade Lusíada* (Lusophone Community) as the way out of the colonial crisis. This solution was announced by Spínola on 15 May, during his inauguration as president of the republic. This position, according to Almeida Santos, the then minister of territorial coordination, was Spínola's offer to the guerrillas in exchange for a ceasefire. However, the military situation had deteriorated to a point where the Portuguese were no longer in a position to impose any kind of pre-requisite for negotiations.

* * *

In actual fact, 25 April did not signal a clear orientation towards decolonization. And it was not only Spínola who was recycling the proposal for a "community" and trying to impose it on the colonies. The programme of the MFA, for example, contained no reference to decolonization.

It was with almost empty hands that a Portuguese delegation, led by Mário Soares and António de Almeida Santos, met with the guerrillas on 25 May 1974 to negotiate a ceasefire. Leading the PAIGC side was Pedro Pires who, in the hierarchy of the party, was not among the most prominent figures. The meeting, which took places at the Hyde Park Hotel in London, rapidly reached an impasse. To the Portuguese, the problem with Guinea's independence was that it did away with any supposed principle that Portugal could invoke to justify postponing independence for Angola and Mozambique. It was these territories which the Portuguese negotiators were concerned about, rather than Guinea, where the Portuguese army had lost the war.

The PAIGC was sure of its goals. In line with the principles which had animated the war for liberation, the party intended to annex Cape Verde as an act of independence, so that Portugal need only transfer sovereignty over these territories to the PAIGC. Nationalists were ready to go back to war if this possibility was not taken seriously.

Spínola was reluctant to give power to the guerrillas, and negotiations were broken off with no date announced for a second round. But

Spínola would try to solve things his way. He distributed his portrait in Bissau and announced his intention to visit the city in order to name the Congress of the People of Guinea as the institution to which he would transfer sovereignty. The guerrillas, outraged by another attempt at manipulation from Spínola, let him know that they were not responsible for his security there. Pressed by a number of internal groups, above all the MFA, Spínola was forced to speak out in favor of the decolonization of the Portuguese territories. In July 1974, the *Republic Gazette* finally published the famous Constitutional Law 7/74, consecrating the principle of decolonization in the Portuguese constitution.

Negotiations continued in Algiers, where, assisted by a regime which was itself the product of revolution, the guerrillas finally succeeded in imposing their will and forced Portugal to recognize the independence of Guinea. However, against the desires of some, it was established that Cape Verde and Guinea, countries which had been part of the same struggle, would obtain independence according to different processes.

With the signing of the peace agreement and the beginning of the process of decolonization, Portugal recognized the PAIGC as the legitimate representative of the populations of both countries. And the subsequent journey of the party until it formed the governments in both countries has more to do with this recognition than with its own implantation in the territories. The way the PAIGC took power in Cape Verde, as in Guinea, is one of the mysteries associated with the dynamic of the liberation movements. Jean Ziegler, using the example of Cuba to explain the ascension of the PAIGC, commented that there were eighty-one Cuban fighters who set off to the island on board the *Granma* in December 1956 to overthrow Fulgêncio Batista, and 700 who entered Havana on 6 January 1959. In relation to Cape Verde, there were exactly thirty-three—"not one more"—commanders and leaders of the PAIGC who disembarked in Sal and who would later form the republic, whereas in Guinea the number was not above 1,500— women and men who left the bush and the various cities in Guinea-Conakry and Senegal to triumphantly enter Bissau.

In Guinea, the taking of power was almost automatic. The PAIGC had successfully neutralized the opposition, formed by elements of the FLING (*Frente de Libertação Nacional da Guiné*—Front for the

EPILOGUE

National Liberation of Guinea). The fact of practically winning the war, for allegedly having liberated two thirds of the territory and proclaimed the independence in the interior, gave them an authority which was not easily challenged. In Cape Verde, however, the situation was different.

In Cape Verde, the PAIGC had a legitimacy that could only be claimed indirectly; it had won it on the African coast, in Guinea, whose struggle for independence had moved few Cape Verdeans. Unlike Guinea, Cape Verde had a very well-structured civil society, with an established press and a number of observers interested in overseeing the direction the country was heading.

The PAIGC militants who arrived in Praia on 11 October 1974 were well received by members of the party, the vast majority of whom had never had any contact with the leaders. However, before their arrival in the archipelago, other political forces were already establishing themselves, among them the UPICV of Leitão da Graça and the UDC of João Baptista Monteiro, a political formation which united intellectuals of São Vicente and defended the independence of Cape Verde as part of the framework of a federation with Portugal.

Before the arrival of the PAIGC to the archipelago, some of its clandestine operatives, including Jorge Querido—probably anticipating what Cabral would have done—had created the *Frente Ampla Anti-Colonial* (Broad Anti-Colonial Front), with the stated objective of becoming an umbrella organization for all the nationalist forces. However, this organization had never functioned because within the party, the idea that power could be shared with other organizations whose legitimacy did not come from the struggle against fascism was inconceivable.

Relations between the PAIGC and other political formations were worsening to the point that Cabral's men had to resort to violence to impose themselves and silence other groups. Aristides Pereira explains this:

> [C]onsidering the imminence of the elections for the Legislative Constituent Assembly and the various rumors which referred to the possibility of landing members of the Cape Verdean diaspora on the islands to try to restore the political domination of the PAIGC, this ended up taking the adequate measure to reinforce the conquests which

have been made, namely the creation of committees of vigilance and popular militias, which served to silence the pretensions of the propaganda against the independence of the archipelago.

The elections, organized by Portugal on 30 July 1975, were only contested by the PAIGC, and the results dictated the constitution of the Legislative Assembly. The PAIGC occupied fifty-six seats and, as Guinea was already independent by then, tried to form a bi-national state.

Notwithstanding their unity, once independence was attained, Cape Verde and Guinea followed different routes. Unity, although it formed Article 4 of both constitutions, had more of an effect in Guinea, where power was shared by Cape Verdeans and Guineans, than in Cape Verde, where there were no Guineans in the structure of the government. In Cape Verde, after some initial agitation which prompted the introduction of extreme and arbitrary measures to prevent loss of power, Cabral's party exercised power in a more moderate manner. The PAIGC ruled the country until 1991 when, with an exemplary electoral process, the *Movimento para a Democracia* (Movement for Democracy—MPD) won the first multiparty elections held in the country.

The moderation of the PAIGC was motivated by internal and external factors. Among the internal factors was that the island had been the theater of dialogue, on the account of its very active civil society, which forced every government to negotiate a consensus. Externally influencing the PAIGC was the fact that Cape Verde depended to a large extent on international aid. And all leaders had learned from Cabral that the best ideology to have was not to have one at all.

Cape Verdeans took pragmatism to the extreme. The government honored all the agreements that the *Estado Novo* had made with South Africa for the use of the International Airport of Sal, which as a stopover point amassed revenues that accounted for 31 per cent of GDP, or 25.4 million USD a year. And even with the pressure from governments such as Angola and Mozambique, the principal external victims of Apartheid, the Cape Verdeans refused to change their minds. They said no to Agostinho Neto when he asked the Cape Verdeans in 1975 to close the airport to the South Africans and to allow Cuban forces to use it to aid the units of the MPLA in Angola, which were trying to prevent the advance of the South Africans towards Luanda. Pedro Pires man-

EPILOGUE

aged to negotiate with both parties and, in a rare gesture of civility, the airport was used simultaneously by Cubans and South Africans.

With no need to make this sort of concession, and without counting upon a critical mass inside and outside the party, Guinea, with Luís Cabral as the president, moved to construct socialism in Africa. Seduced by the Soviets, Cabral's brother began an industrialization programme which dragged the country into the dream of mechanization. Among his most ambitious projects was the construction of assembly plants for EGA automobiles and Pansau mattresses, initiatives that were set in motion at the cost of improvements in agriculture, the basis of the Guinean economy.

Due to these differences in political position—between the pragmatic and the revolutionary—both countries were drifting apart, reaching the point where unity became more of a nuisance than an advantage. It was therefore with a certain relief, at least as far as unity was concerned, that the news that Luís Cabral's unity government had been overthrown by Nino Vieira, on 14 November 1980, reached Praia.

The coup d'état led by Nino Vieira was rightly depicted by foreign observers, including by *Jeune Afrique* correspondent Augusta Conchiglia, as the second death of Cabral. Ultimately, the coup had been justified as a way to put unity to rest, setting aside the Cape Verdean element. However, other reasons must also be considered. First of all, Guinea had become a dictatorship, where there was no other forum through which certain kinds of claims could be addressed. Secondly, with independence the influence of the military had not ceased to grow.

The *coup d'état* allegedly only caused two casualties: Otto Schacht and António Buscardini. It was allegedly sparked by the discovery of 500 bodies of Guinean commandos that the government of Luís Cabral had executed and buried in mass graves. The revelation of these mass executions was used by Nino Vieira to show the foreign press the atrocities of Cabral's regime. Nino Vieira, however, was not innocent in this process: when the commandos were captured, he himself had been the minister of defense. But key here was the relevance of Nino Vieira's gesture itself. Unearthing from the mass graves the truth of the crimes of a government in the service of unity between Guinea and Cape Verde was also a way to put an end to Cabral's dream. For implicit in these discoveries was the idea that these crimes only occurred due to the pressures of a forced and futile unity.

NOTES

INTRODUCTION

"... most successful military campaign against colonialism." See Cann, *Counterinsurgency in Africa*, p. 12.

"...hundreds of thousands of settlers to the colony." Only after the war started did the Portuguese relax migration policies from the mother country to the colony, which considerably increased the white population in Angola and Mozambique. For a discussion on migration policies in the last fifty years of colonial rule (from 1920 to 1974), see Castelo, *Passagens para África*.

"...answer-question dialectics." Scott owes this concept to a number of other thinkers, primarily Quentin Skinner. For Skinner's discussion of the relationship between answers and questions, see the preface to *The Foundation of Modern Political Thought*. For a discussion by Scott on Skinner's concept, see *Conscripts of Modernity*.

"... within the movement." See Manji and Fletcher (Jr.), *Claim No Easy Victories*, p. 9.

"Earlier biographies of Cabral ..." For early works on Cabral, see, for example, Andrade, *Amílcar Cabral* and Ignatiev, *Amílcar Cabral*.

"... only available in Portuguese." Lara Pawson's *In the Name of the People: Angola's Forgotten Massacre* is not only one of the few attempts to unmask these fabrications, but also a rare study of this topic in English. Taking issue with the romantic descriptions by writers such as Basil Davidson of the revolutionary process in Lusophone Africa, Pawson sheds light on the unfolding of the tragic events of May 1977 in Angola, when after just two years of independence the ruling party quashed a military coup by killing thousands of its own militants.

"... strongly contributed to the concoction of these lies ..." Mário de Andrade claimed that the MPLA had authored the attacks on the colonial prisons in Luanda on 4 February 1961 when this national movement was practically non-existent. Bittencourt has written on this, calling attention to the role of

NOTES

propaganda in the armed struggle, or more precisely to "propaganda as a form of struggle". See Bittencourt, *Estamos Juntos!*, p. 95.

"...he was a 'reluctant soldier'". Rabaka, *Concepts of Cabralism*, p. 192.

"...which produced a great deal of noise." Medeiros, *A Verdadeira Morte de Amílcar Cabral*.

"... within the movement that led to the assassination of Cabral." Soares, *Amílcar Cabral:Vida e morte de um revolucionário africano*.

"...death sentences he authorized in Cassacá." Santos, *Amílcar Cabral: Um Outro Olhar*.

"...subaltern colonizers in Guinea." Burbank and Cooper, "The Empire Effect".

"... not wished to secede from Portugal ..." During the tumultuous political times from the Carnation Revolution of 24 April 1974 to the independence of Cape Verde on 5 July 1975, the PAIGC had to share the political space with many other forces, some of which (such the UDC) "defended a Cape Verde integrated into the Portuguese territory, in the same way as Azores and Madeira." Furtado, "Cabo Verde e as quatro décadas de independências," p. 864.

1. BETWEEN GUINEA AND CAPE VERDE

"... and Sierra Leoneans." For a description of these processes of conquest, see Mark and Horta, *The Forgotten Diaspora*.

"... signing treaties with the local potentates..." Honório Pereira Barreto (1813–1859) was the son of João Pereira Barreto and Rosa de Carvalho Alvarenga, whose family, the Alvarenga, controlled the military administration in Zinguinchor for most of the seventeenth century. For a discussion on the social and cultural environment of Guinea at that time, see Havik, *Silences and Soundbites*.

"... in Canhabaque was completed." Bowman, "Abdul Njai," p. 463.

"'... and mestizo traffickers, from Cape Verde.'" Pélissier, *História da Guiné I*, p. 41.

"... locally published government gazette." Mendy and Lobban Jr, *Historical Dictionary of the Republic of Guinea-Bissau*, p. xlvii.

"... they were called *assimilados*—assimilated." During most of the Portuguese presence in Africa, particularly in Angola and Mozambique, there were three groups of people. The whites, the indigenous (the vast majority) and the *assimilados*. Although the status of *assimilados* was abolished in 1961, the cultural effects of such a division have never disappeared.

"... the majority of the posts in public administration." Oliveira, *A Imprensa Cabo-Verdiana*, p. 140.

"His mother was born in Santiago..." The origins of Cabral's mother have for many years eluded researchers, including myself. Thanks to José Maria

NOTES

Almeida, who has found Iva Évora's birth certificate, it has been possible to establish a number of important details regarding her birth. See Monteiro, http://www.buala.org/pt/a-ler/quem-foi-a-mae-de-amilcar-cabral (in Portuguese).

"… no more than 10,000 *reís*." Cabral, *Memórias e Reflexões*, p. 18.

"… Jorge Frederico Velez Coroço …" Caroço's first term in office was from June 1921 until November 1923 and the second from April 1924 until December 1926. His name is also associated with the first effort to institutionalize elementary education in Guinea.

"'… pacify the natives …'" Mendy, *Colonialismo Português em África*. See the English version.

"… hungry for civilization and madly in love …" Cabral, *Memórias e Reflexões*, p. 171.

"… any form of authority." Cabral, ibid., p. 155.

"… his despicable editorial …" Cabral, ibid., pp. 127–8.

"Pressure was mounting from a group of Guineans …" The *Liga Guineense* (Guinean League), founded in December 1910, was the first voluntary association in Guinea-Bissau before the territory came under "Portuguese occupation." It was dissolved five years later, when its leaders were arrested and accused of being behind the revolt of the Papel ethnic group against the Portuguese. See Mendy and Lobban Jr, *Historical Dictionary of the Republic of Guinea-Bissau*, pp. 253–4.

"'… precious supplement to his meagre salary.'" Cabral, *Memórias e Reflexões*, p. 156.

"… celebrated by much of the population …" Caetano, *Minhas memórias de Salazar*, p. 125.

"… reforms necessary to balance the budget." Rosas and Brito, *Dicionário de História do Estado Novo*, pp. 863–4.

"… not convertible into Portuguese escudos." Da Cruz, *A Crise de Angola*.

"'stability rather than growth'". Smith, "António Salazar and the reversal of Portuguese colonial policy," p. 653.

"… right to self-determination." Manela, *The Wilsonian Moment*.

"'… old structures of organization.'" Duarte Silva, *Salazar e Salazarismo*, p. 140.

"… based on social-Darwinism." Alexandre, "Ideologia Colonial". In F. Rosas and J. M. Brandão de Brito, *Dicionário de História do Estado Novo*.

"'… who already consider themselves as such.'" Duarte Silva, *Salazar e o Salazarismo*, p. 140.

"… a category of natives who were not citizens …", "'erudition and customs'". Moreira, *O Ocidente e o Ultramar Português*, p. 14. For a better understanding of how the *indigenato* was created, particularly in relation to the legal contributions of Adriano Moreira, see Moreira, *Administração de Justiça aos Indígenas*.

"… this was outright slavery." These are some of the findings by the American

NOTES

sociologist Edward Ross, who travelled to Angola in 1924 on behalf of the Temporary Slavery Commission of the League of Nations. See Ross, *Report on Employment of Native Labor in Portuguese Africa*.

"... if the cost of labor was reduced to a bare minimum." For the relationship between prices and costs of production, see, for instance, Anne Pitcher, "Sowing the Seeds of Failure."

"'... did not reach their full capacity.'" Santos, *Quase Memórias*, p. 65.

"'... with many barbaric words.'" Cabral, *Memórias e Reflexões*, p. 27.

"... than a lawyer." Author interview with Luís Cabral, Lisbon, 17 March 2000.

"'... adversity of fortune.'" Andrade, *Amilcar Cabral*, p. 20.

"On her return to Cape Verde ..." *Nô Pintcha, Lembranças de Iva Evora, Mae de Amílcar Cabral*, p. 3.

"... in visiting her children ..." Monteiro, *Testemunho de um Combatente*, p. 177.

"... almost cost him his vision." Author interview with Arminda and Armanda Cabral, Bissau, 21 June 2000.

"... various sports and cultural activities." Associacão dos Antigos Alunos do Ensino Secundário de Cabo Verde, *Comemorações do 75º aniversário da Criação do Liceu de Cabo Verde*, pp. 47–8.

"... they were natives of Cape Verde)." Oliveira, *A Imprensa Cabo-Verdiana 1820–1975*, p. 405.

"... *tostões* per hour ..." Cabral, *Seminário de Quadros*.

"... to stave off her family's hunger..." The powerful verses by Aimé Césaire that Andrade had in mind when he writes on Cabral's childhood read: "...and my mother whose legs, for our tireless hunger, pedal, pedal, both by day and by night, and I am even awakened by night by these tireless legs pedaling the night and by the Singer, bitterly biting into the soft flesh of the night as my mother pedals, pedals for our hunger everyday, every night." See Césaire, *Notebook of a Return to My Native Land*, p. 83.

"... on the verge of bankruptcy." Author interview with Osvaldo Lopes da Silva, Mindelo, 30 June 2000.

"... his womanizing tendencies." In *The Fortunate Isles*, Davidson mentions that Juvenal Cabral may have fathered sixty-two children.

"... the size of his household." Author interview with Osvaldo Lopes da Silva, Mindelo, 30 June 2000.

"... the school fund ... one third of his retirement fund." Cabral, *Entre professores primários*, pp. 8–13.

"'... my literary career (vanity?).'" Cabral, *Nos Intervalos da Arte da Minerva*, p. 3.

"... Cape Verdeans of his generation." Chabal, *Amílcar Cabral*, p. 33.

"... a member of the *Claridosos* ..." The name *Claridoso* comes from the Portuguese *claridade* (light). It was a cultural and literary movement which emerged in Cape Verde in the 1930s and marked the beginning of literary modernism in Cape Verde.

NOTES

"... social and political issues." Cabral, *Apontamentos sobre a poesia de Cabo Verde*, p. 6.
"'... with their feet nailed to the land.'" Ibid.
"... corrected by senior officials." Andrade, *Amílcar Cabral*, p. 8.

2. THE YEARS IN LISBON

"... most viable solution to these problems" Lopes, *Cabo Verde: As causas da Independência*.
"Article 73 of the Charter inscribed in international law the inalienable right of people to self-determination." This is particularly clear in its point b, which states: "b. to develop self-government, to take due account of the political aspirations of the peoples, and to assist them in the progressive development of their free political institutions, according to the particular circumstances of each territory and its peoples and their varying stages of advancement"; http://legal.un.org/repertory/art73.shtml
"... two teams each of eleven players." Andrade, *A Geração de Cabral*, p. 10.
"... Mission of Overseas Students." Caldeira, *Sou um simples africano*, p. 78.
"... who had been with him from the start." Chabal, *Amílcar Cabral*, p. 35.
"... the best student of colonial technology." Cabral, *Estudos Agrários*, p. 5.
"...the same cultural references as his Portuguese counterparts." Chabal, *Amílcar Cabral*, p. 34.
"... under the title of *Portugal Ultramarino* (Overseas Portugal)." Faria, *A Linha Estreita da Liberdade*, p. 32.
"... did not try to integrate them", "... issues that affected them." *Présence Africaine*, "Des étudiants d'Afrique Portugaise," pp. 237–8.
"'... full pockets and an empty stomach.'" Rosas, *História de Portugal*, p. 352.
"... courtyards and shacks" and "'... such incredible promiscuity.'" Op. cit. Rosas, p. 99.
"... in converstaion with Michel Laban." Laban, *Mário Pinto de Andrade*, p. 58.
"... re-Africanization of spirits..." Cabral, *A Unidade Política e Moral*, p. 2. For a better understanding of what Cabral's generation meant by "re-Africanization of spirits", see Andrade, *Amílcar Cabral e a reafricanização dos espíritos*, pp. 8–9.
"'... with courteous manners'", "... send their offspring to schools in Lisbon." Du Bois, "Pan-Africa in Portugal", p. 170.
"'... slaves, men, life and men's aspirations.'" Andrade, *Amílcar Cabral*, p. 33.
"... from Lisbon to Luanda and vice versa." Rocha, *Angola*, p. 94.
"... by the Guinean Keita Fodeba." Lara, *Documentos e comentários para a História do MPLA*, p. 32.
"'... of the old generation of the 1920s'". Laban, *Mário Pinto de Andrade*, p. 72.

NOTES

"... São Tomean community in Lisbon." Seibert writes that the twelve-room flat did not belong to Januário Espírito Santo but it was rented by his sister, Andreza, who in turn sublet the accommodation to African students, mostly from São Tomé. Seibert, *Comrades, Clients and Cousins*, p. 55.

"'the progress of black man.'" Laban, *Mário Pinto de Andrade*, p. 72.

"... founded in 1947 and directed by Alioune Diop." Laban, *Mário Pinto de Andrade*, p. 75.

"... hundreds are thought to have perished." Seibert, *Comrades, Clients and Cousins*, p. 87.

"... never been any communist plot." Op. cit. Seibert, p. 69.

"'... we thought he would die'", "'skin allergy'". *Nô Pintcha*, "Lembranças de Iva Évora, mãe de Amilcar Cabral," p. 3.

"... not in the same class." For the correspondence between Amílcar Cabral and Maria Helena, see Cabral, Souto and Elísio, *Cartas de Amílcar Cabral a Maria Helena*.

"... with a person of color", "... was dating a white, Portuguese woman." Duarte, "Amílcar Cabral visto pela viúva," p. 19.

"... lower than in Alabama." Anderson, "Portugal and the End of Ultra-Colonialism 2."

"... united we fight Amílcar ...", "'... without talking to anyone.'" Cabral, *Crónicas da Libertação*, p. 19.

3. ENGINEER AND CLANDESTINE MILITANT

"... the *Campanha do Trigo* ..." This was a major agricultural campaign in Portugal aimed at curtailing wheat imports into Portugal. A number of authors have emphasized the fascist undertones of the campaign, since it came with a new discourse on the role of peasants and the need to attach them to the land. See Pais, de Lima, Baptista, de Jesus, and Gameiro, "*Elementos para a História do fascismo nos campos*".

"... 80 per cent of the cultivated land." Cabral, *Estudos Agrários*, p. 122.

"... failed to materialize." In this regard, Patrick Chabal quotes Cabral as saying: "it was not accidental that we went to Guinea, nor was it a result of material necessity. Everything was thought out and calculated step by step. We had opportunities to work elsewhere in the colonies or even in Portugal. It was the same for other comrades from other colonies who chose to return to their countries. It was, therefore, decided with the aim of contributing to the preparation of the people for the struggle against colonialism." However, this version of events is not accurate, and Cabral is doing what a number of his biographers—including Chabal—are also guilty of: reading his life retrospectively, as if Cabral could have calculated step by step the events he was part of and

NOTES

thus the direction his life would take. In fact, according to the correspondence between Cabral and Maria Helena, his first wife, Cabral tried to obtain a number of jobs. He tried the *Junta do Café* (Coffee Board in Cape Verde), and he was even given reports from the board to prepare for the nomination. He also tried to get a position at the *Junta de Investigações Coloniais* (Board for Colonial Investigation) through his professor Botelho Costa, which would only happen after his return to Lisbon in 1955. For Chabal's quotation of Cabral's plans, see Chabal, *Amílcar Cabral*, p. 47. For Cabral's letters to Maria Helena in which he describes his job hunting, see Cabral, Souto and Elísio, *Cartas de Amílcar Cabral a Maria Helena*, p. 302.

"... would later become the PAIGC." For a critical analysis of the founding of the PAIGC, and one that challenges the official narrative of the formation of this national movement, see, Soares, *Amílcar Cabral*, pp. 189–96.

"Recently built ..." Cabral, Souto and Elísio, *Cartas de Amílcar Cabral a Maria Helena*, 24 September 1952, pp. 348–9.

"'... we saw in the colony'". Lopes, *Terra Ardente*, p. 37.

"... a handful of Bissau's inhabitants ..." Cabral, *Estudos Agrários*, p. 182.

"... had already been delivered." Cabral, *Estudos Agrários*, p. 93.

"...been delivered..." Cabral, *Estudos Agrários*, p. 93.

"...more political and risky work." Laban, *Mário Pinto de Andrade*, p. 100; Cabral, *Crónicas da Libertação*, p. 31.

"... get up and dance." Author interview with Helena Iva Cabral, Lisbon, 25 March 2000.

"'... whites-only zone.'" Pereira, *Uma Luta, um partido, dois países*, p. 33.

"... infiltrated by the police", "... would only weaken the project." Cabral, *Crónicas da Libertação*, p. 31.

"... disembarked at the Port of Bissau." Cabral, *Seminário de Quadros*.

"... to complete his nationalist project." As discussed, Cabral tried to find jobs in other places such as the *Junta do Café*, and he was not convinced that Guinea was his best option. He mentioned in his correspondence to Maria Helena that "Guinea can go to hell". Cabral, Souto and Elísio, p. 338.

"... to perform another activity." Cabral, *Estudos Agrários*, pp. 302–3.

"'... let him be put in jail'", "... to visit his family." Ignatiev, *Amílcar Cabral*, pp. 93–4.

"'... never to return to Guinea." Duarte, *Amílcar Cabral visto pela viúva*, p. 19.

"'... Sports and Recreational Association of Bissau.'" PIDE/DGS, p. 4415, f. 34.

"... motivated by professional disillusionment." Ibid.

"'... direction to his life'", "'... more early to Cabral?'" Azevedo, "A proposito da dimensão humana de Amílcar Cabral," p. 11.

"'... life was going well.'" Cabral, *Crónicas da Libertação*, p. 56.

"... any form of internal resistance." Macey, *Frantz Fanon*, p. 367.

NOTES

"... on 29 September, it became independent." For a historical discussion of this period, see the masterful three-volume biography of de Gaulle, *De Gaulle*, by Jean Lacouture, particularly the chapter "une communité en transit," pp. 568–89.

"'... return to Africa for good.'" Cabral, *Crónicas da Libertação*, p. 59.

"'... the Anticolonial Movement is founded.'" Lara, *Um Amplo Movimento*.

"... 'small' amounts ..." Cabral, in Lara, *Um Amplo Movimento*, pp. 153–5.

"... to dodge the police," "'... nothing was found against him'", "'cadre of the interior'", "... without looking for them." Lara, "Letter to MAC", pp. 74–5.

"'... he asked for secrecy'", "... 'awkwardness' of the situation ..." Lara, *Um Amplo Movimento*, pp. 74–5.

"'... jumpstart the armed struggle.'" Andrade, "Fanon et l'Afrique Combattante", pp. 253–4.

"... to export the 'Algerian model' ..." Macey, *Fanon*, pp. 370–1.

"... in the war against the Algerian nationalists." Andrade, *Fanon*, p. 254.

"... in the famous *Processo dos 50* (Trial of the 50)." Cunha, "Processo dos 50."

"'... for our trusted people.'" Lara, "Report by Amílcar Cabral to MAC", in Lara, *Um Amplo Movimento*, 3rd ed., p. 107.

"... stamped at the airport." Cabral, letter to Lara, in op. cit. Lara, pp. 160–1.

"...analyzed with careful attention." Barden, letter to Lara, in Lara, *Um Amplo Movimento*, pp. 160–1.

"'... the basis of an Angolan source.'" Da Cruz, letter to Lara, in Lara, *Um Amplo Movimento*, p. 186.

"'... undertaken his mission.'" Lara, letter to da Cruz, in Lara, *Um Amplo Movimento*, p. 159.

"... comprised all the nationalist movements" Lara, letter to da Cruz, in Lara, *Um Amplo Movimento*, p. 180.

"... representatives of all organizations." Da Cruz, letter to Lara, in Lara, *Um Amplo Movimento*, p. 254.

"... as the 'messenger' ..." Andrade, "Fanon et l'Afrique Combattante", p. 254.

"... formality of a date of birth." Cabral, *Crónicas da Libertação*, p. 29.

"... would the letters 'GC' be added ..." Soares, *Amílcar Cabral (1924–1973): Vida e Morte de um Revolucionário Africano*, pp. 190–6.

"'... after the independence of Guinea.'" Menezes, letter to Lúcio Lara, in Lara, *Um Amplo Movimento*, p. 248.

"'... of *Casa Gouveia's* boats.'" Rema, *História das Missões Catoóicas da Guiné*, p. 885.

"... by the waters of the Geba river." Mendy and Lobban Jr, *Historical Dictionary of the Republic of Guinea-Bissau*, p. 89.

"... outside of the urban centers." Cabral, *Seminário de Quadros*, p. 9.

NOTES

"... from mere protest nationalism to revolutionary nationalism." Bragança, "La longue marche d'un Révolutionnaire Africain," p. 9.
"... out of the city", "the Front for the Liberation of Guinea and Cape Verde", "... for the time to leave." Cabral, *Crónica da Libertação*, pp. 74–7.

4. SHATTERING THE WALLS OF SILENCE

"'... in a position to help others.'" Lara, *Um Amplo Movimento*, p. 331.
"'... the girl and life.'" Duarte, "Amílcar Cabral visto pela viúva," p. 20.
"'calm her down'." Letter from Amílcar Cabral to Mário de Andrade, in Lara, *Um Amplo Movimento*, p. 358.
"... on Blainville street." PIDE/DGS, 7533.
"'... quite worried.'" Duarte, "Amílcar Cabral visto pela viúva," p. 20.
"'... than anywhere else.'" Letter from Cabral to Lara, in Lara, *Um Amplo Movimento*, p. 360.
"'... settle the matter for good.'" Lara, *Um Amplo Movimento*, p. 360.
"'... get along with the Portuguese.'" Davidson, *Liberation of Guiné*, p. 12.
"... shattering the wall of silence regarding the Portuguese colonial question." Op. cit. Davidson, p. 9
"... charges of terrorism." Rocha, *Angola*, p. 28.
"'private matters'", "'... not from us as individuals'", "'... sacrifice for them.'" Lara, *Um Amplo Movimento*, p. 403.
"... akin to slavery." For a discussion of labor schemes in Portugal, see Nevinson, *A Modern Slavery*.
"'natural laziness of Africans'" Ennes, "Trabalho Indígena".
"'...law of Portuguese citizens.'" Moreira, *O Ocidente e o Ultramar Português*, p. 21.
"... luso-tropicalism ..." Castelo, "O modo português de estar no Mundo".
"... multiracial society in the colonies." Freyre, *Aventura e rotina*.
"... that of South Africa during Apartheid ..." Anderson, "Portugal and the End of Ultra-Colonialism 2," p. 111.
"... white and black people stayed in separate wards ..." Anderson, "Portugal and the End of Colonialism 2," p. 110.
"... exclusively frequented by whites", "... show themselves in public." Cabral, "The Facts About Portugal's African Colonies," in *Unity and Struggle*, p. 23.
"... were refused entry." Santos, *Quase Memórias*, p. 64.
"... in central urban areas." Anderson, "Portugal and the end of Ultra-Colonialism," p. 110.
"'... on miracles to survive.'" Cabral, "The Facts About Portugal's African Colonies," in *Unity and Struggle*, p. 26.
"'... the case has alarmed the Portuguese.'" Letter from Viriato da Cruz to Lúcio Lara, Conakry, 3 March 1960, in Lara, *Um Amplo Movimento*, 3rd ed., p. 337.

NOTES

"'use of force'". Cabral, "The Facts About Portugal's African Colonies," in *Unity and Struggle*, p. 27.

"... seats in the General Assembly of the United Nations..." PIDE/DGS, ANTT, n° PI 60–65.

5. A UNITED FRONT

"'... medicines out of hospitals.'" Markovitz, *Léopold Sédar Senghor and the Politics of Negritude*, p. 22.

"... the company of his family." Luís Cabral, *Crónicas da Libertação*.

"'... which she had shared from the beginning.'" Cabral, *Crónicas da Libertação*, pp. 137–8.

"'cornerstone for liberation'". Cabral, *Seminário de Quadros*.

"'... contribution to Africa unity.'" Luís Cabral, *Crónicas da Libertação*, p. 45.

"... instead of the use of violence." For a discussion on political rivalries among nationalist groups in Senegal and Guinea, see Dhada, *Warriors at Work*.

"'... idea of organizing a new party.'" Ferreira, "Relatório do Consulado Português em Dakar," AHDMNE-PAA, box 462.

"'war of extermination'". Ibid.

"...was rather far-fetched." Lopes, *Cabo Verde*, pp. 122–3.

"Cabral countered that ..."The PIDE seems to agree. PIDE/DGS, 5418.

"... bribing people into to joining them." Ibid.

"... met to discuss strategies." Ibid., p. 508.

"... the United States delegation." Lewis, *W.E.B. Du Bois*, p. 505.

"'black consciousness in international law.'" Ibid., p. 507.

"... from there to Accra, Ghana." For a full description of the students' flight from Lisbon, see Nicoll, "The great escape that changed Africa's future," https://www.theguardian.com/world/2015/mar/08/great-escape-that-changed-africas-future

"... work for the political bureau of the party." Lopes, *Cabo Verde*, pp. 111–3.

"... the skills required to fight the Portuguese." Author interview with Bobo Keita, Praia, 13 May 2000.

"... from gymnastics to the use of weapons." *Nô Pintcha*, "Um encontro marcado em Setembro 1959."

"... to be the future of the country." Author interview with Bobo Keita, Praia, 13 May 2000.

"... the same people who had just attempted to kill him." Davidson, *Liberation of Guinea*, pp. 52–4.

"... with weapons and ammunition to desert." Cabral, *Seminário de Quadros*.

"... under the weight of his briefcases", "Cabral's growing diplomatic weight." Cabral, *Crónicas da Libertação*, p. 128.

NOTES

6. MODES OF MAKING WAR

"... upon their return to the country." Andrade, "Fanon et l'Afrique," pp. 253–5.
"... on the support of the popular masses." Fanon, *The Wretched of the Earth*.
"... sweep through the entire country." Wolff, *Peasant Wars of the Twentieth Century*, pp. 152–3.
"... saturated with Maoism." Castanheira, *Quem mandou matar Amílcar Cabral?*, p. 37.
"'... can create them.'" Guevara, *Guerrilla Warfare*, p. 13.
"... which could come from anywhere." Afonso and Gomes, *Guerra Colonial*, p. 99.
"... of exports in 1948." Da Mota, *Guiné Portuguesa*, p. 145.
"... it was trying to eliminate: the traditional." Cabral, *Textos políticos*, pp. 8–9.
"... (compound to compound)", "'political and economic unit.'" Hawthorne, *Planting Rice and Harvesting Slaves*, p. 34.
"'... ferociously to conquer them.'" Cabral, *A Arma da Teoria*, p. 7.
"... than they were by the Portuguese." Lopes, *Etnia, Estado e Relações de Poder na Guiné-Bissau*, p. 34.
"'subaltern roles of supporters of colonialism.'" Ziegler, *Contre l'ordre du monde*, p. 271.
"... higher dimension of the human." Fanon, *Wretched of the Earth*, p. 143.
"... control of workers and peasants." Cabral, "The Weapon of Theory".
"... an act 'of rage and despair'". Castanheira, *Quem mandou matar Amílcar Cabral*, p. 20.
"... 15 per cent of the national territory." Guerra, *Memórias das guerras coloniais*, p. 214.
"... rivers and canals which started there." Cabral, *Unidade e Luta*, p. 41.
"... captured by the PIDE." Pontes and Marinho, *O Seculo XX Portugues*.
"... as the PAIGC would later claim." Cabral, *Unidade e Luta*, p. 24.
"... known as 'stabilized resistance.'" Troung Chinh, cited in Anderson, "Portugal and the End of Ultra-Colonialism 3", p. 97.
"'bite and escape'". Guevara, *La Guerra de Guerrillas*, p. 18.
"'between victory and defeat.'" Cabral, *Contribuição ao estudo do pensamento*, p. 5.
"'Return to Sources'", "... to resist colonial repression", "'primitive population'", "'tribal mentality'". Cabral, "National Liberation and Culture."
"... in front of the populations they had abused." Ziegler, p. 314.
"... many other Cassacá Congresses." Cabral, *Contribuição ao Estudo do Pensamento*, p. 7.

NOTES

7. THE CAPE VERDEAN QUESTION

"… from 17–20 July 1963." PAIGC, *O Desenvolvimento da Luta em Cabo Verde*.
"'… a Portuguese product.'" Cabral, Souto and Elísio, *Cartas de Amílcar Cabral a Maria Helena*, p. 291.
"… the Portuguese provinces in Europe." Lopes, *Os Bastidores da Independência de Cabo Verde*, p. 136.
"… extension of the Portuguese provinces in Europe." Lopes, *Cabo Verde*, p. 136.
"'… of a human aggregate'", "'ethnic group'". Andrade, *Amílcar Cabral*, p. 34.
"… got a cold reception." Author interview with Lilica Boal, Praia, 24 July 2000.
"… the few who stayed with the party …" Author interview with Lilica Boal, Praia, 24 July 2000.
"… the first foco of insurrection." Author interview with Pedro Pires, Praia, 17 May 2000.
"… rigourously monitored." PIDE/DGS, ANTT, "Possíveis actividades do PAIGC em Cabo Verde", p. 283.
"… possessing propaganda materials." AHDMNE-PAA, box 445.
"… send the photographed documents to Lisbon." AHDMNE-PAA, box 1310, "Política Ultramarina—agitação nas províncias ultramarinas."
"… totally unarmed against PIDE brutality." Monteiro, *Testemunho de um combatente*, pp. 95–6.

8. A STATE INSIDE THE COLONY

"'low intensity conflict.'" See Kitson, *Low Intensity Operations*.
"… against the attacks of the colonial army." Venter, *Portugal's Guerrilla War*, p. 24.
"… for their logistics and information …" Davidson, *The Liberation of Guiné*, p. 109–10.
"'unattainable to the enemy'". Guevara, *Guerrilla Warfare*, (1961), p. 110.
"'… was not the symbol of oppression.'" Lipinska, "Deux semaines dans le maquis de la Guinée-Bissau", p. 30.
"'… central base of the south.'" Cabral, *Crónicas da Libertação*, p. 220.
"'… in developing countries'", "… aid to the poorest countries in the world." AHDMNE-PAA, box 485, "Política ultramarina—agitação nas províncias ultramarinas."
"… if they were in the interior of the territory." Author interview with Amélia Araújo, Praia, 16 July 2000.
"… tuning into the guerrilla one", "…listening conditions were perfect." Author interview with Amélia Araújo, Praia, 16 July 2000.
"… in Portuguese newspapers themselves." Lopes, *Os Bastidores da Independência de Cabo Verde*, p. 163.

NOTES

"'true sons of Guinea'", "'... expel the Cape Verdeans.'" Cabral, *Vamos reforçar a nossa vigilância, para desmascarar os agentes do inimigo: Para defendermos o Partido e aluta para continuarmos a condenar ao fracasso todos os planos dos criminosos colonialistas portugueses.*

"... comply with the instructions of their leader." AHDMNE-PAA, box 463, "Política ultramarina—agitação nas províncias ultramarinas" (67369).

"This, at least, was the thesis defended ..." Jim Hoagland, "Portugal's 'unwinnable' war", *The Washington Post*, 21 February 1971.

"... instructions of their leader", "... left behind by the Portuguese administration", "... close to Delaba" "... stolen engines from PAIGC boats ..." Dhada, pp. 74–95.

"... retaliations from the natives of Guinea." PIDE/DGS, ANTT, "Informação n 79 SC/CI (2)".

9. WINNING IN POLITICS WITHOUT LOSING THE WAR

"... assets of Portuguese in Africa." Cunha, *O Ultramar, a Nação, e o "25 de Abril"*, p. 91.

"'... experiment with the federative solution.'" Caetano, *Depoimento*, p. 169.

"'... a step into independence.'" Caetano, *Minhas memórias de Salazar*, p. 708–9.

"... faced by African continent.'" Oliveira, "Uma mão cheia de nada?"

"'... to move past the domino theory ...'" MacQueen, "Portugal's first domino".

"... minimal effect on the Portuguese economy", "'... would be exterminated ...'" Spínola, *Por uma Guiné Melhor*. Some of the excerpts I reproduce here did not make it into the aforementioned source; I gathered them from Dutra Faria, a journalist of the Agência Nacional de Informação (National Agency for Information).

"'... meeting certain needs of the population.'" Chakhotin, *The Rape of the Masses*, pp. 3–32.

"... to Algeria as observers." Cann, *Counterinsurgency in Africa*.

"The officials assembled by Spínola ..." MacQueen p. 214.

"... such as the PIDE inspector Fragoso Allas ..." Antunes, *A Guerra de África*, p. 510.

"... change the course of the war at any cost." Antunes, *O Factor Africano*, p. 73.

"'... prepation of land for cultivation ...'", "'... but about persuasion.'" Spínola, *Por uma Guiné Melhor*, pp. 136–8.

"... or recede to a red one." Antunes, *A Guerra de África*, p. 384.

"'... to the poles of progress." Spínola, *Por uma Guiné Melhor*, p. 182.

"... to destory the guerrilla units." Antunes, *O Factor Africano*, pp. 782–3.

"'... lose the will to fight.'" Antunes, *A Guerra de África*, p. 384.

NOTES

"... such as Abdul Injai." For more information on Abdul Injai, see Bowman, "Abdul Njai: Ally and Enemy of the Portuguese in Guinea-Bissau."
"'... without despondency or dismay.'" Aragão, *Tropas Negras*, p. 23.
"... and vocational education." Spínola, *Por uma Guiné Melhor*, p. 44.
"any 'cultural content.'" Wolf, *Peasant Wars*, p. 25.
"... institutions of tribal power." For an exhaustive discussion on the making of tribal-related political identity see Mamdani, *Citizen and Subject*.
"'... forms of European life.'" Belchior, *Os Congressos do Povo da Guiné*, pp. 14–17.
"'... the chief of the tribalized.'" Mamdani, *Citizen and Subject*.
"... hailed internationally as a victory of the movement." Venter, *Portugal's Guerrilla War*, p. 147.
"... questioning the war effort." Dhada, p. 580.
"'... benefits of foreign material support.'" Spínola, *Por uma Guiné Melhor*, p. 248.
"... as Portuguese as Your Excellency.'" PIDE/DGS, ANTT, 5445.
"... weaponry and sometimes even fuel ..." Dhada, p. 91.
"'... validity of this policy.'" AHDMNE-PAA, box 463, "Política ultramarina—agitação nas províncias ultramarinas".
"'... subversive pamphlets, printouts, and correspondence." AHDMNE-PAA, box 463, "Política ultramarina—agitação nas províncias ultramarinas".
"... Teixeira Pinto, Farim, and São Domingo." AHDMNE-PAA, box 463, "Política ultramarina—agitação nas províncias ultramarinas".
"... collective desertions from the movement." Cabral, *Sobre a situacao da Luta e suas perspectivas*, p. 14.
"... hacked up the bodies with machetes." Cabrita, "Desaparecidos em combate," *Expresso*.
"'... thought they could buy us.'" Cabral, *Demasquons les messonges et les crimes des colonialistes portuguais*.
"... sent his intelligence officer?" Cabral, *Crónicas da Libertação*, p. 397.
"'... to both planes.'" Marinho, *Operação Mar Verde*, p. 15.
"'... I found honorable to Portugal.'" Ibid., p. 66.
"... sinking three PAIGC boats ..." Antunes, *A Guerra de África*, p. 514.
"... armed with 40mm canons." Cabral, *Tirons toutes les leçons de l'agression criminelle perpétrée par les colonialistes Portuguais contre le Peuple de la République de la Guiné*, p. 4.
"... launched by the Portuguese forces." United Nations, "Report of the Special Mission of the Security Council Established Under Resolution 294 (1971)," http://casacomum.org/cc/visualizador?pasta=07066.092.013#!1
"... coerced into taking part in the operation." Marinho, *Operação Mar Verde*, p. 102.
"'... had to fend for themselves.'" Antunes, *A Guerra de África*, p. 515.
"... which he kept on his person ..." Kaké, *Sékou Touré*, p. 147.

NOTES

"... to the Italian communist daily *L'Unitá*." AHDMNE-PAA, box 1311.
"... ten-year statute of autonomy." MacQueen, p. 220.
"'... in a position of clear superiority.'" Antunes, *Carta Particulares a Marcello Caetano*, p. 156.

10. TOWARD INDEPENDENCE

"... the side of the defending forces." Kitson, *Low Intensity Operations*, p. 21.
"'... Portuguese domination in our land.'" Cabral, "Decididos a resistir", in an interview with *Tricontinental*, in Fonseca and Pires, *Amílcar Cabral*, pp. 131–48.
"... infiltration by volunteer recruits." Urdang, *Fighting Two Colonialisms*, p. 49.
"... positions occupied in the territory." Cabral, *Unidade e Luta*, p. 171.
"'positive neutrality'" Worsley, *The Third World*, p. 133.
"'... militarily occupied by a foreign power.'" Cabral, *Unity and Struggle*, p. 221.
"... true situation in the Portuguese colonies." Cabral, *Crónicas da Libertação*, p. 188.
"... donated USD 20,000 to Cabral's party." AHDMNE-PAA, box 25, 26 July 1971.
"... Christian upbringing they had all shared." Castanheira, "A Amiga Italiana de Cabral", pp. 42–3.
"'... stop supporting the colonial war.'" Cabral, "Sur la situation de notre lutte armée de libération nationale".
"'destroying the work of integration in Africa.'" Castanheira, "Segredos de uma audiência", p. 47.
"'... proven Marxist affiliation.'" Ibid.
"'... did not know who they were.'" Ibid., p. 54.
"... Portuguese government considered everything 'clarified.'" Da Cruz, *O Estado Novo e a Igreja Católica*, p. 213.
"... important donation of medical supplies ..." Cabral, *A condição da ajuda que nos recebemos e que não deve haver nenhumas condições*, p. 55.
"... closing the door to them." Antunes, *Nixon e Caetano*, pp. 225–6.
"'... risk to the free world.'" Foreign Affairs, "Report on Portuguese Guinea and the Liberation Movement," *House of Representatives*, Ninety-First Congress, Washington DC, Government Printing Office, 1970, p. 95.
"'... against the Portuguese domination.'" Committee on Foreign Affairs, "Report on Portuguese Guinea and the Liberation Movement," p. 71.
"... requests for the return of military equipment." Mahoney, *JFK: Ordeal in Africa*, p. 171.
"... bombs produced in the US." Mahoney, *JFK: Ordeal in Africa*, pp. 195–7.
"'... weapons and other assistance.'" Committee on Foreign Affairs, "Report on Portuguese Guinea and the Liberation Movement," p. 71.
"... understand the questions he was asked." AHDMNE-PAA, box 1311.

NOTES

"'... on the question of ideology.'" Ibid.
"... Peralta in November 1968." Saraiva, "Cubano prisioneiro de Guerra", p. 16.
"... Cubans fighting on their side." For a discussion of the involvement of Cubans in wars in Africa and particularly in Guinea-Bissau, see Piero Gleijeses, *Conflicting Missions*, pp. 186–213, and Daniel dos Santos, *Amílcar Cabral: Um Outro Olha*, pp. 214–5.
"'we have survived'". AHDMNE-PAA, box 1311.
"... superiority of the colonial air force." Dhada, p. 177.
"'who failed to stir any interest'". AHDMNE-PAA, box 1311.
"... in the sectors of Cubacaré and Tombali." Cabral, "L' Agression terroriste portugaise contre la Mission Spéciale des Nations Unies".
"... was a political and military victory." Ibid.
"... figures recorded in the census untrustworthy." Rudebeck, *Guinea-Bissau*, p. 144.
"'... local organs of regional power.'" AHDMNE-PAA, box 1311.
"... from January to August 1972." Rudebeck, *Guinea-Bissau*, p. 162.

11. THE KILLING OF CABRAL

"'... so close to getting there.'" Author interview with Lilica Boal, Praia, 24 July 2000.
"'betrayal cancer.'" Rooney, *Kwame Nkrumah*.
"'... a militant to continue the work.'" Malley, "Venger Cabral."
"... and Vaz and Miguel Embaná ..." Soares, *Amílcar Cabral*, pp. 394–5.
"... the modest sum of 10,000 *escudos* to each ..." PIDE/DGS, ANTT, (2), 7477.
"'had the best opportunity.'" Lopes, *Os Bastidores da Independência de Cabo Verde*, p. 200.
"'... and liquidate Amílcar Cabral.'" PIDE/DGS, ANTT, (2), box 7477.
"... to insert 'African agents' into the party", "... internally destabilize the organization", "'... in its backbone: its unity.'" Cabral, *Vamos reforçar a nossa vigilância, para desmascarar os agentes do inimigo: Para defendermos o Partido e aluta para continuarmos a condenar ao fracasso todos os planos dos criminosos colonialistas portugueses*, pp. 1–6.
"'coup d' état of the Guineans'", "'essential positions of responsibility.'" Ibid.
"... reintegrate with the guerrillas", "... Portuguese police since 1969", "... a single navy ship." Castanheira, *Quem mandou matar Amílcar Cabral?*, pp. 122–7.
"'... that later on become big errors.'" Cabral, *L'Agression terroriste portuguaise contre la Mission Spéciale des Nations Unies*, p. 11.

NOTES

"... Cabral's agenda to his associates." Castanheira, *Quem mandou matar Amílcar Cabral?*, p. 122.

"... form a PAIGC without the Cape Verdeans." PIDE/DGS, ANTT, 3018.

"... he would be in trouble." Author interview with Osvaldo Lopes da Silva, Mindelo, 30 June 2000.

"... and the militants in transit ...", "... able to do so, she was killed." Lopes, *Os Bastidores da Independência de Cabo Verde*, pp. 206–7.

"'... to discuss no matter what.'" Ignatiev, *Amilcar Cabral*, p. 239.

"... arrest all the *brumedjos* (Cape Verdeans)." I have been able to reconstruct Cabral's final moments and the events that followed thanks to interviews with Amélia Araújo, Lilica Boal, and Alcides Évora.

"... Radio Bissau and street protests." Author interview with Osvaldo Lopes da Silva, Mindelo, 30 June 2000.

"... on 18 May 1972." Blessis, "Qui a tué Amílcar Cabral?", p. 56.

"... who was 'extremely receptive.'" Spínola, *Portugal e o Futuro*, p. 27.

"'... impediments to the meeting with Cabral.'" Spínola, *País sem Rumo*, p. 43.

"'... could have on the struggle.'" *A Capital*, "Quem matou Amílcar Cabral?", 22 January 1973, p. 17.

"'... partition of the Portuguese province of Guinea.'" *Diário de Notícias*, "Dirigente dos Terroristas do PAIGC—Assassinado em Conacry", p. 1.

"... annex Guinea into its territory." AHDMNE-PAA, box 1051.

"... ancestry which has been disputed ..." Kaké, p. 20.

"'... a meter from the gate of his house'", "... conspirators could be detained." Oramas, *Amílcar Cabral: Para Além do seu tempo*, pp. 149–50.

"... would end up backing the coup." Alata, *Prison d'Afrique*, pp. 218–19.

"'... taking part in its execution.'" Oramas, *Amílcar Cabral: Para Além do seu tempo*, p. 156.

"... had his fingernails and toenails pulled out." Castanheira, *Quem mandou matar Amílcar Cabral*, p. 95.

"... express orders to not refer to the name of the nationalist." Author interview with Helena Iva Cabral, Lisbon, 25 March 2000.

"'... for another part of your country.'" *Nô Pintcha*, "President Sekou Toure", p. 8.

EPILOGUE: (DIS-)CONTINUING AMÍLCAR CABRAL

"'... Cabral thinks for us.'" Lopes, *Os Bastidores da Independência*, p. 455.

"'... carried on the work he had delineated...'" Aristides Pereira, *Uma Luta, um partido, dois países*, p. 244.

"... before the arrival of the land–air missiles." Venter, pp. 2–3.

"... to guantee the security of the event." Lopes, *Os Bastidores da Independência*, p. 235.

NOTES

"... territories administered by Portugal." Lopes, *Os Bastidores da Independência*, p. 243.

"Only later would Cabral reconsider it ..." Cabral, "Le Testement Politique de Cabral," pp. 34–7.

"'... Guinea and Cape Verde are only one.'" Cabral, *Unidade e Luta*, p. 128.

"... the breakdown of combat morale ..." Maia, *Capitão de Abril*, p. 64; Vasconcelos, "O Inferno de Guidage, p. 29.

"... a war of aggression against the Guinean population." Oliveira, "Uma mão cheia de nada?"

"... leading to the formation of the MFA." Maia, p. 67.

"'not one more'". Ziegler, pp. 28–9.

"... umbrella organization for all the nationalist forces." Lopes, *Os Bastidores da Independência*, pp. 275–6.

"'... against the independence of the archipelago.'" Pereira, *Uma Luta*, p. 283.

"... refused to change their minds." Lopes, *Os Bastidores da Independência*, p. 478.

"... used simultaneously by Cubans and South Africans." Lopes, *Os Bastidores da Independência*, p. 480.

BIBLIOGRAPHY

Texts:

A Capital, "Quem matou Amílcar Cabral?", 22 January 1973.
Alata, Jean-Paul, *Prison d'Afrique*, Paris, Éditions du Seuil, 1976.
Alexandre, Valentim, "Ideologia Colonial," in Fernando Rosas and José Maria Brandão de Brito, *Dicionário de História do Estado Novo: M–Z*, vol. 2, Lisbon, Bertrand Editora, 1996.
Anderson, Perry, "Portugal and the End of Ultra-Colonialism," *New Left Review*, no. 15, 1962, pp. 83–102.
———, "Portugal and the End of Ultra-Colonialism 2," *New Left Review*, no. 16, 1962, pp. 88–123.
———, "Portugal and the End of Ultra-Colonialism 3," *New Left Review*, no. 17, 1962, pp. 85–114.
Andrade, Mário Pinto de, "Amílcar Cabral e a reafricanização dos espíritos: um depoimento de Mário Pinto de Andrade", *Nô Pintcha*, 12 September 1976.
———, *Amílcar Cabral*, Paris, Maspero, 1980.
———, "Fanon et l'Afrique combattante," in *Mémorial International*, Paris, Présence Africaine, 1983.
Afonso, Aniceto and Carlos de Matos Gomes (eds), *Guerra Colonial*, Lisbon, Editorial Notícias, 2000.
Antunes, José Freire, *Cartas Particulares a Marcello Caetano*, vol. 1, Lisbon, Publicações Dom Quixote, 1985.
———, *O Factor Africano (1890–1990)*, Lisbon, Bertrand Editora, 1990.
———, *Nixon e Caetano: promessas e abandono*, Lisbon, Difusão cultural, 1992.
———, *A Guerra de África, 1961–1974*, Lisbon, Bertrand Editora, 1995.
Aragão, Francisco, *Tropas Negras: As Forças Ultramarinas na Defesa Nacional*, Lisbon, s.n., 1926.
Azevedo, Ário de, "A propósito da dimensão humana esta em Estudos

BIBLIOGRAPHY

Agrarios", *Estudos Agrários*, Lisbon, Instituto de Investigação Científica e Tropical/Instituto Nacional de Estudos e Pesquisas, 1988.

Belchior, Manuel, *Os Congressos do Povo da Guiné*, Lisbon, Ed. Arcadia, 1973.

Bittencourt, Marcelo, *Estamos Juntos!: O MPLA Ea Luta Anticolonial (1961–1974)*, Luanda, Kilombelombe, 2008.

Blessis, Sophie, "Qui a tué Amílcar Cabral?", *Jeune Afrique*, 16 November 1983.

Bowman, Joye L., "Abdul Njai: Ally and Enemy of the Portuguese in Guinea-Bissau, 1895–1919," *The Journal of African History*, vol. 27, no. 3, 1986, pp. 463–79.

Bragança, Aquino de, "Le Complot Contre Cabral", *Afrique/Asie*, February 1973.

———, "La longue marche d'un Révolutionnaire Africain," *Afrique/Asie*, 5 October 1973.

Burbank, Jan and Frederick Cooper, "The Empire Effect." *Public Culture*, vol. 24, no. 2 (67), 2012, pp. 239–47.

Cabral, Amílcar, *Nos Intervalos da Arte da Minerva*, Cidade de Praia, s.n., circa 1937–8.

———, "Apontamentos sobre poesia de Cabo Verde", in *Cabo Verde: Boletim de propaganda e informação* (Praia), no. 28, 1 January 1952.

———, *Sobre a situação da Luta e suas perpectivas*, Conakry, PAIGC, 1965.

———, "The Weapon of Theory." Address delivered to the first Tricontinental Conference of the Peoples of Asia, Africa and Latin America held in Havana in January 1966, https://www.marxists.org/subject/africa/cabral/1966/weapon-theory.htm (last accessed 13 November 2020).

———, *Seminário de Quadros*, Conakry, PAIGC, 1969.

———, "Démasquons les messonges et les crimes des colonialistes Portuguais, renforçons le parti et la lutte afin d'accélérer la libération totale de notre peuple," Conakry, Mimeo, September 1970.

———, "Sur la situation de notre lutte armée de libération nationale," Conakry, Mimeo, October 1970.

———, *Tirons toutes les leçons de l'agression criminelle perpétrée par les colonialistes Portuguais contre le Peuple de la République de la Guiné*, Conakry, PAIGC, 1971.

———, *L'Agression terroriste portugaise contre la Mission Spéciale des Nations Unies*, Conakry, PAIGC, 1972.

———, *Vamos reforçar a nossa vigilância, para desmascarar os agentes do inimigo: Para defendermos o Partido e aluta para continuarmos a condenar ao fracasso todos os planos dos criminosos colonialistas portugueses*, Conakry, PAIGC, 1972.

———, "Le Testement Politique de Cabral," *Jeune Afrique*, 10 February 1973, pp. 34–7.

———, "National Liberation and Culture," *Transition*, no. 45, 1974, pp. 12–17.

BIBLIOGRAPHY

———, *Unidade e Luta: Obras Escolhidas*, Lisbon, Seara Nova, 1976.
———, *Textos políticos*, Porto, Edições Afrontamento, 1976.
———, *A condição para a ajuda que nós recebemos é que não deve haver nenhumas condições*, Bissau, PAIGC, 1977.
———, "The Facts About Portugal's African Colonies," in *Unity and Struggle: Speeches and Writings*, New York, Monthly Review Press, 1979.
———, *Unity and Struggle: Speeches and Writings*, New York, Monthly Review Press, 1979.
———, *A Arma da Teoria: Breve análise da estrutura social da Guiné e de Cabo Verde: Fundamentos e objectivos da Libertação Nacional em relação à estrutura social*, Bissau, Departamento de Informação e Cultura do CC do PAIGC, 1984.
———, *Estudos Agrários*, Lisbon, Instituto de Investigação Científica Tropical, 1988.
Cabral, Iva, Márcia Souto and Filinto Elísio (eds), *Cartas de Amílcar Cabral a Maria Helena*, Lisbon, Rosa de Porcelana Editora, 2016.
Cabral, Juvenal, *Entre professores primários: um caso inédito*, Praia, Minerva, 1944.
———, *Memórias e Reflexões*, Praia, Instituto da Biblioteca Nacional, 2002.
Cabral, Luís, *Crónicas da Libertação*, Lisbon, O Jornal, 1984.
Cabral, Vasco, *Contribuição ao Estudo do Pensamento de Amílcar Cabral*, Bissau, PAIGC, 1984.
Cabrita, Felícia, "Desaparecidos em combate", *Expresso*, 29 April 1995.
Caetano, Marcelo, *Depoimento*, Rio de Janeiro, Editora Record, 1974.
———, *Minhas memórias de Salazar*, Rio de Janeiro, Editora Record, 1977.
Caldeira, Alfredo (ed.), *Amílcar Cabral: Sou um simples africano*, Lisbon, Fundação Mário Soares, 2000.
Cann, John, *Counterinsurgency in Africa: The Portuguese Way of War (1961–1964)*, Warwickshire, Helion & Company Ltd, 2012.
Castanheira, José Pedro, *Quem mandou matar Amílcar Cabral?*, Lisbon, Relógio d'Água, 1995.
———, "Segredos de uma audiência", *Expresso*, 15 July 1995.
———, "A Amiga Italiana de Cabral," *Expresso*, 1995.
Castelo, Cláudia, *"O modo português de estar no Mundo": O Luso-tropicalismo e a Ideologia Colonial Portuguesa (1933–1961)*, Porto, Edições Afrontamento, 1998.
———, *Passagems para África: o Povoamento de Angola e Moçambique com Naturais da Metrópole (1920–1974)*, Porto, Edições Afrontamento, 2007.
Césaire, Aimé, *Notebook of a Return to My Native Land*, trans. by Mireille Rosello and Annie Pritchard, Newcastle, Bloodaxe Books, 1995.
Chabal, Patrick, *Amílcar Cabral: Revolutionary Leadership and People's War*, Cambridge, Cambridge University Press, 1983.

BIBLIOGRAPHY

Chakhotin, Sergei, *The Rape of the Masses: The Psychology of Totalitarian Political Propaganda*, New York, Haskell House Publishers, 1971.

Committee on Foreign Affairs, "Report on Portuguese Guinea and the liberation movement: Hearing before the Subcommittee on Africa of the Committee on Foreign Affairs, House of Representatives; Ninety-First Congress," *African Pamphlet Collection*, Washington DC, Government Printing Office, 1970.

Cruz, Domingos da, *A Crise de Angola*, Lisbon, Imprensa Lucas, 1928.

Cruz, Manuel Braga da, *O Estado Novo e a Igreja Católica*, Lisbon, Editorial Bizâncio, 1998.

Cunha, Anabela, "Processo dos 50: memórias da luta clandestina pela independência de Angola," *Revista Angola de Sociologia*, no. 8, 2011, pp. 87–96.

Cunha, Joaquim Moreira da Silva, *O Ultramar, a Nação, e o "25 de Abril"*, Coimbra, Atlântida Editora, 1977.

Davidson, Basil, *The Liberation of Guiné: Aspects of an African Revolution*, Harmondsworth, Penguin, 1969.

———, *The Fortunate Isles: A Study in African Transformation*, Trenton NJ, Africa World Press, 1989.

Dhada, Mustafah, *Warriors at Work: How Guinea Was Really Set Free*, Boulder CO, Colorado University Press, 1993.

Diário de Notícias, "Dirigente dos Terroristas do PAIGC—Assassinado em Conacry", 22 Janeiro 1973.

Duarte, António, "Amílcar Cabral visto pela viúva," *História*, no. 61, November 1983.

Duarte Silva, A.E., *Salazar e o Salazarismo*, Lisbon, Publicações Dom Quixote, 1989.

———, *Independência da Guiné-Bissau e a Descolonização Portuguesa: Estudo da História, Direito e Política*, Porto, Edições Afrontamento, 1997.

Du Bois, W.E.B., "Pan-Africa in Portugal", *The Crisis: A Record of Darker Races*, vol. 4, no. 27, February 1924.

———, "The Negro Mind Reaches Out," in *The New Negro*, Alain Le Roy Locke (ed.), pp. 384–414, New York, Arno Press, 1968.

Ennes, António, "Trabalho Indígena," in *Antologia Colonial Portuguesa*, Lisbon, Agência Geral das Colónias, 1949.

Faria, António, *A Linha Estreita da Liberdade: A Casa dos Estudantes do Império*, Lisbon, Colibri, 1977.

Ferreira, Luiz Gonzaga, "Relatório do Consulado Português em Dakar", in AHDMNE-PAA, box 442, "Organizações nacionalistas: PAIGC/PAICV."

Fonseca, Luís and Olívio Pires (eds), *Amílcar Cabral: A raízes que a luta criou: Internvenções, entrevistas reflexões, e artigos*, Lisbon, Fundação Amílcar Cabral, 2018.

Fraser, C. Gerald, "Amilcar Cabral Death for A Symbol Of Hope," *The New*

BIBLIOGRAPHY

York Times, 28 January 1973, https://www.nytimes.com/1973/01/28/archives/death-for-a-symbol-of-hope-the-world.html

Freyre, Gilberto, *Aventura e rotina: Sugestões de uma Viagem à procura das Constantes Portuguesas de Caráter e Ação*, Rio de Janeiro, J. Olympo, 1953.

Furtado, Carlos Alves, "Cabo Verde e as quatro décadas de independência: dissonâncias, múltiplos discursos, reverberações e lutas por imposições de sentido à sua história recente," *Estudos Ibero-Americanos*, vol. 42, no. 3, 2016, pp. 855–87.

Gleijeses, Piero, *Conflicting Missions: Havana, Washington and Africa 1959–1976*, Chapel Hill NC and London UK, The University of North Carolina Press, 2002.

Guerra, João Paulo, *Memórias das guerras coloniais*, Porto, Edições Afrontamento, 1994.

Guevara, Che, *Guerrilla Warfare*, Middlesex, Penguin Books, 1961.

———, *La Guerra de Guerrillas*, Tafalla, Txalaparta, 1998.

Havik, Philip J., *Silences and Soundbites: The Gendered Dynamics of Trade and Brokerage in the Pre-colonial Guinea Bissau Region*, Münster, Lit Verlag, 2004.

Hawthorne, Walter, *Planting Rice and Harvesting Slaves: Transformations along the Guinea-Bissau Coast 1400–1900*, Portsmouth NH, Heinemann, 2003.

Hoagland, Jim, "Portugal's 'unwinnable' war heats up," *The Washington Post*, 21 February 1971.

Ignatiev, Oleg, *Amílcar Cabral*, Moscow, Edições Progresso, 1984.

Kaké, Ibrahima Baba, *Sékou Touré: le héros et le tyran*, Paris, Groupe Jeune Afrique, 1987.

Kitson, Frank, *Low Intensity Operations: Subversion, Insurgency and Peace-Keeping*, Harrisburg, Stackpole Books, 1971.

Laban, Michel, *Mário Pinto de Andrade: Uma entrevista dada a Michel Laban*, Lisbon, João Sá da Costa, 1997.

Lacouture, Jean, *De Gaulle: Le Politique*, vol. 2, Paris, Éditions du Seuil, 1985.

Lara, Lúcio, *Documentos e comentários para a História do MPLA: até Fev. 1961*, Lisbon, Publicações Dom Quixote, 2000.

———, *Um amplo movimento...: Itinerário do MPLA através de documentos e anotações de Lúcio Lara*, vol. I, Luanda, Associação Tchiweka de Documentação, 2017.

———, *Um amplo movimento...: Itinerário do MPLA através de documentos e anotações de Lúcio Lara*, vol. II, Luanda, ed. Lúcio Lara, 2006.

———, *Um amplo movimento...: Itinerário do MPLA através de documentos e anotações de Lúcio Lara*, vol. III, Luanda, ed. Lúcio Lara, 2008.

Lewis, David, *W.E.B. Du Bois: The Fight for Equality and the American Century 1919–1963*, New York, Holt, 2000.

Lipinska, Suzanne, "Deux semaines dans le maquis de la Guinée-Bissau", *Africasia*, vol. 16, 1970.

BIBLIOGRAPHY

Lopes, Carlos, *Etnia, Estado e Relações de Poder na Guiné-Bissau*, Lisbon, Edições 70, 1982.

Lopes, José Vicente, *Cabo Verde: Os Bastidores da Independência de Cabo Verde*, Praia, Spleen, 2002.

———, *Cabo Verde: As Causas da Independência, e, O Estado e a Transição para a Democracia na África Lusófona*, Praia, Spleen, 2003.

Lopes, Noberto, *Terra Ardente: Narrativas da Guiné*, Lisbon, Editora Marítimo-Colonial, 1947.

Macey, David, *Frantz Fanon: A Biography*, New York, Picador, 2001.

MacQueen, Norrie, "Portugal's first domino: 'Pluricontinentalism, and Colonial War in Guiné-Bissau," *Contemporary European History*, vol. 8, no. 2, 1999, pp. 209–30.

Mahoney, Richard D., *JFK: Ordeal in Africa*, Oxford and New York, Oxford University Press, 1983.

Maia, Salgueiro, *Capitão de Abril: Histórias da Guerra do Ultramar e do 25 de Abril: Depoimentos*, Lisbon, Editorial Notícias, 1992.

Malley, Simon, "Venger Cabral," *Afrique/Asie*, 19 February 1973.

Mamdani, Mahmood, *Citizen and Subject: Contemporary Africa and the Legacy of Late Colonialism*, Princeton, Princeton University Press, 1996.

Manela, Erez, *The Wilsonian Moment: Self-Determination and the International Origins of Anticolonial Nationalism*, Oxford and New York, Oxford University Press, 2007.

Manji, Firoze and Bill Fletcher Jr., *Claim No Easy Victories: The Legacy of Amilcar Cabral*, Québec, Council for the Development of Social Science Research in Africa and Daraja Press, 2013.

Marinho, António, *Operação Mar Verde*, Lisbon, Temas e Debates, 2006.

Mark, Peter and José da Silva Horta, *The Forgotten Diaspora: Jewish Communities in West Africa and the Making of the Atlantic World*, Cambridge, Cambridge University Press, 2011.

Markovitz, Irving, *Léopold Sédar Senghor and the Politics of Negritude*, Portsmouth NH, Heinemann, 1969.

Medeiros, Tomás, *A verdadeira morte de Amílcar Cabral*, Lisbon, Althum, 2012.

Mendy, Peter Karibe, *Colonialismo Português em África: A Tradição de Resistência na Guiné-Bissau (1879–1959)*, Bissau, INEP, 1994.

———and Richard A. Lobban Jr, *Historical Dictionary of the Republic of Guinea-Bissau*, Lanham MD, Toronto and Plymouth UK, The Scarecrow Press, 2013.

Monteiro, Eurídice, "Quem foi a mãe de Amílcar Cabral?", *Buala*, 16 September 2014, http://www.buala.org/pt/a-ler/quem-foi-a-mae-de-amilcar-cabral (last accessed 18 February 2018).

Monteiro, Pedro, *Testemunho de um combatente*, Mindelo, Centro Cultural Português, 1995.

BIBLIOGRAPHY

Moreira, Adriano, *Administração da Justiça aos Indígenas*, Lisbon, Agência Geral do Ultramar, 1955.

———, *O Ocidente e o Ultramar Português*, Rio de Janeiro, Irmãos Pongetti, 1961.

Mota, A. Teixeira da, *Guiné Portuguesa*, Lisbon, Agência Geral do Ultramar, 1954.

Nevinson, Henry, *A Modern Slavery*, New York, Harper, 1906.

Nicoll, Ruaridh, "The great escape that changed Africa's future," *The Guardian*, 8 March 2015, https://www.theguardian.com/world/2015/mar/08/great-escape-that-changed-africas-future

Nô Pintcha, "Um encontro marcado em Setembro 1959: Recordação de Chico Té," 12 September 1976.

———, "President Sékou Touré," 4 December 1976.

———, "Lembranças de Iva Évora, mae de Amílcar Cabral," 12 September 1978.

Oliveira, João Nobre de, *A Imprensa Cabo-Verdiana: 1820–1975*, Macau, Fundação de Macau, 1998.

Oliveira, Pedro Aires, "Uma mão cheia de nada? A política externa do marcelismo", *Penélope*, no. 26, 2002, pp. 93–122.

Oramas, Oscar, *Amílcar Cabral: Para Além do seu tempo*, Lisbon, Hugin, 1998.

Pacheco, Carlos, *MPLA: Um Nascimento Polémico (as Falsificações Da História)*, Lisbon, Vega, 1997.

PAIGC, *O Desenvolvimento da Luta em Cabo Verde—Reunião de Quadros Responsáveis*, Dakar, Bureau de Dakar do PAIGC, 1963.

Pais, José Machado, Aida Maria Valadas de Lima, José Ferrerira Baptista, Maria Fernanda Marques de Jesus and Maria Margarida Gameiro, "Elementos Para a História Do Fascismo Nos Campos: A 'Campanha Do Trigo': 1928–38 (I)," *Análise Social*, 1976, pp. 400–74.

———, "Elementos Para a História Do Fascismo Nos Campos: A 'Campanha Do Trigo': 1928–38 (II)," *Análise Social*, 1978, pp. 321–89.

Pawson, Lara, *In the Name of the People: Angola's Forgotten Massacre*, London, I.B. Tauris, 2014.

Pélissier, René, *História da Guiné I: Portugueses e Africanos na Senegâmbia, 1841–1936*, Lisbon, Editorial Estampa, 1997.

Pereira, Aristides, *Uma Luta, um partido, dois países: Guiné-Bissau e Cabo Verde*, Lisbon, Editorial Notícias, 2002.

Pitcher, M. Anne. "Sowing the Seeds of Failure: Early Portuguese Cotton Cultivation in Angola and Mozambique, 1820–1926," *Journal of Southern African Studies*, vol. 17, no. 1, 1991, pp. 43–70.

Pontes, Joana and Luís Marinho, *O Século XX Português Series*, Lisbon, SIC, 2002.

Présence Africaine, "Situation des Étudiants Noirs dans le Monde: Des Étudiants d'Afrique Portugaise," vol. 14, 1953, pp. 223–40.

BIBLIOGRAPHY

Rabaka, Reiland, *Africana Critical Theory: Reconstructing the Black Radical Tradition, from W.E.B Du Bois and C.L.R James to Frantz Fanon and Amílcar Cabral*, London, Lexington Books, 2010.

———, *Concepts of Cabralism: Amilcar Cabral and Africana Critical Theory*, London, Lexington Books, 2014.

Rema, Henrique Pinto, *História das Missões Católicas da Guiné*, Braga, Editorial Franciscana, 1982.

Rocha, Edmundo, *Angola: Contribuição ao estudo da génese do nacionalismo moderno angolano (1950–1964)*, Luanda, Kilombelombe, 2003.

Rooney, David, *Kwame Nkrumah: The Political Kingdom in the Third World*, London, I.B. Tauris, 1988.

Rosas, Fernando, *História de Portugal: O Estado Novo (1926–1974)*, vol. VII, Lisbon, Editorial Estampa, 1998.

Ross, Edward, *Report on Employment of Native Labor in Portuguese Africa*, New York, Abbott Press, 1925.

Rudebeck, Lars, *Guinea-Bissau: A Study of Political Mobilization*, Uppsala, Scandinavian Institute of African Studies, 1974.

Santos, António de Almeida, *Quase Memórias: do Colonialismo e da descolonização*, vol. I, Lisbon, Casa das Letras, 2006.

Santos, Daniel dos, *Amílcar Cabral: Um Outro Olha*, Lisbon, Chiado Editora, 2014.

Saraiva, José Manuel, "Cubano Prisioneiro de Guerra," *Expresso*, 16 March 1996.

Scott, David, *Conscripts of Modernity: The Tragedy of Colonial Enlightenment*, Durham NC, Duke University Press, 2004.

Seibert, Karl Gerhard, *Comrades, Clients and Cousins: Colonialism, Socialism and Democratization in São Tomé and Príncipe*, Leiden, Brill, 2006.

Skinner, Quentin, *The Foundation of Modern Political Thought*, Cambridge, Cambridge University Press, 1998.

Smith, Alan K., "António Salazar and the Reversal of Portuguese Colonial Policy," *The Journal of African History*, vol. 15, no. 4, 1974, pp. 653–67.

Soares, Julião, *Amílcar Cabral:Vida e morte de um revolucionário africano*, Lisbon, Edição de Autor, 2016.

Spínola, António de, *Por uma Guiné Melhor*, Lisbon, Agência Geral do Ultramar, 1970.

———, *Portugal e o Futuro*, Lisbon, Editora Arcádia, 1974.

———, *País sem Rumo: Contributo para a história de uma revolução*, Lisbon, SCIRE, 1978.

Telepneva, Natalia, "Our Sacred Duty: The Soviet Union, the Liberation Movements in the Portuguese Colonies, and the Cold War, 1961–1975," PhD Thesis, The London School of Economics and Political Science (LSE), 2014.

BIBLIOGRAPHY

United Nations, "Report of the Special Mission of the Security Council Established Under Resolution 294 (1971)," Security Council, Official Records, Twenty-sixth year, Special Supplement no. 3, http://casacomum.org/cc/visualizador?pasta=07066.092.013#!1 (last accessed 14 November 2020).

Urdang, Stephanie, *Fighting Two Colonialisms: Women in Guinea-Bissau*, New York, Monthly Review Press, 1979.

Vasconcelos, Francisco de, "O Inferno de Guidage," *Público*, 5 October 1995.

Venter, Al. J., *Portugal's Guerrilla War: The Campaign for Africa*, Cape Town, Malherbe, 1973.

Wolf, Eric R., *Peasant Wars of the Twentieth Century*, New York, Harper and Row, 1969.

Worsley, Peter, *The Third World*, Chicago, University of Chicago Press, 1970.

Ziegler, Jean, *Les rebelles: Contre l'ordre du monde*, Paris, Éditions du Seuil, 1983.

Author interviews:

Alcides Évora, Praia, 25 July 2000.
Amélia Araújo, Praia, 16 July 2000.
Ana Maria Cabral, Praia, 29 July 2000.
Anne Blanchard, Paris, 30 March 2000.
Aristides Pereira, Praia, 9 May 2000.
Arminda and Armanda Cabral, Bissau, 21 June 2000.
Bobo Keita, Praia, 13 May 2000.
Helena Iva Cabral, Lisbon, 25 March 2000.
Lilica Boal, Praia, 24 July 2000.
Luís Cabral, Lisbon, 17 March 2000.
Mário Fonseca, Praia, 5 June 2000.
Olívio Pires, Praia, 19 July 2000.
Osvaldo Lopes da Silva, Mindelo, 30 June 2000.

Archives:

Arquivo Histórico Diplomático do Ministério dos Negócios Estrangeiros, Política África-Ásia (AHDMNE-PAA), Lisbon, Portugal.
Arquivo Nacional da Torre do Tombo (ANTT), Lisbon, Portugal.

INDEX

Abidjan, Côte d'Ivoire, 66
Accra, Ghana, 70, 78, 101, 127
Acto Colonial (1933), 25–6, 95
Addis Ababa, Ethiopia, 182
adjacencies, 33–4, 129–30
Afonso, Aniceto, 112
AFRICA.CONT, 15
African Awakening (Davidson), 81
African Research Group, 179
Africasia, 137
Afrique/Asie, 187, 190
Afro-pessimism, 13
Aftonbladet, 139
age system, 104, 114
agricultural census (1947), 60–62
Agricultural Society of Cassequel, 64
Alabama, USA, 51, 83
Alatas, Jean-Paul, 197
de Albergaria, Bernardo Teixeira, 179
Alcântara, Lisbon, 39, 43, 51
Aleluia, Tiago, 127
Alentejo, Portugal, 47, 53–4, 55
Alexandre Albuquerque Square, Praia, 49
Alfama, Lisbon, 39
Algeria, 101, 105, 108, 109, 110, 131, 132, 133, 166

Cabral assassination commission (1973), 198
Guinea-Bissau peace negotiations (1974), 209–10
War of Independence (1954–62), 65, 69, 96, 153, 155, 156
All-African People's Conference
 1958: 109
 1960: 78–9
Allas, Fragoso, 153
Almada, Dulce, 141, 194, 206
d'Almeida, Bebiano, 127
Alouette helicopters, 137
Amado, Jorge, 44
Amboim, Angola, 64
American Auto Workers, 177
American War of Independence (1775–83), 180
Amico, Bruna, 138
amulets, 123
Amura Fortress, Bissau, 200
Ana Mafalda, 56
Anderson, Perry, 83, 84
Andrade, Costa, 37
de Andrade, Ernestina Soares, 20
de Andrade, Herculano, 131
de Andrade, Lucette, 65
de Andrade, Mário Pinto

INDEX

Cabral, relationship with, 4, 13, 28, 30, 50, 51, 130
  on Casa de África, 45
  on Centro do Estudos Africanos, 46
  Conakry, life in, 79
  Fanon, relationship with, 69, 109
  Lisbon, life in, 39, 43, 44, 45
  Luanda prison raids (1961), 98
  on luso-tropicalism, 83
  Maître École staging (1954), 44
  and Movimento Anti-Colonial, 67, 69
  poetry publication, 43
  Présence Africaine, writing in, 46, 68, 83, 138
  on propaganda, 5
  on protonationalism, 41
  on student population, 35
Angola, 14, 79, 151
  assimilados, 18
  Cabral in, 8, 63–4, 69–70, 109
  Cape Verdean migration, 19, 20, 55
  CIMADE escape incident (1961), 101
  Civil War (1975–2002), 212
  Communist Party, 68
  Creole elite, 40
  education in, 30
  European migration, 81, 113
  FNLA, 1, 100
  Galvão report (1947), 84–5
  Independence (1975), 13
  land expropriation in, 61, 116
  mixed race people in, 83, 84
  Movimento Anti-Colonial, 67–8
  PAIGC and, 99
  political organizations, dating of, 71
  protestant missions in, 35

  shipping routes, 43
  South Africa, relations with, 212
  students from, 35, 37, 39, 43–7
  Tunisia recruitment mission (1959), 69–70
  Vatican, relations with, 176
  War of Independence (1961–74), 1, 97–8, 99, 106
Angolan Company of Agriculture, 64
Antananarivo, Madagascar, 66
Anthologie de la Nouvelle Poésie Nègre et Malgache, 42, 43
Antologia da Poesia Negra de Expressão Portuguesa, 43
António, Mário, 38
Aragão, Francisco, 155
Araújo, Adriano, 90
Araújo, Amélia, 107–8, 139, 140, 141, 193, 194
Araújo, Gomes, 118
Araújo, José, 108, 127, 141, 193, 199, 206
Argentina, 19
assimilados, 18, 40, 46–7, 58, 84, 122
Associação de Estudantes Negros, 40
Atlantic Charter (1941), 92
Aventura e Rotina (Freyre), 83
Awolowo, Abafemi, 94
Azeredo, Carlos, 153
de Azevedo, Ário, 63, 64, 67
Azores, 34, 129

Bafatá, Guinea-Bissau, 21, 22, 158, 184
Baginha, Fernando, 199
Balanta people, 60–61, 104, 112–15, 140, 144
Bana, António, 103
Banco de Portugal, 27

INDEX

Banco Nacional Ultramarino, 24, 117
Banda, Hastings, 94
Bandung Conference (1956), 96, 171
Barata, Nunes, 153
Barbosa, Aristides, 190, 191, 197
Barbosa, Rafael, 75, 90, 102, 106, 160–61, 190, 194
Barden, AK, 70
Barreto, Honório, 17, 41
barter system, 61, 144–5
Batepá massacre (1953), 46–7
Baticã, Francisco, 146
Batista, Fulgencio, 170, 210
Beafada people, 140
Beato, Lisbon, 39
Beaumont, Jacques, 100
beetroot, 69
Beijing, China, 110
Beira Alta, Portugal, 19
Belchior, Manuel, 157
Belgian Congo (1908–60), 81, 86
Belgium, 81
Ben Bella, Ahmed, 108
Bentivoglio, Eugenio, 138
Berlin Conference (1884–5), 11, 17
bi-groups, 137, 143, 150
Biafada people, 21
Bijagós, Guinea-Bissau, 164
Bingham, Jonathan, 179
Bissagos Islands, Guinea-Bissau, 184
Bissará, Guinea-Bissau, 161
Bissau, Guinea-Bissau, 22, 30, 86, 100
 amnesty (1969), 160, 162, 190, 194
 Cabral assassination (1973), 200
 Cabral in, 55–62, 72–5, 101
 elections (1972), 184
 militant migration from, 101–2
 PIDE raids (1961), 106
 Pidjiguiti massacre (1959), 71, 74, 86, 109, 140
bissilões, 56
'bite and escape', 121, 169
Black Orpheus' (Sartre), 42
Blanco, José, 153
blood tax, 127
Boal, Augusto, 147
Boal, Lilica, 127, 131, 187, 194
Boé, Guinea-Bissau, 199
Boké, Guinea-Conakry, 107, 144
Bolama, Guinea-Bissau, 182, 184
Boletim de Informação e Propaganda de Cabo Verde, 48, 56
Bolivia, 132
Bolor massacre (1878), 18
Bonn, Germany, 101
Borja, Horácio Sevilha, 182
de Bragança, Aquino, 74, 105, 190
Brazil, 40, 44, 82, 97
Brazzaville, Congo-Brazzaville, 66, 141
Breton, André, 42
Brigada de Estudos e Defesa Fitossanitária dos Produtos Ultramarinos, 63
de Brito, Rebordão, 164, 165
Bulgaria, 173
Burbank, Jane, 11
Burma, 96
Buscardini, António, 199, 213

Cabo Verde (Lopes), 6
Cabral, Amílcar
 agricultural census (1947), 60–62
 agronomy, career in, 1, 4, 8, 28, 32, 34, 48, 53–4, 55
 aliases, 4, 80
 All-African People's Conference (1960), 78–9

245

INDEX

Angola, visits to, 8, 63–4, 69–70, 109
Asian tour (1972), 181
assassination (1973), 3–4, 6, 7, 9–10, 12–13, 22, 145, 190–201, 209
assassination plots, 148, 188–9
birth (1924), 7, 20–21
Bissau, life in, 55–62, 72–5, 101
on betrayal, 187–8
Cassacá Congress (1964), 9–10, 121–5, 136–7, 139, 143, 147, 148
Centro do Estudos Africanos, 44–7, 49
Conakry, life in, 2, 8–9, 12, 22, 87–90, 101–8, 160, 189
da Cruz, relationship with, 68–9
Cuba visit (1968), 133
cult of personality, 203–4
desertions, views on, 162
diplomacy, 104–5, 108, 171–83
education, 7–8, 28, 29–30, 31–2, 35–52
elections (1972), 183–5
famines, experience of, 7, 32, 33
father, relationship with, 28
free speech, lack of, 3
da Graça, relationship with, 92
Guevara, meeting with (1965), 180
Guinea-Conakry independence (1958), 65, 67
Independence Proclamation (1973), 181–2
judicial system, views on, 147
Larbac *nom de plume*, 38
Lisbon, life in, 4, 8, 13, 32, 33–52, 57, 59, 62–5
London visit (1960), 79–86
luso-tropicalism, views on, 83

marriage to Ana Maria, 88, 203
marriage to Maria Helena, 35, 50–52, 88
Marxism, 8, 11–12, 54, 103, 173, 174
nationalism, 4, 8–9, 11, 31–2, 55, 59, 65, 117
Négritude, 8, 42–3, 49
Nkrumah's death (1972), 187–8
Northern Front assassinations (1970), 162–3
Operação Mar Verde (1970), 164–7, 183, 194, 195, 197
PAIGC founding, 7, 9, 47, 71–3
Paris arrest (1968), 133
passports, 80, 133
on peasants, 103
PIDE plot document (1973), 22
Pidjiguiti massacre (1959), 71, 74, 86, 109
poems, 4, 8, 31–2
Political Testament (1973), 206
Pope, audience with (1970), 174–7
race, views on, 130
radio broadcasts, 49–50
Salazar, letter to (1960), 23
Senegal operations, 87, 90–92
skin allergy, 50
Soviet Union visits (1970, 1972), 179–80, 181, 204
supernatural, views on 123
Sweden visit (1972), 181
on 'tribal mentality', 122
Tricontinental Conference (1967), 117
Tunisia recruitment mission (1959), 69–70
two circles theory, 171
UN activity (1972), 181, 182
USA visits (1970, 1972), 177–81

INDEX

War of Independence (1963–73), *see* Guinea-Bissau War of Independence
war preparations, 99–108
weapons smuggling, 105–8
writing of, 4, 7, 22, 31, 38, 48, 49, 53–4, 81, 84–5, 172
Cabral, Ana Luísa, 88
Cabral, Ana Maria, 88, 141, 193
Cabral, António, 28, 57
Cabral, Armanda, 28, 52, 57
Cabral, Arminda, 28, 35, 52, 57
Cabral, Fidélis Almada, 107, 148, 188, 199
Cabral, Helena Iva, 57
Cabral, João Caracciolo, 81, 105
Cabral, Juvenal, 7, 19–23, 27–31, 34, 48, 51–2, 55
Cabral, Lucette, 107
Cabral, Luís, 21, 28, 30, 52, 57, 62, 67, 88, 131, 148
  on African unity, 90
  Amílcar's death (1973), 200
  arrest (1961), 107
  arrest warrant (1961), 100
  Casa Gouveia, work at, 57, 100, 117
  Guinea-Conakry independence (1958), 65, 67
  on Northern Front negotiations (1970), 163
  on PAIGC founding, 72
  presidential election (1973), 206
  Soviet Union, relations with, 213
Cabral, Maria Helena, 35, 50–52, 56, 60, 62, 63, 77, 88, 106
Cabral, Vasco, 107, 121, 125, 127, 148, 188, 193, 199, 204
Cabral Generation, 39
Cacine, Guinea-Bissau, 22
Caetano, Marcelo, 23, 98, 150–51, 167, 182
amnesty (1969), 160
Carnation Revolution (1974), 207, 208
  at Colonial College, 98
  on communism, 178
  Senegal, negotiations with (1971–2), 167–8, 194
  Vatican, relations with, 176, 177
Calvão, Alpoim, 164, 165, 166
Câmara Municipal de Lisboa, 15
da Câmara, Maria Baptista, 30–31
Campanha do Trigo (1929–38), 54
Canhabaque, Guinea-Bissau, 17
Cani, Inocêncio, 145, 191, 193, 199, 209
Cantanhez, Guinea-Bissau, 120
Cap Skirring, Senegal, 167, 194
Cape Verde, 5, 6, 7, 48
  adjacency status debate, 33–4, 129–30
  assimilados, 18
  Bolor massacre (1878), 18
  Creole, 18
  Dakar meeting (1963), 127–8
  droughts in, 7, 19, 23, 32, 33, 48, 53
  CIMADE escape incident (1961), 101
  Claridosos, 10, 32
  education in, 19, 20, 23, 29, 35
  elections (1975), 212
  Guinea, relations with, *see* Cape Verde–Guinea relations
  identity, 10
  Independence (1975), 14, 210, 212
  lançados, 17, 18
  migration from, 11, 19, 48, 55
  population surplus, 18
  Portugal, relations with, 10–11, 17–19, 21, 58, 117, 128
  slave trade and, 11, 89, 128

247

INDEX

soil erosion in, 33, 55
South Africa, relations with, 212–13
student associations from, 37
War of Independence period (1963–73), 12, 14, 127–34, 141–2, 209, 210–12
Cape Verde–Guinea relations, 9–11, 14, 17–19, 75, 213
  adjacency status and, 33–4, 129–30
  colonization and, 11, 17–19, 21, 22, 58, 92, 117
  Cabral assassination (1973), 190–94, 199, 200–201, 203, 205
  Creole and, 18
  Dakar meeting (1963), 127–8
  independence and, 14, 211–12
  juridical status and, 18
  migration and, 11, 19, 48, 55
  PAIGC and, 9, 34, 73, 89, 91–2
  slavery and, 11, 89
  War of Independence (1963–73), 12, 14, 127–34, 141–2, 159
Capital, A, 195
Carmona, Óscar, 23, 129
Carnation Revolution (1974), 168, 207–8
Caroço, Jorge Frederico Velez, 20
Carrasco, Urbano, 153
de Carvalho, Otelo Saraiva, 153
Casa de África, 45, 59
Casa dos Estudantes de Angola (CEA), 37, 45
Casa dos Estudantes do Império (CEI), 8, 37–8, 44, 50, 51
Casa Gouveia, 57, 61, 100, 113, 117
Casa Grande and Sanzala (Freyre), 83

Casa Nosoco, 74
Casamance Basin, 195
Casaroli, Agostino, 177
Cassacá Congress (1964), 9–10, 121–5, 136–7, 139, 143, 147, 148
Cassamá, Awa, 192
Cassamá, Bacar, 58
Cassequel Properties, 64
Cassurães, Portugal, 19
Castanheira, José Pedro, 6–7
de Castro, Artur, 45
de Castro, Fernanda, 36
Castro, Fidel, 108, 110, 132
Catchungo, Guinea-Bissau, 162
Catholicism, 19, 24, 129, 171, 174–7, 208
Catió, Guinea-Bissau, 182
Centro do Estudos Africanos, 44–7, 49
Cerejo, Pedro, 15
Certeza, 32
Césaire, Aimé, 42
Ceylon, 96
Chabal, Patrick, 32, 36
Chakotin, Sergei, 152–3
Chaliand, Gérard, 138
Chantre, Honório, 132
Chaves, Portugal, 50
Chelas, Lisbon, 39
Chiang Kai-Shek, 116
China, 25, 78, 104, 105, 106, 110–11, 112, 115–16, 173, 181, 195
Chissano, Joaquim, 192, 193, 199
Chiume, Kanyama, 80
Chona, Mainza, 80
Christian democracy, 174
Churchill, Winston, 92
civilization, 26, 27, 34, 58, 82, 128, 130
Claridosos, 10

248

INDEX

Club Radiofónico de Portugal, 37
Clube Marítimo, 44
Có, Vicente, 91
cocoa, 41
coconuts, 144
coffee, 64
Coimbra, Portugal, 23, 24, 37, 43
Cold War (1947–91), 96, 152, 171, 177–8
Coloboi, Guinea-Conakry, 107
Colombo Conference (1954), 96
Colonial Act (1933), 25–6, 95
Colufi river, 21
Comité inter-mouvements auprès des évacués (CIMADE), 100
Committee of African Organizations, 80
communism, 42, 43, 47, 50, 57, 68, 166, 171, 173, 174, 178, 183
Communist Party of Angola, 68
Communist Party of France, 42
Communist Party of Italy, 175
Communist Party of Portugal, 43, 57
Como, Guinea-Bissau, 9, 119–20, 143
Companhia União Fabril (CUF), 113, 151
Compania de Comandos Africanos, 164, 165, 167
Comunidade Lusíada, 209
Conakry, Guinea-Conakry, 66, 79, 99–108, 146
  Cabral in, 2, 8–9, 12, 22, 87–90, 101–8, 160, 189
  Cabral assassination (1973), 3–4, 6, 7, 9–10, 12 13, 22, 145, 190–201, 209
  Escola Piloto, 146–7, 160, 187, 192, 194, 200
  Operação Mar Verde (1970), 164–7, 183, 194, 195, 197

concessionaires, 61, 82, 113, 116
Conchiglia, Augusta, 213
Concilio Vaticano II (1962–5), 174
Concordata (1940), 176
CONCP, 105, 106, 171
Conference of Solidarity with the People of Portuguese Colonies (1970), 175
Confissões de Zé Badiu (Cabral), 27
Congo
  Belgian (1908–60), 81, 86
  French (1882–1960), 66
  Republic of (1960–), 70, 86
Congress of Black Writers and Artists (1959), 69
Congressos dos Povos da Guiné, 157
Conscripts of Modernity (Scott), 2–3
Conselho Executivo da Luta (CEL), 191, 199
Conselho Nacional de Cabo Verde (CNCV), 206
Constitutional Law 7/74, 210
'Continuar Cabral', 204
Conversas em Família, 177
Cooper, Frederick, 11
Correia, Adelina, 22, 30
Correia, Mendes, 36
da Costa, António Lopes, 19
da Costa, Botelho, 53, 63
da Costa, Jorge Moreira, 153
Côte d'Ivoire, 66, 105
cotton, 27, 64
counterinsurgency, 152–4, 163
Creole, 18, 27–8, 104, 140
Crimmi, Bruno, 138
Croese, Sylvia, 15
crops, 60–61, 82, 113
da Cruz, Viriato, 8, 13, 38, 44, 68–9, 70, 72, 79, 85, 87, 99, 109
Cuba
  Angolan War (1975–91), 212

249

INDEX

Cabral assassination commission (1973), 198
Cabral's visit (1968), 133
  doctors from, 147
  education in, 131
  Guevara's death (1967), 132–3
  Operação Mar Verde (1970), 166
  PAIGC, relations with, 103, 133, 147, 170, 180
  Revolution (1953–9), 110–11, 112, 115, 121, 210
  Tricontinental Conference (1966), 117, 180
Cuba, Portugal, 53
Cubacaré, Guinea-Bissau, 182
cult of personality, 203–4
da Cunha, Pedro, 132
Curaçao, 97
Czechoslovakia, 88, 106, 173

D'jai, Mamadou, 191, 193
Dahl, Birgitta, 138–9
Dakar, Senegal
  Cabral in, 75, 77, 87, 91, 131
  education in, 147
  de Gaulle's visit (1958), 66
  Graça in, 92
  PAIGC in, 99, 100, 101, 108, 117, 127–8, 131
  Red Cross in, 141
Daman, 99, 176
Dar-es-Salaam, Tanzania, 171
Davidson, Basil, 81, 137
death penalty, 9, 148, 162
Debray, Régis, 111
Delaba, Guinea-Bissau, 144
Delgado, Humberto, 24
Democratic Movement for the Portuguese Colonies, 67–8
Depoimento (Caetano), 168
Derwinski, Edward, 179–80

detribalization, 116
Development Plan (1967–73), 156
Dhada, Mustafah, 143, 144
Diagne, Blaise, 93–4
Diário de Notícias, 195
Diário Popular, 153
Dias, Luciana, 15
Diawara, Manthia, 15
Diggs, Charles, 177–8, 181
Diop, Alioune, 46, 68, 175
Diop, Majhemout, 97
Direcção Geral de Segurança (DGS), 190
Directório Revolucionário Ibérico de Libertação (DRIL), 97
Diu, 99, 176
Dodds, Richard, 138
droughts, 7, 19, 23, 32, 33, 48, 49, 53
Du Bois, William Edward Burghardt, 40–41, 45, 93–4
Duarte, Abílio, 72, 117, 127

East Germany, 173
Eastern Bloc, 173, 174
eau de cologne, 50
Ecuador, 182
education
  colonial period, 13, 19–20, 23, 28, 29
  in Cape Verde, 19, 20, 23, 28, 29, 35
  literacy, 50, 122, 139, 145
  PAIGC and, 103, 119, 122, 144, 145–7, 148, 173
  in Portugal, 8, 32, 35–47, 50, 51, 100
EGA, 213
Egypt, 25, 93, 96, 198
elections (1972), 183–5
Em Defesa da Terra (Cabral), 49, 53
Embaná, Miguel, 148, 188

INDEX

empire, 11
Ennes, António, 82
Ervedosa, Carlos, 37
Escola Piloto, Conakry, 146–7, 160, 187, 192, 194, 200
Escola Politécnica, Conakry, 200
Escola Superior Colonial, Lisbon, 98
do Espírito Santo, Alda, 32, 45, 46, 51
do Espírito Santo, Januário da Graça, 45, 47
do Espírito Santo, Julieta, 51
do Espírito Santo, Salustino da Graça, 47
Estação Agronómica Nacional, 53
Estado Novo (1933–74), 27, 40, 44, 45, 47, 51, 149, 150, 156
   Campanha do Trigo (1933–38), 54
   Carnation Revolution (1974), 207, 208
   Catholicism and, 176, 208
   luso-tropicalism, 82–4
   multiculturalism and, 51
   political activism in, 44, 72
Estatuto do Indígenato (1926), 26, 58, 82, 98, 157
Ethiopia, 93, 96, 182
Étudiants Africains Parlent, Les, 46
Évora, Alcides, 193, 198
Évora, António Pinhel, 19
Évora, Iva Pinhel, 7, 19, 28–9, 50, 51–2, 57, 200

Fabião, Carlos, 153, 168
Facts About Portugal's African Colonies, The (Cabral), 81, 85, 172
famines, 7, 19, 23, 32, 33, 48, 53, 157
Fanon, Frantz, 69, 81, 109, 113, 117–18

Faria, Dutra, 151
Farim, Guinea-Bissau, 161
Fati, Mussa, 75
Fazenda Nhia, 64
Fazenda São Francisco, 64
Fazenda Tentativa, 64
Felupes people, 152
Fernandes, Gil, 179
Ferreira, Vicente, 41
Fletcher, Bill, 3
Florida, USA, 97
foco theory, 109, 111, 132
Fodéba, Keita, 44
football, 58
For a Better Guinea, 145, 155, 161
Forças Armadas Revolucionárias do Povo (FARP), 137, 143, 146, 192
forced labor, 26, 46–7, 82, 94
Forro people, 46–7
Fortes, Fernando, 72
FRAIN, 79, 81, 86, 87, 105
France, 18, 25–6, 65–7
   Algerian War (1954–62), 65, 69, 96, 153, 155, 156
   CIMADE escape incident (1961), 100–102
   communism in, 42
   Diagne and, 94
   Fifth Republic established (1958), 66
   Ghana, relations with, 101
   Guinea independence (1958), 65–7, 87–8, 96–7
   Indochina War (1946–54), 95–6
   intellectuals in, 42
   Loi Defferre (1956), 66, 96
   migration to, 18
   neo-colonialism, 65, 151
   PAIGC, relations with, 131–2, 137–8, 173
   Paris Peace Conference (1919), 25, 93

INDEX

Pires in, 131–2
Portugal, relations with, 131–2, 137
Franco, Francisco, 100
Frankfurt, Germany, 69
freedom of speech, 3, 173
Freetown, Sierra Leone, 188
Frente Ampla Anti-Colonial, 211
Frente de Libertação da Guiné (FLG), 90
Frente de Libertação da Guiné e de Cabo Verde (FLGC), 90
Frente de Libertação de Moçambique (FRELIMO), 1, 177, 192, 193, 199
Frente de Libertação Nacional da Guiné (FLING), 210–11
Frente Nacional de Libertação de Angola (FNLA), 1, 100
Frente Unida de Libertação (FUL), 194
Freyre, Gilberto, 82–3
Front de libération nationale (FLN), 101, 109
Fulamory, Guinea-Bissau, 199
Fulani people, 60–61, 113, 114, 116, 140, 152, 154–5, 157–8, 195, 196
Fundação Tchiweka, 15

Gabu, Guinea-Bissau, 158
Galvão, Henrique, 84–5, 97
da Gama, Inácio Soares, 191, 197
Garin, Vasco, 180
de Gaulle, Charles, 65–7, 96–7
Gaye, Cheikh, 182
Geba river, 21
Germany, 65, 78, 81, 101, 152–3, 173
Ghana, 65, 70, 78, 86, 94, 96, 101, 188
Ghibo, Bakary, 197

Gleijeses, Piero, 180
Glissanti, Marcella, 175
Goa League, 81
Goa, 30, 99, 105, 176
Goan League, 105
Goan People's Party, 105
gold, 26
Gold Coast, 96
Gomes, Afonso, 131
Gomes, Lourenço, 127, 199
Gorgulho, Carlos, 46–7, 58
Gouvernement provisoire de la République algérienne (GPRA), 69, 105, 109
Grã-Cruz da Ordem Militar da Torre e Espada, 24
da Graça, Leitão, 92, 211
Graça, Lisbon, 39
Granada TV, 138
Granja Experimental de Pessubé, 8, 56
Granma, 210
griots, 124
groundnuts, 60–61, 113
Guarda Nacional Republicana (GNR), 208
Guerra de Guerrillas, La (Guevara), 111, 136
Guerra, Sofia Pomba, 57
Guevara, Ernesto 'Che', 110, 111, 121, 132–3, 136, 169, 204
Guidage, Guinea-Bissau, 205
Guilege, Guinea-Bissau, 205
Guinea-Bissau
  agricultural census (1947), 60–62
  Algiers Accords (1974), 209–10
  Bolor massacre (1878), 18
  Cape Verde, relations with, *see* Cape Verde–Guinea relations
  CIMADE escape incident (1961), 101–2

252

INDEX

coup d'état (1980), 213
education in, 23
elections (1972), 183–5
geography of, 112, 141
identity, 10
Independence Proclamation (1973), 178, 181–2, 206–7
job posts in, 21, 55
National Assembly, 183, 185
Pidjiguiti massacre (1959), 71, 74, 86, 109, 140
Plano de Fomento (1967–73), 156
political organizations, dating of, 71
population census (1971), 183, 185
UN accession (1973), 207
War of Independence (1963–73), *see* Guinea-Bissau War of Independence
Guinea-Bissau (Crimmi and Lucas), 138
Guinea-Bissau War of Independence (1963–73), 1–2, 5, 9–10, 12, 108, 109–201
 air campaigns, 137, 143, 145, 146, 149, 154, 170, 173, 182–3, 204–5
 Algiers Accords (1974), 209–10
 amnesty (1969), 160, 162, 190, 194
 Balanta and, 60, 113–15, 144
 bi-groups, 137, 143, 150
 Cabral assassination (1973), 3–4, 6, 7, 9–10, 12–13, 22, 145, 190–201, 209
 Cape Verde and, 12, 14, 127–34, 141–2, 159
 Cassacá Congress (1964), 9–10, 121–5, 136–7, 139, 143, 147, 148
 Como campaign (1964), 119–20
 Congressos dos Povos da Guiné, 157–8
 corruption and, 145
 counterinsurgency, 152–4, 163
 desertions, 159, 162
 education and, 145–7, 173
 elections (1972), 183–5
 FARP, 137, 143, 146
 France and, 131–2, 137–8
 health services and, 147, 173
 Independence Proclamation (1973), 178, 181–2, 206–7
 liberated zones, 3, 5, 12, 137, 138, 142–7, 170, 173, 177–8, 183, 185
 as 'low-intensity conflict', 135
 Madina do Boé Congress (1973), 205
 Mandinka and, 116, 155
 Northern Front negotiations (1970), 162–3
 Operação Ametista Real (1973), 205
 Operação Mar Verde (1970), 164–7, 183, 194, 195, 197
 People's Warehouses, 144–5
 population census (1971), 183, 185
 propaganda and, 138–42, 145
 Rádio Libertação, 139–41
 refugees, 158, 183
 stabilized resistance phase, 121, 169
 Tite attack (1963), 1, 9, 108, 118
 UN Special Mission (1972), 182–3
Guinea-Conakry, 2, 8
 Cabral in, 2, 8–9, 12, 22, 86, 87–90, 189
 Cabral assassination (1973),

253

INDEX

3–4, 6, 7, 9–10, 12–13, 22, 145, 190–201, 209
Escola Piloto, 146–7, 160, 187, 192, 194, 200
Independence (1958), 65–7, 87–8, 96–7, 195
Operação Mar Verde (1970), 164–7, 183, 194, 195, 197
PAIGC in, 99–108
Pereira in, 100

Haitian Revolution (1791–1804), 40
Hamilcar Barca, 21
Havana, Cuba, 117, 132, 170, 180, 210
health services, 147, 148, 173
Hegel, Georg Wilhelm Friedrich, 42
helicopters, 137, 145, 149, 154, 170
herbicides, 173
Hoagland, Jim, 143
Hoje e Amanhã (Cabral), 38
Hong Kong 156
Honorin, Michel, 138
Horta, Elisa, 51
Houphouët Boigny, Félix, 105
human rightsm 173
hut tax, 26

Ignatiev, Oleg, 4, 28, 62
Ilha de Santo Nome (Tenreiro), 44
ilustres coloniais, 82
impost de palhota, 26
imposto de sangue, 127
Imprensa Nacional, 8, 32
In Defense of Land (Cabral), 49, 53
India, 25, 37, 78, 82, 93, 95, 96, 99, 105, 176
indígenas, 46–7, 58, 128
indigenato, 58, 82, 128, 130

Indochina, 95–6
Indonesia, 93, 96
Injai, Abdul, 155
Instituto Superior de Agronomia (ISA), 8, 35, 50, 53, 63, 64
International Labour Organization (ILO), 27
International Union of Telecommunications, 142
irās, 122
Islam, 123, 157
Israel, Paolo, 15
Italy, 69, 138, 175

Januário, José, 165
Japan, 181
Jeune Afrique, 181, 206, 213
Jewish people, 17, 39
John XXIII, Pope, 174
Johnson, Wallace, 94
Jones, Leroy, 181
Jonjon, 188
Junta de Investigações do Ultramar, 63
Junta de Salvação Nacional, 208

Kalashnikovs, 164
Kamel, Belkhiria, 182
Kandjafra, Guinea-Bissau, 199
Karla boats, 191
Kaurane, Guinea-Bissau, 199
Keita, Bobo, 101
Keïta, Fodéba, 108
Keita, Modibo, 105
Kennedy, John Fitzgerald, 100, 178
Kenya, 94
Kenyatta, Jomo, 94
Kirumira, Edward, 15
kola nuts, 144

Laban, Michel, 5, 39

INDEX

Labanta Negro (1966 documentary), 138
Labéry, Henri, 90, 91
Lachol, 188
Lafayette, Gilbert du Motier, Marquis, 180
Lala Quema (1964 documentary), 138
Lança, Marta, 15
lançados, 17
Landau, George, 181
Lar do Combatente, 102
Lara, Lúcio, 13, 67, 68, 69, 70, 77, 99, 109
Lara, Ruth, 69
Lara, Tchiloia, 15
Laurinda, Nha, 131
League of Nations, 27
Lefgren, Folke, 182
Leite, António, 131
Lenin, Vladimir, 173, 179–80
Lewis, David, 93
liberated zones, 3, 5, 12, 137, 138, 142–7, 170, 173, 177–8, 183, 185
Liberation of Guiné, The (Davidson), 138
Liberia, 93, 96, 167
Libertação, A, 139
Libya, 96, 166
Liceu Gil Eanes, São Vicente, 7, 29–30, 31–2, 35, 57, 146
Liga Académica Internacional dos Negros, 40
Lima, Isidoro Manuel, 188
de Lima, Manuel Monge, 153
limpet mines, 164
Lincoln University, 181
Lipinska, Suzanne, 137
Lisbon, Portugal
  Cabral in, 4, 8, 13, 32, 33–52, 57, 59, 62–5

Carnation Revolution (1974), 207
CIMADE escape incident (1961), 100
da Cruz in, 68–9
Movimento Anti-Colonial in, 67–8
Neto in, 79
poverty in, 38–9, 52
students in, 8, 32, 35–47, 50, 51, 100
literacy, 50, 122, 139, 145
Loi Defferre (1956), 66, 96
London, England, 79–86, 87, 89, 94
Loock, Nel-Mari, 15
Lopes, Januário, 167
Lopes, José Vicente, 6, 192
Lorraine, 131
Luanda, Angola, 13, 30, 55, 68, 97, 176
Lucas, Uliano, 138
Lugard, Frederick, 156
luso-tropicalism, 82–4
Lutte Armée en Afrique (Chaliand), 138
da Luz, Silvino, 128, 132

Macanha people, 140
Macau, 30, 37
de Macedo, Augusto Divo, 188
Machado, Humberto, 43, 68
Machado, Júlia, 43
Macmillan, Harold, 97
Madagascar, 66
Madeira, 30, 34, 129
Madina do Boé, Guinca-Bissau, 112, 148, 178
  Congress (1973), 205, 206
Madina do Boé (1967 documentary), 138
Magalhães, José, 40

255

INDEX

Magalhães, Osório, 162–3
Maia, Salgueiro, 207
Maître École (Fodéba), 44
maize, 60
Makerere Institute of Social Research, 15
malaria, 62
Malawi, 80, 94
Malayan Emergency (1948–60), 153, 155
Mali, 70
Malley, Simon, 187
Mamdani, Mahmood, 15, 157
Manchester, England, 94
Mande Empire, 115, 155
Mandinka Empire (1878–98), 196
Mandinka people, 116, 140, 155, 157–8, 196
Mané, Ansumane, 148
Mangana, Valentino, 198
Manjaco people, 152
Manji, Firoze, 3
Manufacturing Union Company, 113, 151
Mao Zedong, 110–11, 144, 173, 204
Mapa Cor-de-Rosa, 195
maquisards, 123
Margarido, Alfredo, 38
Margeretha, 188
Mariazinha em África (de Castro), 36
Markovitz, Irving, 87–8
Marquis of Sá da Bandeira
Marret, Mario, 138
Martins, Júlio, 39
Marvila, Lisbon, 39
Marxism, 8, 11–12, 39, 42, 44, 54, 103, 153, 173
Massip, José, 138
da Mata, Marcelino, 164
de Matos, Carlos, 112
de Matos, Norton, 43

Mausoleum of Camayenne, Conakry, 199
Mecca, 157
Medeiros, Tomás, 5
Mello Geraldes Prize, 36
de Melo e Alvim, Diogo, 62, 71
de Melo, Fontes Pereira, 18
Mendes, Francisco, 206
de Menezes, Hugo Azancot, 8, 41, 51, 73, 79, 80, 89
Mercantil Lda, 63
Mesquita, Alberto Marques, 37
mezinhos, 123
Michigan, USA, 177
Mindelo, São Vicente, 188
Ministry of Colonies (Portugal), 37, 44
Ministry of Rural Economy (Guinea-Conakry), 87
Miranda, Nuno, 32
Miranda, Tomás, 32
Mission of Overseas Students, 35
Mississippi, USA, 83
mixed race people, 82–4
Mocidade Portuguesa, 37
Mohamed V, King of Morocco, 105
Monde, Le, 85
Mondlane, Eduardo, 100, 138, 177
Monrovia, Liberia, 167
Montanha prison, Conakry, 147, 192
Monteiro, Armindo, 26
Monteiro, Eurídice, 15
Monteiro, João Baptista, 211
Monteiro, Pedro, 28, 134
Monteiro, Telmo Crato, 51
Moreira, Adriano, 26, 98, 150, 156
Morés, Guinea-Bissau, 138
Morocco, 79, 88, 96, 105–8, 206
Moselle, Lorraine, 131

INDEX

Moumié, Félix, 97
Mourão, Fernando, 37–8
Movimento Anti-Colonial (MAC), 8, 67–71, 72, 78, 79, 89
Movimento das Forças Armadas (MFA), 207, 209, 210
Movimento de Libertação da Guiné e de Cabo Verde (MLGCV), 90, 91
Movimento de Libertação dos Territórios sob Domininação Portuguesa, 89
Movimento para a Democracia (MPD), 212
Movimento Popular de Libertação de Angola (MPLA), 9, 13–14, 47, 71, 72, 79, 105
  Cape Verde, relations with, 212
  CIMADE escape incident (1961), 101
  CONCP and, 105
  FRAIN and, 87
  in Guinea-Conakry, 87, 97, 98
  PAIGC, relations with, 99, 141
  Viva Angola Combatente, 141
Mozambique, 79, 151
  assimilados, 18
  Cape Verdean migration, 19, 20
  CIMADE escape incident (1961), 100
  Creole elite, 40
  education in, 30
  European migration, 81, 113
  forced labor in, 26
  FRELIMO, 1, 177, 192, 193, 199
  land expropriation in, 61, 116
  mixed race people in, 83, 84
  Mondlane assassination (1970), 177
  political organizations, dating of, 71
  protestant missions in, 35
  South Africa, relations with, 212
  students from, 35, 37
  UDENAMO, 105
  War of Independence (1964–74), 1
Muaca, André, 176
multiculturalism, 51, 82–4

Nagata, Yutaka, 182
Nagonia, Koba, 191
Namorado, Joaquim, 44
Nangue, Francisco Gomes, 167
Nanjing, China, 104
napalm, 118, 173, 179
Nascimento, Irénio, 165
National Assembly, 183, 185
National Association for the Advancement of Colored People (NAACP), 93
National Campaign Committee for Goa, 105
nationalism, 4, 8–9, 11, 31–2, 42, 79
Native Law, 58
Navy of Guinea-Bissau, 191–2, 193
Nazi Germany (1939–45), 65, 81, 152–3
Négritude, 8, 42–3, 49
Negro, O, 40
Nehru, Jawaharlal, 93, 95, 99
Nelli, Piero, 138
Netherlands, 173
Neto, Agostinho, 13, 32, 38, 43–4, 46, 47, 68, 69, 79, 174, 212
Neves, Baeta, 63
Neves, José, 15
das Neves, Manuel, 97
New Christians, 17
New York Times, 180, 181
New York, USA, 94, 179

INDEX

Nigeria, 94, 156
Nix, Robert, 179
Nixon, Richard, 178
Nkrumah, Kwame, 70, 90, 94, 187–8
Nô Pintcha, 204
Nogueira, Franco, 151
Non-Aligned Movement, 96, 171, 182
North Atlantic Treaty Organization (NATO), 69, 137
North Korea, 181
Northern Front, 106, 124, 162, 205
Norway, 182
Nos Intervalos da Arte da Minerva (Cabral), 31
Nossa Senhora da Graça, Guinea-Bissau, 20
Nossa Terra (1966 documentary), 138
Nostis et Nobiscum (1849), 174
Nyasaland (1907–64), 94

Oliveira, Carlos, 44
Operação Ametista Real (1973), 205
Operação Mar Verde (1970), 164–7, 183, 194, 195, 197
Oramas, Oscar, 196–7, 198
Orfeão Académico de Coimbra, 84
Organization of African Unity (OAU), 78, 89, 94, 167, 182, 188
Oslo, Norway, 182
Osservatore Romano, 176
Overseas Ministry, 56

Pacheco, Carlos, 14
Pádua, Mário, 147
Paesi Nouvi, 175
PAIGC-Actualités, 160

PAIGC, *see* Partido Africano para a Independência da Guiné e Cabo Verde
Pakistan, 96
palm oil, 103
Pan-African Congress
  First (1919), 93
  Second (1921), 94
  Third (1923), 40, 45
  Fourth (1927), 94
  Fifth (1945), 94
Pandit, Vijaya, 93
Pansau, 213
Paris Match, 97
Paris, France, 42, 78, 100
Paris Peace Conference (1919), 25, 93
Parti Africain de l'Indépendance (PAI), 97
Parti de la Fédération de l'Afrique, 70
Parti Démocratique Africain, 66
Parti Démocratique de Guinée (PDG), 73, 199
Partido Africano para a Independência da Guiné e Cabo Verde (PAIGC), 1, 3, 55, 71–3, 87
  Algiers Accords (1974), 209–10
  All-African People's Conference (1960), 79
  Angolan War (1961–74), 99
  arrests (1961), 107, 161
  Balanta and, 60, 113–15, 144
  Cabral assassination (1973), 3–4, 6, 7, 9–10, 12–13, 145, 190–201
  Cabral assassination plot trial (1967), 148, 188
  Cassacá Congress (1964), 9–10, 121–5, 136–7, 139, 143, 147, 148

INDEX

communism and, 173, 174, 177, 178, 183
Conselho Executivo da Luta (CEL), 191, 199
corruption, 145
Dakar meeting (1963), 127–8
death penalty, use of, 9, 148, 162
desertions, 159, 162
diplomacy, 104–5, 108, 171–83
Eastern Bloc, relations with, 173, 174
education provision, 103, 119, 122, 144, 145–7, 148, 173
elections (1972), 183–5
ethnic divisions, 117
founding of, 7, 9, 47, 71–3
Guinea-Conakry operations, 89, 97, 99–108
health services, 147, 148, 173
judicial system, 147, 148
Madina do Boé Congress (1973), 205, 206
Mandinka and, 116, 155
Pidjiguiti massacre (1959), 71, 74, 86, 109, 140
People's Warehouses, 144–5
population census (1971), 183
propaganda, 138–41
Rádio Libertação, 139–41
satellite groups, 91
Senegal operations, 90–92, 99
UPICV, relations with, 92
War of Independence (1963–73), *see* Guinea-Bissau War of Independence
war preparations, 99–108
weapons smuggling, 105–8
Western nations, relations with, 131–2, 137–9, 140, 173–81
Partido Africano para Independência, 71

Partido Comunista Angolano, 68
Partido Comunista Português, 43, 57
Paul VI, Pope, 174–7
Pauw, Cristoff, 15
Pavlov, Ivan, 152
peasants, 103, 111, 116, 144
People's Warehouses, 144–5
Peralta, Pedro Rodríguez, 180
Pereira, Aristides, 100, 117
 arrest (1961), 107, 108
 Cabral assassination (1973), 192, 193, 197
 Cabral assassination plot trial (1967), 148, 188
 Cabral, relationship with, 57
 on Cape Verde–Guinea relations, 58, 211–12
 on cult of personality, 203–4
 Dakar meeting (1963), 127–8
 general secretary appointment (1973), 199, 205
 PAIGC founding, 72–3
Pereira, Carmen, 137
Pereira, Fernando, 15
Pereira, Joaquim, 162–3
Pessubé Farm, Guinea-Bissau, 8, 56
PIDE, *see* Polícia Internacional e de Defesa do Estado
Pidjiguiti massacre (1959), 71, 74, 86, 109, 140
Pilot School, Conakry, 146–7, 160, 187, 192, 194
Pimentel, Alberto Gomes, 115
Pink Map (1885), 195
Pinto, César Correia, 21
Pinto, Teixeira, 17, 21
Pio, Nicolau, 131
Pires, Pedro, 101, 127, 131–2, 134, 206, 209, 212–13
Pius XI, Pope, 174

INDEX

Plano de Fomento (1967–73), 156
poetry, 4, 8, 27, 31–2, 37, 43, 44
Poland, 192
Polícia de Segurança Pública (PSP), 160, 208
Polícia Internacional e de Defesa do Estado (PIDE), 6–7, 109
  and Angolan nationalists, 69
  and Barbosa, 161
  and Batepá massacre (1953), 47
  Bissau raids (1961), 106
  and Cabral, 8, 22, 46, 51, 62, 68, 77, 80, 85–6, 134
  and Cabral assassination (1973), 12–13, 188, 189, 190–91
  and Cape Verde, 92, 133, 134
  and Centro de Estudos Africanos, 46
  and CIMADE escape incident (1961), 100
  and da Cruz, 69
  and death penalty, 148
  and elections (1972), 184
  informants, 72, 92
  and Operação Mar Verde (1970), 166
  and Pires, 131
Popular Assembly, 183, 185
population census (1971), 183, 185
Por uma Guiné Melhor, 145, 155, 161
Port Everglades, Florida, 97
Porto, Portugal, 36
Portugal
  Acto Colonial (1933), 25–6, 95
  Algiers Accords (1974), 209–10
  Angolan War (1961–74), 1, 97–8, 99, 106
  Balanta, relations with, 60, 113–14
  Berlin Conference (1884–5), 11, 17

  Cabral in, 4, 8, 13, 32, 33–52, 57, 59, 62–5
  Cabral assassination (1973), 12–13, 188, 189, 190–91, 194–6, 209
  Caetano government (1968–74), see Caetano, Marcelo
  Campanha do Trigo (1929–38), 54
  Cape Verde, relations with, 10–11, 17–19, 21, 58, 117, 128
  Carnation Revolution (1974), 168, 207–8
  CIMADE escape incident (1961), 100
  Concordata (1940), 176
  Constitutional Law 7/74, 210
  coup d'état (1926), 23
  Estado Novo (1933–74), see Estado Novo
  Estatuto do Indígenato (1926), 26, 58, 82, 98, 157
  France, relations with, 131–2, 137
  Fulani, relations with, 116, 155, 157–8
  Goa annexed (1961), 100
  luso-tropicalism, 82–4
  Mandinka, relations with, 155, 157–8, 196
  Movimento das Forças Armadas (MFA), 207, 209, 210
  Mozambique War (1964–74), 1
  Operação Ametista Real (1973), 205
  Operação Mar Verde (1970), 164–7, 183, 194, 195, 197
  presidential election (1949), 43
  Salazar government (1932–68), see Salazar, António de Oliveira

260

INDEX

Santa Maria hijacking (1961), 97
Senegal, negotiations with (1971–2), 167–8, 194
slavery, 11, 24, 27, 46, 82, 89, 128, 129
UN accession (1955), 95
US military aid, 178, 179
World War II period (1939–45), 35, 38–9
Portugal and the Future (Spínola), 208
Portugal Ultramarino, 37
Portugal's War in Guinea (Venter), 143
Portuguese Empire
  Angola (1575–1975), *see* Angola
  Cape Verde (1462–1975), *see* Cape Verde
  Colonial Act (1933), 25–6, 95
  Constitutional Law 7/74, 210
  Estatuto do Indígenato (1926), 26, 58, 82, 98
  Guinea (1588–1974), *see* Guinea-Bissau
  India (1505–1961), 30, 37, 82, 99, 176
  luso-tropicalism, 82–4
  Macau (1557–1999), 30, 37
  Mozambique (1505–1975), see Mozambique
  Pink Map (1885), 195
  Ultimatum (1890), 195
Portuguese language, 19, 27–8, 129, 140
Praia, Cape Verde, 7, 8, 19, 32, 49, 51, 57, 200, 211
Présence Africaine, 46, 68, 83, 138, 175
price fixing, 41, 61, 82
Prison d'Afrique (Alatas), 197
'Prison Problem Overseas, The' (Moreira), 98

Processo dos 50 (1959), 69
propaganda, 5, 6, 14, 138–41
Protestantism, 35
protonationalism, 40, 41

Quando o Cupido Acerta o Alvo (Cabral), 31
de Queiroz, Eça, 24
Quem mandou matar Amílcar Cabral? (Castanheira), 6–7
Querido, Jorge, 211
Qui Pluribus (1846), 174
Quinara, Guinea-Bissau, 144
Quitafine, Guinea-Bissau, 120, 182
Quran, 123, 148

Rabaka, Reiland, 5
Rabat, Morocco, 88, 105, 106, 107, 108, 206
racism, 36, 42, 51, 82
Radio Bissau, 194
Radio Ghana, 92
Rádio Libertação, 139–41
Radio Moscow, 58
Radio of Cape Verde, 49
radio, 49–50, 139–42
Ramos, Armando, 90
Ramos, Pedro, 107
Ramos, Raul dos Passos, 162–3
Rapazote, João, 15
'rape of the masses', 152
Rassool, Ciraj, 15
Ratoma, Conakry, 192, 193
re-Africanization of spirits', 39–40, 121
Red Cross, 141
refugees, 88, 100, 158, 164, 183
dos Reis Borges, Simôa, 19–20, 22, 30
Rema, Henrique Pinto, 74
Republic Gazette, 210
Republic of Congo, 70, 86

261

INDEX

Rhode Island, USA, 92
rice, 60–61, 103, 113, 144
Roberto, Holden, 98
Roçadas, Carlos, 48
da Rocha, Maximiana Monteiro, 19
da Rocha, Vieira, 41
Rocheteau, Guilherme, 32
Rodrigues, Maria Helena, *see* Cabral, Maria Helena
Rome, Italy, 69, 175
Roosevelt, Franklin, 92
Rosas, Fernando, 39
Rosenthal, Benjamin, 179
Rudebeck, Lars, 184

Sá da Bandeira, Bernardo de Sá Nogueira de Figueiredo, 1st Marquis, 129
Sal, Cape Verde, 210, 212
Salazar, António de Oliveira, 19, 23–7, 42, 54, 82, 88, 208
    brain hemorrhage (1968), 150
    Cabral's letter (1960), 23
    CIMADE escape incident (1961), 100
    on 'civilizing' Africans, 27
    Colonial Act (1933), 25–6
    Goa annexed (1961), 99
    labor policies, 27
    Minister of Finance (1928–40), 23–4
    Minister of the Colonies (1930–31), 25
    Prime Minister appointment (1932), 24
    World War II (1939–45), 38–9
Salim, Salim Ahmed, 181
Samory, Almamy, 196
San Francisco Conference (1945), 92–3, 94
San Sebastian, Spain, 100
Sanca, Albino, 161
Sanches, Manuela Ribeiro, 15
Sanctuary of Fátima, Portugal, 176
Santa Liberdade, 97
Santa Maria, 97
Santiago, Cape Verde, 7, 18, 19, 54–5, 130, 134
Santo Amaro, Lisbon, 39
Santo Antão, Cape Verde, 133
Santos, Almeida, 84, 209
Santos, António de Almeida, 209
Santos, Arnaldo, 32
dos Santos, Daniel, 9–10
dos Santos, Eduardo, 68, 69
dos Santos, Marcelino, 67–8, 105, 174
São Domingo, Guinea-Bissau, 161
São Nicolau, Cape Verde, 19, 20, 29
São Tomé, 40–41, 44, 45, 46–7, 58, 89, 130
    Batepá massacre (1953), 46–7, 58
São Vicente, Cape Verde, 7, 30, 188, 211
Sartre, Jean-Paul, 42, 81
Saúde Maria, Victor, 75, 127, 128
Schacht, Otto, 107, 197, 199, 213
Schultz, Arnaldo, 143, 149–50, 152
Scott, David, 2–3
Seles, Angola, 64
Senegal
    Cabral assassination commission (1973), 198
    Cabral in, 75, 77, 87, 90–92, 131
    de Gaulle's visit (1958), 66
    education in, 147
    Graça in, 92
    Guinea-Bissau, border with, 106, 147
    Guinea-Bissau, migration to, 17

INDEX

Independence (1960), 90, 195, 196
Mali Federation (1959–60), 90, 196
PAIGC in, 71, 73, 75, 77, 86, 87, 90, 99–101, 108, 117, 127, 131
Parti Africain de l'Indépendance (PAI), 97
Portugal, negotiations with (1971–2), 167–8, 194
Red Cross in, 141
refugees in, 158
Senegambians, 17
Senghor, Léopold Sédar, 42, 43, 73, 87, 91, 167–8, 194, 195
seniority system, 104, 114
Setúbal, Portugal, 64
Seydi, Doudou, 91
Sheppard, John, 138
Sierra Leone, 17, 94, 188, 198
Sierra Maestra, Cuba, 112, 132
Silva e Cunha, Joaquim, 98
da Silva, Adriano Duarte, 129
da Silva, Inácio, 90
da Silva, Ivo Carvalho, 19
da Silva, João Carvalho, 19
da Silva, José Nascimento, 188
da Silva, Lopes, 91
da Silva, Osvaldo Lopes, 101, 128, 192
Silveira, Onésimo, 203
slavery, 11, 24, 27, 40, 46, 49, 82, 89, 128, 129
Small Group of Terrorists Attacked, A (1968 documentary), 138
Smith, Alan, 25
Soares, Mário, 209
soccer, 58
social Darwinism, 26, 82
Social Democratic Party of Sweden, 138–9, 181

socialism, 13, 88, 177, 213
Sofia, Bulgaria, 166
Soga, Guinea-Bissau, 164
soil erosion, 48, 53–4, 55
de Sousa, Henrique Teixeira, 29
Sousa, Julião Soares, 7
de Sousa, Noémia, 38, 68, 69
South Africa, 15, 26–7, 83, 97, 143, 164, 170, 212, 213, 212
Soviet Union, 78, 88, 165, 171, 213
and Cabral assassination (1973), 195, 197
Cabral's visits (1970, 1972), 179–80, 181, 204
Cani in, 191
CIMADE escape incident (1961), 101
Cold War (1947–91), 96, 152, 171, 177–8
CONCP foundation (1961), 105
education in, 101, 159
Guinea-Bissau, relations with, 213
Guinea-Bissau War (1963–73), 133, 140, 152, 159, 164, 165, 173, 178
Pires in, 131
UN activity, 95
weapons from, 164, 165, 204
Spain, 100
Spínola, António, 6, 141–2, 143, 145, 150, 151, 152–68
Algiers Accords (1974), 209–10
amnesty (1969), 160, 162, 190, 194
Cabral assassination (1973), 189, 190, 193, 194–5, 209
Carnation Revolution (1974), 208
Comunidade Lusíada plan (1974), 209
Operação Mar Verde (1970), 164–7, 183, 194, 195

INDEX

Portugal and the Future (1974), 208
Senegal, negotiations with (1971–2), 167–8, 194
Sports and Recreational Association of Bissau, 63
stabilized resistance, 121, 169
Stellenbosch Institute for Advanced Studies, 15
strategic hamlets, 154
Strela missiles, 181, 204
Streten, Dimir, 165
Struggle of Mozambique, The (Mondlane), 138
Sudan, 96
sugar beet, 63
sugarcane, 64
supernatural, 122–3
Supreme Council of the Struggle (CSL), 183
Surrealism, 42
Sweden, 78, 138–9, 140, 174, 181, 182

tabanka, 114
Tabanka, Guinea-Bissau, 103
Tage Erlander Fund, 139
Tanzania, 171
Tarrafal prison, Cape Verde, 190
tarrafo, 115, 119
Té, Chico, 101, 102
Teixeira, Óscar, 179
Teixeira Pinto, Guinea-Bissau, 161
Tejo river, 65
Templar, Gerald, 153
Tenreiro, Francisco José, 44, 46
'Testement Politique de Cabral, Le', 206
Third World, 93
Times, The, 160
Timor, 37
Tite, Guinea-Bissau, 1, 9, 108, 118

Tomás, Américo, 150, 208
Tomás, João, 190, 191, 193, 197
Tombali, Guinea-Bissau, 144, 182
Touré, Ahmed Sékou, 8, 9, 66–7, 73, 87, 155, 196
  Cabral assassination (1973), 190, 193, 195, 196–9
  foreign aid and, 88
  Independence (1958), 65–7, 88, 96–7
  Operação Mar Verde (1970), 164–7, 197
  PAIGC, relations with, 91, 105, 107–8
Touré, Mamadou, 161
Touré, Momu, 190, 193, 197
Touré, Samory, 199–200
Trás-os-Montes, Portugal, 50
Trial of the 50 (1959), 69
tribalism, 116, 122, 124, 157
Tricontinental Conference, 117, 180
Tricontinental, 110, 121
Tripoli, Libya, 166
trypanosoma rhodesiense, 115
tsetse flies, 115
tungsten, 39
Tunisia, 69, 78–9, 96, 182
Turpin, Richard, 90

Uganda, 15
Ultimatum (1890), 195
Um Nyobé Ruben, 97
União Democrática de Cabo Verde (UDC), 91, 211
União Democrática Nacional de Moçambique (UDENAMO), 105
União dos Povos da Guiné (UPG), 91
União dos Povos de Angola (UPA), 98

INDEX

União dos Povos para a Independência de Cabo Verde (UPICV), 92, 211
Union of Democratic Control, 81
Union of the Peoples of Cameroon, 97
L'Unitá, 166
United Kingdom, 25–6, 79–86, 92, 153, 154–5, 173, 195
United Nations, 171–2, 179
  Afro-Asiatic group, 171–2
  Almada dossier (1962), 206
  Cabral's speech (1972), 181
  Charter (1945), 34, 42, 93, 94, 95, 171
  Food and Agriculture Organization, 60
  General Assembly, 86, 94, 171–2, 181, 182
  Guinea-Bissau accession (1973), 207
  PAIGC, relations with, 171
  Portuguese accession (1955), 95
  Resolution 1514 (1960), 95, 172
  San Francisco Conference (1945), 92–3, 94
  Security Council, 182
  Special Commission on Portugal (1962), 172
  Special Mission to Guinea (1972), 182–3
United States, 177–81
  All-African People's Conference (1960), 78
  Atlantic Charter (1941), 92
  Cabral's visits (1970, 1972), 177–81
  Cold War (1947–91), 96, 152, 171, 177–8
  colonialism and, 25
  Guevara's death (1967), 132–3
  migration to, 19, 39
  PAIGC, relations with, 177–81
  Portugal, relations with, 178–9
  San Francisco Conference (1945), 92–3, 94
  segregation in, 51, 83
  slavery in, 40
  UPICV in, 92
  Vietnam War (1955–75), 155, 156
  War of Independence (1775–83), 180
  weapons from, 178, 179
  World War II period (1939–45), 25, 39
Universal Exhibition of Porto (1934), 36
University of Porto, 36
University of Syracuse, 180
Urdang, Stephanie, 170

Valério, José, 21
Vamos Conhecer a Nossa Terra, 141
Van Dúnem, José, 43
Vassalo e Silva, Manuel António, 99
Vatican, 171, 174–7
Vaz, George, 105
Vaz, Honório Sanches, 148, 188
Venter, Albertus Johannes, 143, 204–5
Vergès, Jacques, 101
Viana, Gentil, 101
Vidigueira, Portugal, 53
Vieira, Henriette, 131, 194
Vieira, Herculano, 133
Vieira, João Bernardo, 148
Vieira, Luandino, 38
Vieira, Nino, 104, 120, 205, 206, 213
Vietnam, 93, 110, 112, 155, 156, 194

INDEX

Viseu, Portugal, 19
Viva Angola Combatente, 141
Voss e Sá, Ana Maria, *see* Cabral, Ana Maria
Voz de Cabo Verde, 22

Warriors at Work (Dhada), 143
Washington Post, 143, 180
weapons trade, 105–8, 164, 178
Wilson, Woodrow, 25
witchcraft, 9, 122
World Council of Churches, 174
World in Action, 138
World War I (1914–18), 25, 93, 94

World War II (1939–45), 35, 38–9, 65, 81, 92, 96, 174
Wrangler, Christian, 138
Wretched of the Earth, The (Fanon), 69, 81, 117–18

Xabregas, Lisbon, 39

Yaya, Alpha, 199
Yugoslavia, 78, 165, 173

Zaire (1971–97), 198
Zambia, 80, 85
Zeituni, Messaoudi, 197, 198
Ziegler, Jean, 117, 210